Dragon® NaturallySpeaking® FOR DUMMIES®

2ND EDITION

Edward W. [signature]

by Stephanie Diamond

WILEY

John Wiley & Sons, Inc.

Dragon® NaturallySpeaking® For Dummies®

Published by
John Wiley & Sons, Inc.
111 River Street
Hoboken, NJ 07030-5774
www.wiley.com

Copyright © 2011 by John Wiley & Sons, Inc., Indianapolis, Indiana
Published by John Wiley & Sons, Inc., Indianapolis, Indiana
Published simultaneously in Canada

WILEY

About the Author

Stephanie Diamond is a thought leader and management marketing professional with 20+ years of experience building profits in over 75 different industries. She has worked with solopreneurs, small business owners and multibillion dollar corporations.

She worked for eight years as a Marketing Director at AOL. When she joined, there were less than 1 million subscribers. When she left in 2002 there were 36 million. While at AOL, she developed a highly successful line of multimedia products that brought in an annual $40 million dollars in incremental revenue.

In 2002 she founded Digital Media Works, Inc. (DigMediaWorks.com) an online marketing company that helped business owners discover the hidden profits in their business. She is passionate about guiding online companies to successfully generate more revenue and find their company's real value.

As a strategic thinker, Stephanie uses all the current visual thinking techniques and brain research to help companies get to the essence of their brand. In 2011, she founded the Savvy Executive Institute (SavvyExecutiveInstitute.com) where she helps companies accelerate their growth by understanding and communicating their value to customers using all the latest techniques.

Stephanie received a BA in Psychology from Hofstra University and an MSW and MPH from the University of Hawaii. She lives in New York with her husband and Maltese named Colby.

Dedication

To Barry, who makes all things possible.

To my family, for their encouragement and love.

Author's Acknowledgments

It is my great privilege to write this book. I want to offer great thanks to Wiley Publishing, Inc. for lettting me re-introduce Dragon NaturallySpeaking to a waiting audience of smart readers.

The following people were especially important in creating this book, and I offer very sincere thanks:

* To the wonderfully creative group at Wiley, Acquisitions Editor Katie Mohr and Project Editor Pat O'Brien. They made this project a dream!

* To the very sharp folks at Nuance Communications, Peter Mahoney, SVP and GM and Erica Hill, Senior Manager, Corporate Communications, for sharing their knowledge.

* To Matt Wagner, my agent at Fresh Books, for his continued hard work on my behalf.

Finally, thanks to you for choosing this book to learn about Dragon NaturallySpeaking. I wish you enormous joy on your exciting journey into voice recognition.

Publisher's Acknowledgments

We're proud of this book; please send us your comments at http://dummies.custhelp.com. For other comments, please contact our Customer Care Department within the U.S. at 877-762-2974, outside the U.S. at 317-572-3993, or fax 317-572-4002.

Some of the people who helped bring this book to market include the following:

Acquisitions, Editorial, and Vertical Websites

Project Editor: Pat O'Brien

Acquisitions Editor: Katie Mohr

Copy Editor: Debbye Butler

Technical Editor: Eric Guinazzo

Editorial Manager: Kevin Kirschner

Vertical Websites Project Manager: Laura Moss-Hollister

Vertical Websites Project Manager: Jenny Swisher

Supervising Producer: Rich Graves

Vertical Websites Associate Producers: Josh Frank, Marilyn Hummel, Douglas Kuhn, Shawn Patrick

Editorial Assistant: Amanda Graham

Sr. Editorial Assistant: Cherie Case

Cover Photo: © iStockphoto.com / Cary Westfall

Cartoons: Rich Tennant (www.the5thwave.com)

Composition Services

Project Coordinator: Nikki Gee

Layout and Graphics: Joyce Haughey, Lavonne Roberts

Proofreader: Laura Bowman

Indexer: Potomac Indexing, LLC

Publishing and Editorial for Technology Dummies

Richard Swadley, Vice President and Executive Group Publisher

Andy Cummings, Vice President and Publisher

Mary Bednarek, Executive Acquisitions Director

Mary C. Corder, Editorial Director

Publishing for Consumer Dummies

Kathy Nebenhaus, Vice President and Executive Publisher

Composition Services

Debbie Stailey, Director of Composition Services

Contents at a Glance

Table of Contents

Introduction

· ·

*F*inally! Someone has freed you from that medieval torture rack, the keyboard, and its contemporary accessory, the mouse. You've been muttering epithets at your computer. Now you can actually speak to it. Although it still won't take your epithets to heart, it will now at least write them down for your future convenience.

For those who can't type or spell (or at least, not well), and for those whose bodies have been punished by keyboarding, Dragon NaturallySpeaking spells relief (and other words, too). NaturallySpeaking gives your lips their job back: being your principal data output device. In fact, with NaturallySpeaking, you may be able to type faster with your lips than with your fingers. At the same time, you can eliminate spelling errors (and spell checking) from your life. Yes, it's true!

NaturallySpeaking can do great things soon after you open the box, but too often its talents lie hidden. Recognizing speech is one of those human talents that is still very complex to a computer. Recognizing human speech is as much a miracle for a computer as computing the precise value of *pi* is for a human. (Computing the highly abstract value of pie, oddly enough, is much easier for a human.)

NaturallySpeaking borders on being miraculous, but to get really practical results, you have to meet this miracle halfway. Perhaps you have been wondering what all the excitement is about, either because you are thinking of getting NaturallySpeaking or because, so far, NaturallySpeaking hasn't excited you. *Dragon NaturallySpeaking For Dummies* is here to help.

About This Book

This book reveals the stuff you need to know to turn NaturallySpeaking from a technical miracle into a working tool. Following are a dozen things this book can help you do:

- ✔ Discover what NaturallySpeaking can and can't do.
- ✔ Train NaturallySpeaking to recognize your voice.
- ✔ Run NaturallySpeaking in the best way for your application.

- Use voice commands to get the formatting you want.

- Correct NaturallySpeaking when it makes a mistake.

- Add to or customize NaturallySpeaking's vocabulary.

- Speak better for better recognition.

- Control your desktop by voice.

- Transcribe speech from a portable recorder.

- Use playback and text-to-speech tools to help proofread.

- Choose hardware for better performance.

- Create your own dictation shortcuts and custom commands.

Conventions Used in This Book

Ever try to describe something basically simple and discover that the description made it ridiculously complex instead? Well, it's that way with describing NaturallySpeaking commands, so I try to simplify the job by using some typographic conventions. You won't really need to think about the typography much (let alone go to any conventions about it), but in case you're wondering about it, here's what it means:

- I put NaturallySpeaking commands (the ones you speak, not the menu choices) in bold and initial capitals, enclosed in quotation marks, such as "**Scratch That.**"

- When part of a NaturallySpeaking command varies according to what you are trying to do, I indicate the variable part in angle brackets (*<and>*), as in: "**Format That *<font>*.**" The term *<font>* here represents one of the many fonts allowed by that command, like Arial.

- When part of a NaturallySpeaking command is text from an example I discuss, I put that part in italics. For example, **Select *we put that part*** is a command telling NaturallySpeaking to select the text "we put that part."

- Where I want you to pause slightly in a command, I put a comma. For instance, if I tell you to say, "**Caps On, *The Sands of Barcelona,* Caps Off,**" I want you to pause briefly where those commas appear.

Foolish Assumptions

I think you are a person of elevated literary taste and acute discernment, who aspires to converse with computers. Beyond that, I assume certain things about you, my esteemed reader.

I assume you are a new user of NaturallySpeaking, using (or intending to use) version 11.0 of the Home or Premium edition. I also assume you are passably familiar with Microsoft Windows.

I figure you are picking up this book for any of the following reasons:

- ✔ You have installed NaturallySpeaking and are baffled by it.
- ✔ You are impressed by NaturallySpeaking but wonder if you are getting the full benefit of it.
- ✔ You'd like NaturallySpeaking to work more accurately.
- ✔ You can't get all the NaturallySpeaking features to work.
- ✔ NaturallySpeaking works, but not consistently.
- ✔ You don't have NaturallySpeaking, and are wondering if you would like it.

How This Book Is Organized

This book is a *reference* book, which means that you don't have to read it in any particular order. Jump right in wherever something looks good, or find a particular subject in the table of contents (at the front of the book) or the index (at the back of the book).

But this book is *organized* so you can follow it from the first page to the last and learn how to use Dragon NaturallySpeaking from the basic starting point.

It's like two books in one, which makes it one great book.

Part I: Installing and Understanding NaturallySpeaking

If you haven't yet installed, trained, and launched NaturallySpeaking, this short part is the place to begin. This part is also the place to go if you have already launched your application but are a bit confused about the way it works.

Chapter 1 helps you know what to expect so that you can tell whether things are working properly or decide whether you have the NaturallySpeaking edition you need. Chapter 2 guides you through various wizards that attend to the mysteries of training your new NaturallySpeaking assistant.

Part II: Creating Documents and Spreadsheets

Part II is where you get down to the nitty-gritty of dictating, editing, and formatting your documents: what to say, how to say it, and how to correct NaturallySpeaking's errors. See how to start up NaturallySpeaking and use the tools and options available on the NaturallySpeaking menu. Learn how to use the basic word-processing features of the NaturallySpeaking DragonPad.

I also show you how you can use NaturallySpeaking's basic dictation, editing, and formatting features in virtually any application. Then I show you how specific applications enable you to do nearly anything you can do in the NaturallySpeaking DragonPad itself.

Discover how best to use NaturallySpeaking with a variety of applications. You can use Dragon's Natural Language Commands in Word or WordPerfect, and your voice commands can control some of those word processors' special features.

Part II also explains how to use some of the key audio features of NaturallySpeaking Premium: how to proofread by playing back — or reading, in a synthesized voice — your dictation and how to set up NaturallySpeaking to handle recorded speech. In this part, you also discover how to transcribe recorded speech.

Part III: Communicating Online

This is a fun part (perhaps just a bit more than the others). It covers the web and all the things you can do with NaturallySpeaking online. New gadgets are coming out every day. I take a look at some of the most popular ones that are speech enabled.

Part III is a veritable feast of new online connections. You can verbally click links in Internet Explorer, use Outlook to read and answer mail, and post on social networks. You can also fire up your favorite mobile device — iPhone, iPad, iPod touch, BlackBerry, or Android and dictate and send on the go and hands free.

Part IV: Controlling Windows

How important is it to be able to control your environment by voice? Imperative, I'd say. Learning how to navigate in Windows is critically important when you have important things to do. When you learn how to navigate in Windows with NaturallySpeaking, the learning carries over to any Windows application you use. This means that learning to use Word, Excel, Outlook, PowerPoint, and a host of other applications automatically also becomes easier.

Part IV shows you how to get around quickly and efficiently. You can open, resize, and close windows and dialog boxes. And what about launching programs and "mousing" around? It's all covered here.

Part V: Working Smarter

The Holy Grail for companies like Nuance Communications is to get their software to accurately recognize every word you say without becoming noticeably slow. In Part V, you embark on your own quest for better accuracy and speed. I play Professor Henry Higgins to your Liza and suggest ways to speak better. You discover how you can train NaturallySpeaking to adapt to your way of speaking and to recognize more words in your vocabulary. You also decide whether you need to beef up your PC hardware for better performance.

Besides dealing with accuracy, Part V tells you how to handle various changes: upgrading, moving NaturallySpeaking to another computer, and making changes to your voice or environment. It also suggests places to go for help or more information.

Part VI: The Part of Tens

Need a quick solution to a problem or a question? The Part of Tens solves the ten most common problems in several different subjects: dictation errors, command errors, and other common mistakes. While you're making errors, though, you might as well have some fun with NaturallySpeaking. I tell you how to make NaturallySpeaking the hit of your parties (if you have rather geeky parties) by having it perform stupid stunts and watching the results. And you'll find more chapters at `www.dummies.com/go/dragonnaturallyspeaking`.

Icons Used in This Book

Like a Dairy Queen ice-cream Blizzard, *For Dummies* books are packed full of cool, crunchy tidbits. Accordingly, you'll find the text studded with attractive two-color icons, pointing out tips, warnings, reminders, and the like. (Yes, of course, black and white are colors!) Here are the icons you'll find:

Tips are insights and shortcuts that make your life easier, your wit sharper, and your hair more silky and manageable.

You don't have to read paragraphs marked with Technical Stuff, but you'll be a finer, more moral person if you do.

I used to know what this icon was for, but I forget. Oh! It notes a topic that I mention and that you should remember.

This icon marks things that are likely to blow up in your face or at least may cause problems.

Where to Go from Here

The next step depends on what you need right now. If you're stuck on a particular aspect of Dragon NaturallySpeaking right now, look it up in the index and turn straight to that topic. If you are a newbie, why not just turn this page?

Let's get started!

Part I
Installing and Understanding NaturallySpeaking

The 5th Wave   By Rich Tennant

"It's for my wife. Do you have something like Dragon NaturallyInterrupting?"

In this part . . .

If you have a brand-new NaturallySpeaking assistant, this is the place to get your relationship off on the right foot. In this part, we'll tell you what to expect (and not to expect) from your new pal, how to install it snugly into your PC and get it accustomed to your voice, and then how to launch it.

Chapter 1 tells you what you can expect and what your particular member of the Dragon NaturallySpeaking family can do. How accurate should it be? Can it record meetings? Other people? Does it let you control your desktop by voice? Can it slice, dice, and make julienne fries? Chapter 2 tells you how to get it installed and properly trained. Naturally enough, it comes with wizards. Chapter 2 explains how to deal with those. Chapter 3 tells you how to launch NaturallySpeaking and what and where the controls are.

If your new assistant is already trained and ready to go, move on to Part II and start dictating. Otherwise, turn to Chapter 1 and discover what magic is in store for you.

Chapter 1

Knowing What to Expect

*V*oice recognition is used in places like cars, hospitals, and legal offices. Yet, some people are still skeptical about software that enables you to dictate to your computer and get a transcription of what you said. People think it's very cool, but they secretly wonder if it really works.

It works. (And it *is* really cool.) Right out of the box, today's Dragon NaturallySpeaking reports 99 percent accuracy. I bet that's a score you'd like for your own personal output. Well then, read this book and dive right in. You'll be rewarded with higher productivity and hands-free computing.

Sections of this book were written by dictating them into Dragon NaturallySpeaking. It was a lot of fun, and I predict that you will also find NaturallySpeaking to be useful and fun — if you approach it with the appropriate expectations.

Clarifying What NaturallySpeaking Can Do for You

Something about dictating to a computer awakens all kinds of unrealistic expectations in people. If you expect it to serve you breakfast in bed, you're out of luck. I didn't write this book by saying "Computer, write a book about NaturallySpeaking." I had to dictate it word for word, just as I would have had to type it word for word if I didn't have NaturallySpeaking.

So what are realistic expectations? Think of NaturallySpeaking the way that you think about your keyboard and mouse. It's an input device for your computer, not a brain transplant. It doesn't add any new capabilities to your computer beyond deciphering your spoken words into text or ordinary PC commands. If you say, "Go make me a sandwich," NaturallySpeaking will dutifully type "go make me a sandwich" into whatever word-processing application that happens to be open.

Just because your computer can understand what you say, don't expect it to understand what you mean. It's still just a computer, you know.

Here are five specific things you *can* expect to do with NaturallySpeaking, and where to look for more details about how to do them:

- **Browse the web.** If you use Internet Explorer and NaturallySpeaking together, you can cruise around the web without ever touching your keyboard or mouse. Pick a website from your Favorites menu, follow a link from one web page to another, or dictate a URL (web address) into IE's Address box, leaving your hands in your lap the whole time. See Chapter 13 for details.

- **Control your applications.** If you see the name on a menu, you can say it and watch it happen — not just in NaturallySpeaking but in your other applications as well. If your e-mail program has a Check Mail command on its menu, then you can check your e-mail by saying a few words. Anything that your spreadsheet has on a menu becomes a voice command you can use. Ditto for hotkeys: If pressing some combination of keys causes an application to do something you want, just tell NaturallySpeaking to press those keys. See Part II.

- **Control your desktop.** Applications will start running just because you tell them to. Use your voice to open and close windows, switch from one open window to another, and drag and drop stuff from here to there. See Chapter 16.

- **Dictate into a digital recorder and let NaturallySpeaking transcribe it later.** You need NaturallySpeaking and a digital (or very good analog) recorder. See Chapter 11.

- **Write documents.** NaturallySpeaking is darn good at helping you write documents. You talk, it types. If you don't like what you said (or what NaturallySpeaking typed), tell NaturallySpeaking to go back and change it. You can give vocal instructions to make elements bold, italic, large, small, or set in a particular font. Chapters 4, 5, and 6 explain what you need to know to write documents in the NaturallySpeaking DragonPad itself. If you want to dictate into Microsoft Word or Corel WordPerfect, see Chapter 9. For all other applications, see Chapter 8.

Now, I happen to think that's plenty to get excited about. I can make my own sandwiches, thank you.

Figuring Out What NaturallySpeaking Can't Do

Even with NaturallySpeaking, your computer's capability to understand English is more limited than what you can reasonably expect from a human. People use a very wide sense of context to figure out what other people are saying. We know, for instance, what the teen behind the counter at Burger King means when he asks, "Wonfryzat?" (That's fast-food-employed teen-speak for "Do you want fries with that?") We'd be completely confused if that same teenager walked up to us at a public library and asked, "Wonfryzat?"

NaturallySpeaking figures things out from context, too, but only from the *verbal* context (and a fairly small verbal context at that). It knows that "two apples" and "too far" make more sense than "too apples" and "two far." But two- to three-word context seems to be about the extent of the software's powers. (I can't say exactly how far it looks for context, because Nuance, the manufacturer, is understandably pretty hush-hush about the inner workings of NaturallySpeaking.) It doesn't understand the content of your document, so it can't know that words like "Labradoodles" and "Morkies" are going to show up just because you're talking about dogs.

Consequently, you can't expect NaturallySpeaking to understand every form of speech that humans understand. In order to work well, it needs advantages like these:

- ✔ **Familiarity.** Each person who dictates to NaturallySpeaking has to train it individually so that NaturallySpeaking can build an individualized user model. (See Chapter 2.) So NaturallySpeaking can't transcribe the voice mail that other people leave for you.

- ✔ **Who is talking?** Each time before you start dictating, you need to iden- tify yourself so that NaturallySpeaking can load the right user model.

- ✔ **One user at a time.** NaturallySpeaking only loads one user model at a time, so it can't transcribe a meeting during which several people talk, even if it has user models for all of them.

- ✔ **Constant volume.** You can't plunk a microphone down in the middle of the room and then pace around while you dictate.

    Wear a good microphone (like the one that comes with NaturallySpeaking) and position it the same way every time you use it.

    Don't mumble or let your voice trail off.

    It does a pretty good job with accents, though, as long as you're consistent.

- ✔ **Reasonable background noise.** Humans may be able to understand you when your favorite drummer is blasting away on your speakers or the blow dryer is on. They may be reading your lips at least part of the time, and they can guess that you are probably saying, "Turn that thing down!" NaturallySpeaking lacks in the lip-reading department, as well as in the capability to make obvious situational deductions.

- ✔ **Reasonable enunciation.** You don't have to start practicing "Moses supposes his toeses are roses," but you do need to realize that NaturallySpeaking can't transcribe sounds that you don't make. See Chapter 17 for an in-depth discussion of this issue.

- ✔ **Standard turn-of-the-millennium English prose.** If you want to be the next James Joyce, stick to typing. You can have some fun by trying to transcribe Shakespeare or things written in other languages, but it isn't going to work very well (unless you do some really extensive training). On the other hand, NaturallySpeaking is just the thing for writing books, blog posts, reports, short stories, and letters to Mom.

Doing the Fun Stuff

NaturallySpeaking comes out of the box not knowing anything about you. It has to work as well for a baritone with a Scottish accent as for a mezzo-soprano with a slight lisp. It needs time to figure out how you talk.

How long? If everything goes smoothly, as it probably will if you have compatible hardware and follow the instructions in Chapter 2, something like 40 minutes will probably pass between the time you take the shrink-wrap off the box and the time you dictate your first word. Allocate 10 minutes or so of that time to read to your computer so it can analyze your voice and pronunciation. Nuance has shortened this training and has succeeded admirably!

Training continues for as long as you keep using NaturallySpeaking. It makes mistakes, you correct them, and it learns. That's the process. It gets better and better the more frequently you use it.

The exact error rate depends on many factors: how fast your computer is, how much memory it has, how good your microphone is, how quiet the environment is, how well you speak, what sound card your computer has, and so on.

NaturallySpeaking is 99 percent accurate out of the box and it gets better as long as you keep correcting it. Don't be lazy.

Selecting the Right NaturallySpeaking Product

NaturallySpeaking is not a single product; it's a family of products. And like most families, some members are richer than others. Depending on the features you want, you can pay a hefty price for software. You get what you pay for.

In spite of their socioeconomic differences, this family gets along pretty well. The products are all based on the same underlying voice recognition system, so they create the same kinds of user files. This fact has two consequences for you as a user:

- ✔ The products are all about equally accurate at transcribing your speech.
- ✔ It's easy to upgrade to a better version.

  You can start out with the inexpensive Home edition, test out whether you like this whole idea of dictation, and then move up to a full-featured version without having to go through training all over again.

Which edition is best for you depends on why you're interested in NaturallySpeaking in the first place. Are you a poor typist who wants to be able to create documents more quickly? A good typist who is starting to worry about carpal tunnel syndrome? A person who can't use a mouse or keyboard at all? A busy executive who wants to dictate into a recorder rather than sit in front of a monitor? Is price an important factor to you? Do you need NaturallySpeaking to recognize a large, specialized vocabulary? Do you want to create macros that enable you to dictate directly into your company's special forms?

The more features you want, the more you should expect to pay.

Expanding the use of speech recognition

Speech recognition software is entrenched in many private sector industries. Dragon NaturallySpeaking serves several industries, including the following:

- ✔ **Financial:** NaturallySpeaking helps financial people manage their paperwork and meet compliance requirements.
- ✔ **Legal/Medical:** Transcription and documentation play a major role in keeping things moving in the legal and medical fields. NaturallySpeaking significantly cuts the time needed to produce various documents.
- ✔ **Insurance:** This one is self-explanatory. Anything that cuts down on paperwork in the insurance industry is clearly a public service.

The public sector uses Dragon NaturallySpeaking as follows:

✔ **Education:** It is well documented that NaturallySpeaking can help level the playing field for students who face learning challenges. Teachers are able to provide better learning experiences to all their students.

✔ **Accessibility:** NaturallySpeaking makes a major contribution to people who are challenged by the use of a keyboard or mouse. The software provides access to the Web and opens up the world to people who might otherwise be denied digital access.

✔ **Public Safety:** Dragon's capability to save time on paperwork frees up law enforcement professionals to do the work that keeps us safe.

The latest generation of the NaturallySpeaking family

The current generation of NaturallySpeaking, version 11.0, was released in the second half of 2010. In addition to the usual bug fixes and incremental improvements that you expect in a new version of an application, NaturallySpeaking 11.0 brings the following five major enhancements:

✔ **Improved accuracy:** Every facet of NaturallySpeaking works faster by cutting down on the time required for the program to recognize dictation and produce output.

✔ **New interface:** The creation of the Sidebar, the use of an improved "Results" display, and a context-sensitive Help system make it easier for the user to find and use the right commands.

✔ **Faster response time:** Response to commands is faster and makes dictating less about stopping and starting. You can pay attention to longer phrases with pauses in between.

✔ **Shortcuts for common commands:** Nuance has anticipated many of the common commands that you want to use and has created shortcuts for them.

✔ **Shorter training time:** Initial training time is approximately 4 minutes. This is a drastic reduction in the time you need to get up and running.

Here is the current lineup of some of the NaturallySpeaking products, with a few comments about their features:

✔ **NaturallySpeaking Home:** This entry-level edition is perfect for people who hate to type. It is as accurate as the more expensive editions, enables control of the Windows desktop, includes a Dictation Box for dictating into other applications, and enables you to browse the web by voice. The Home version includes Full Text Control for a small number of applications and some Natural Language Commands for Word and WordPerfect. It doesn't support Excel and playback of your own voice for corrections. The Home edition is perfect if you're planning to dictate only the first draft of documents, which you then polish using a mouse and keyboard. This version probably isn't the best choice for people with physical disabilities.

✔ **NaturallySpeaking Premium:** Premium includes all the Home edition's features, plus a few extras. It enables you to select a piece of your document and play back your own dictation, a great feature when you are trying to correct a mistake that either you or NaturallySpeaking made 20 minutes ago. It also opens the possibility of dictating into a recorder and letting NaturallySpeaking transcribe it later. See Chapter 11.

✔ **NaturallySpeaking Professional:** This edition is the one to get if you're personally committed to using voice recognition for everything or if you're a manager planning to convert your entire office to NaturallySpeaking. The Professional edition has everything Nuance could think of to make your experience easier, including two great features: You can build your own specialized vocabularies and create your own voice command macros. Or, more precisely, the office geek can construct specialized vocabularies and commands tailored to match the way his office works, and then everyone else in the office can use them too.

✔ **NaturallySpeaking Legal and NaturallySpeaking Medical:** At heart, these two editions begin with the Professional edition, but Nuance has done some of the work that I describe about the office geek in the preceding bullet:

  • The Medical edition comes out of the box knowing the names of obscure diseases, body parts, and pharmaceuticals.

  • The Legal edition knows *amicus curiae, habeas corpus,* and a bunch of other Latin legal terminology that would make the Professional edition throw up its proverbial hands.

✔ **Dragon NaturallySpeaking for the Mac:** I cover the NaturallySpeaking Windows products in this book, but Nuance also has a collection of products for the Mac, including Dragon Dictate, MacSpeech Scribe, MacSpeech Dictate Legal, and MacSpeech Dictate Medical. If you know some Mac users, tell them to check these out. (For use with mobile devices, including the iPhone, iPod, or iPad, see Chapter 15.)

In addition to these off-the-shelf products, you can also have NaturallySpeaking installed on your office network. This corporate option goes beyond the scope of what I cover in this book. If you're interested in this option, contact Nuance directly. Training programs for your staff are also available.

Training NaturallySpeaking

I admit it: Training a new piece of software is a strange idea. Other computer programs don't need to be trained. When you get a new word processor, it doesn't have to watch you type for awhile before it catches on. New spreadsheets do their adding and subtracting perfectly well straight out of the box, without any instruction from you. And personally, I'm happier knowing that Quicken *didn't* learn how to balance a checkbook by watching me do it.

So why does NaturallySpeaking need to be trained before it understands your speech? The simple answer is that speech recognition is probably one of the hardest things your computer does. Humans may not think speech recognition is hard, but that's because they are good at it. Michael Jordan probably has trouble understanding why the rest of us think it's so hard to dunk a basketball.

This section explains why deciphering speech is hard for computers and how the training program helps NaturallySpeaking overcome these difficulties. I hope that understanding these issues will give you confidence during the training process (described in Chapter 2) that it really works.

What's so hard about recognizing speech, anyway?

If 3-year-olds can recognize and understand speech (other than the phrase "go to bed"), why is it so hard for computers? Aren't computers supposed to be smart?

Well, yes and no. Computers are very smart when it comes to brain-straining things like playing chess and filling out tax returns, so you may think they'd be whizzes at "simple" activities like recognizing faces or understanding speech. But after about 50 years of trying to make computers do these simple things, programmers have come to the conclusion that a skill isn't simple just because humans master it easily. In fact, our brains and eyes and ears are chock-full of sophisticated sensing and processing equipment that still runs rings around anything we can design in silicon and metal.

We humans think it's simple to understand speech because all the really hard work is done before we become conscious of it. To us, it seems as if English words just pop into our heads as soon as people open their mouths. The unconscious (or preconscious) nature of the process makes it doubly hard for computer programmers to mimic. If we don't know exactly what we're doing or how we do it, how can we tell computers how to do it?

To get an idea of why computers have such trouble with speech, think about something they're very good at recognizing and understanding: touch-tone phone numbers. Those blips and bloops on the phone lines are much more meaningful to computers than they are to people. Several important features make the phone tones an easy language for computers, as I discuss in the following list. English, on the other hand, is completely different.

- ✔ **The touch-tone "vocabulary" has only 12 "words" in it.** After you know the tones for the ten digits plus * and #, you're in. English, on the other hand, has hundreds of thousands of words.

- ✔ **None of the words sound the same.** On the touch-tone phone, the "1" tone is distinctly different from the "7" tone. But English has homonyms, such as *new* and *gnu,* and near homonyms, like *merrier* and *marry her.* Sometimes entire sentences sound alike: "The sons raise meat" and "The sun's rays meet," for example.

- ✔ **All "speakers" of the language say the words the same way.** Push the 5 button on any phone, and you get exactly the same tone. But an elderly man and a 10-year-old girl use very different tones when they speak; and people from Great Britain, Canada, and the United States pronounce the same English words in very different ways.

- ✔ **Context is meaningless.** To the phone, a 1 is a 1 is a 1. How you interpret the tone doesn't depend on the preceding number or the next number. But in written English, context is everything. It makes sense to "go to New York." But it makes much less sense to "go two New York" or "go too New York."

What's a computer to do?

In order to work effectively for you, a speech-recognition program like NaturallySpeaking needs to combine four vastly different areas of knowledge. It needs to know a lot about speaking in general, about the spoken English language in general, about the way your voice sounds, and about your word-choice habits.

How NaturallySpeaking knows about speech and English in general

Dragon NaturallySpeaking gets its general knowledge from the folks at Nuance, some of whom have spent most of their adult lives analyzing how English is spoken. NaturallySpeaking has been programmed to know in general what human voices sound like, how to model the characteristics of a given voice, the basic sounds that make up the English language, and the range of ways that different voices make those sounds. It has also been given a basic English vocabulary and some overall statistics about which words are likely to follow which other words. (For example, the word *medical* is more likely to be followed by *miracle* than by *marigold.*)

How NaturallySpeaking learns about your voice

NaturallySpeaking learns about your voice by listening to you. During the training process, you read out loud some text selections that NaturallySpeaking has stored in its memory. Because it already knows the text that you're reading, NaturallySpeaking uses this time to model your voice and learn how you pronounce words.

NaturallySpeaking goes on learning about your voice every time you use it. When you correct a word or phrase that NaturallySpeaking has guessed wrong, NaturallySpeaking adjusts its settings to make the mistake less likely in the future.

To help NaturallySpeaking learn better, correct it whenever it's wrong. At times, it may seem simpler just to select the incorrect text, delete it, and start over. But NaturallySpeaking doesn't learn when you do this. It thinks that you have merely changed your mind, not that its interpretation was incorrect.

How NaturallySpeaking learns your word-choice habits

Initially, NaturallySpeaking learns how you choose words from the Vocabulary Builder phase of training. It may seem as if NaturallySpeaking is just learning how you say some unusual words. But, in fact, Vocabulary Builder is worthwhile even if no new words are found, because NaturallySpeaking analyzes how frequently you use common words and which words are likely to be used in combination.

NaturallySpeaking comes out of the box knowing general facts about the frequency of English words, but Vocabulary Builder helps sharpen those models for your particular vocabulary.

For example, if you want to use NaturallySpeaking to write letters to your mother and you let it study your previous letters to Mom, then NaturallySpeaking will learn that the names of your other family members appear much more frequently than they do in general English text. It is then much less likely to misinterpret your brother Johan's name as *John* or *yawn*.

Onward to general training!

By enabling you to install NaturallySpeaking, your computer has taken on one of the hardest tasks a PC ever faces. It needs your help. If you endure training with patience and persistence, and if you gently but firmly correct your NaturallySpeaking assistant whenever it makes a mistake, you'll be rewarded with a computer that takes your verbal orders and transcribes your dictation without complaint (and even without a coffee break, unless you need one).

But I read in a magazine. . . .

Quite a few magazine and newspaper articles have been written about voice recognition in general, and Dragon NaturallySpeaking in particular. Almost all of them contain an example that's something like this: A guy says into a microphone, **"Send e-mail to Bob about Friday's meeting. Period. Bob, comma, glad you're going to be there. Period."**

As if by magic, an e-mail application opens, a message window appears, Bob's e-mail address is pulled out of an address book somewhere, "Friday's meeting" is entered on the subject line, and the following text is entered into the message body: **"Bob, glad you're going to be there."**

The example is completely legitimate, as you can see in Chapter 12. But you need to keep something in mind: If you say, **"Do the numbers on February's revenue receipts,"** your spreadsheet just sits there.

Like any good magician's trick, more appears to be happening than actually happens. The computer has not suddenly been granted intelligence that rivals that of a human. The Nuance programmers have created a handful of scripts for doing everyday tasks, like generating e-mail messages and entering new events into a calendar program. They've made the commands sound like the instructions you would give a personal assistant, and they've set things up so that a lot of similar-sounding commands produce the same result. But if you say, **"Zip a message off to Bob,"** nothing happens.

Impressive? Yes. Magic? Not quite. It's still just a computer. To learn about the terminology related to this almost magic, see the glossary at the end of this book.

Chapter 2

Installing Dragon and Basic Training

*B*y now, you have chosen the version of Dragon NaturallySpeaking that is best for you, you have concluded that your hardware configuration is appropriate, and you are sitting in front of your computer ready to get started. It's exciting to anticipate using a tool that can make you more productive every day!

But, before you can start saving all that time, you need to install the program, create a User Profile, and train the software. Installing NaturallySpeaking is easy. In most cases, you just put the DVD into your DVD-ROM drive and follow the directions on the screen. Setting up your profile is really quick, too. You will be asked several questions about whether you have an accent or what age range you are in, but the good news is that they're all questions you know the answers to.

The training process is also quick and straightforward. You have to read aloud some text and a choice of some well-known material and you're done. After that, the program will work on its own to improve accuracy and you can help it along. I cover that in later chapters. In the late 1990s, training NaturallySpeaking was a long, boring process. But fear not! Those days are over. By the end of this chapter, you will be ready to start dictating your project plan for that next great startup!

Installing Dragon NaturallySpeaking on Your Computer

Whether you're installing NaturallySpeaking for the first time or installing over a previous version, the process is easy. If you have User Profiles from NaturallySpeaking version 9 or 10, the Upgrade Wizard finds those User Profiles and sets them up in version 11. Otherwise you are guided through the creation of a new User Profile. Follow these steps:

1. **Find the envelope that contains the installation DVD.**

   The DVD in the white envelope has a label with a serial number on it. The serial number will enable you to activate the program so keep it handy. You'll see duplicates of the number in a peel-off label format for your convenience.

2. **Paste the duplicate serial numbers in places that you can easily access.**

   For safekeeping, peel two of them off (leaving one on the envelope) and put them on your software receipt, in the front of this book, or in a file folder where you'll be able to find them again.

   Now is a good time to plug in the microphone. Microphones other than those with a USB (including the headset microphones that come with NaturallySpeaking editions) plug into your computer's sound card. If you have a desktop computer, turn the computer so that you can see the back where all the cables are. If you're like me, this is a place you don't enjoy visiting.

   Because many people feel this way, Nuance has thoughtfully provided a user guide in the box for the headset included with the software. Look at the side of the sheet that has the operating guide. Your computer likely has color-coded jacks for the microphone and the headset along with small icons showing a mic and a headset. The headset has two color-coded plugs that correspond to the ones on the headset. Insert the plugs into the jacks as shown in the photo they supply.

3. **Put the installation DVD into your DVD drive.**

   The Windows AutoRun feature starts running the installation program automatically. See Figure 2-1.

   If you wait 30 seconds or so and nothing happens, don't worry. Nothing is wrong. Do this instead: Double-click the Computer icon on the Windows desktop. When the Computer window opens, find the icon corresponding to your DVD-ROM drive and double-click it. Find the setup. exe file in the DVD-ROM window and double-click it. Now you are exactly where you would be if it had started automatically. It will take a minute to prepare the files.

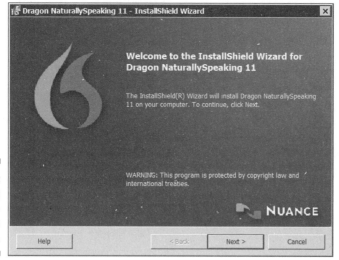

Figure 2-1:
Beginning
the instal-
lation
process.

4. **Click Next, as shown in Figure 2-1.**

   The InstallShield Wizard starts. The End User License Agreement appears.

5. **Click the radio button that says "I accept the terms in the license agreement" if you agree, and then click Next in the License Agreement window.**

   You are presented with the customer information window. See Figure 2-2.

6. **Type in your username and serial number where prompted and click Next.**

   The serial number will never have any letter *O*s in it. If you see something that looks like an *O,* it's always a zero.

7. **Choose which components of Dragon NaturallySpeaking to install.**

   The screen displays two radio button choices, Typical/Complete or Custom.

   Unless you are an advanced user, select Typical/Complete.

8. **Choose the Destination Directory.**

   The wizard suggests `C:/ProgramFiles/Nuance/NaturallySpeaking11`, which is the logical choice. If you agree, do nothing. If you'd like to choose a different folder, click the Browse button. A Choose Directory window appears. Select the folder you want. After you select the folder you want, click the OK button in the Choose Directory window.

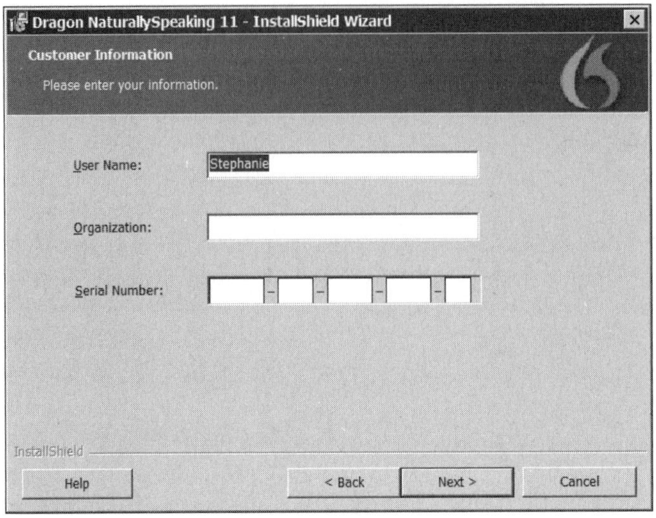

Figure 2-2:
Type in your
username
and serial
number.

9. **Click Next.**

   A Ready to Install the Program window appears; its purpose is to make sure you didn't make a mistake on the choices you made. You can click Back to return to the preceding screen and change the choices you made there.

10. **Click Install.**

    The files are copied to your hard drive, as shown in Figure 2-3. This may take several minutes. When all the files are copied, a screen appears and you are asked to choose a way to register the software.

11. **Click one of the three radio buttons to register.**

    You can choose Register Online, Print Registration Form, or Remind Me in 7 days. Make your choice based on your needs.

12. **Click OK.**

    A screen informs you that the wizard has completed installing your files. A check box that is automatically selected will look for program updates when the setup is complete.

13. **Uncheck the check box in Step 12 if you don't want to look for updates.**

    I recommend that you leave it checked so that you start your training with the most up-to-date files.

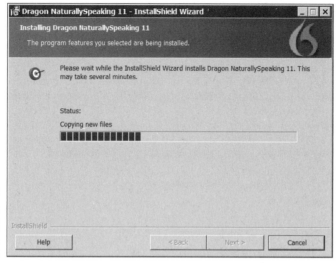

Figure 2-3:
Installing
files.

14. **Click Finish.**

After a pause, a screen pops up prompting you to activate the software, as show in Figure 2-4. You can either activate it now or within five more uses. Activation is required to use the program after the fifth use.

Figure 2-4:
Choose
when to
activate
your soft-
ware.

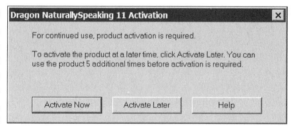

15. **Click the Activate Now button.**

You are presented with two options, "activate automatically," or "activate manually." If you click "activate automatically" you must be connected to the web. This is done to verify that you are using a valid serial number. No personal information is sent. If you don't choose to activate now, you will be prompted the next five times you use the software.

If you need a break, you can take it now before you start to give the program its first workout. Take a moment to congratulate yourself on taking the first step to greater productivity and hands-free dictation!

If you checked your system requirements before you installed the program it is unlikely that you will get an alert screen like the one shown in Figure 2-5. But if you do, this screen alerts you that you don't have enough computer resources (probably RAM) to run some of the external programs listed with Natural Language commands and that performance will be slower. If you see this screen, go to the Dragon Help menu in the upper-right corner of the interface menu bar and choose Performance Assistant to help you increase your speed and change options.

Figure 2-5:
Resources
are insuf-
ficient to
run all the
features
of Dragon
Naturally
Speaking.

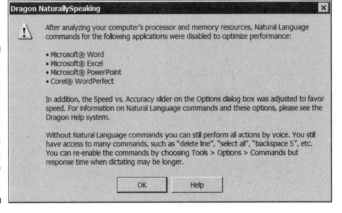

Creating a User Profile

If you wonder how NaturallySpeaking 11 maintains a 99 percent accuracy rate, the secret is in the User Profile. The profile learns your unique speech patterns and word choices. But, as with any good assistant, you need to provide NaturallySpeaking with clear, accurate instructions for it to follow. The User Profile Wizard captures how you speak, your style, and how you input your information.

The User Profile asks you to:

✔ Choose a username so that NaturallySpeaking can set up its filing system for the speech files you create during the training process.

✔ Choose your age group.

✔ Pick the region of the world in which you live.

✔ Determine whether you have one of Dragon's recognized accents.

✔ Tell it how you will talk to the computer (setting up your microphone).

This list may sound daunting, but the User Profile Wizard guides you through the process quickly. And you only have to set up this User Profile once for yourself. There are other User Profile options, including adding a dictation source to an existing profile. I tackle those later.

Running the New User Wizard

To get yourself properly introduced to your new software, you use a User Profile Wizard. You can start the wizard in one of two ways:

- ✔ Automatically, the first time you run NaturallySpeaking after installation, by clicking the Dragon icon on your desktop

- ✔ By choosing Start⇨All Programs–>Dragon NaturallySpeaking 11.0 from the Windows Start menu

You can also set up a new User Profile manually by going to the DragonBar and choosing Profile⇨New User Profile and then clicking the new button in the "New User Profile" window. The wizard will open.

To start the process of choosing a username and testing and configuring your microphone, follow these steps:

1. **Click Next on the Creating a User Profile screen.**

   The Create User screen appears. The wizard wants to know the following information:

   • **Your User Profile name:** This name will appear on future lists and menus so that you can tell NaturallySpeaking which user you are. So pick a name you will recognize as your own. Type it into the text box in the center of the screen and click Next.

   Your username is case sensitive. Be aware of that when you make a choice. If you type your name as **Tom** with a capital T, you won't be able to use **tom** later.

   • **Your age group:** The wizard is not just being nosy. Age plays a part in how your voice sounds. No one is looking. Make your choice from the drop-down list, as shown in Figure 2-6. Click Next.

   • **Identification of the words you say:** It's important for NaturallySpeaking to prepare files that are specific to your region of the world. Again, choose from the drop-down list. Click Next.

   • **The way you pronounce your words:** I'm sure we all agree that it's the other person who has an accent. But there really are identifiable accents depending on where in the world you first learned to

speak (see Figure 2-7). It's important for NaturallySpeaking to prepare files that are specific to your region of the world. Choose an
accent from the drop-down list and click Next.

- **How you talk to your computer:** You need to identify whether
  you're going to speak directly into a microphone (and what kind)
  or use a recorder. As shown in Figure 2-8, you have a choice of
  Mic-In Jack, USB, Bluetooth, or Line-In Jack. If you want to use the
  headset that came with NaturallySpeaking, then choose Mic-In
  Jack. For now, to make it easy, unless you are sure about your
  recorder, just choose your microphone.

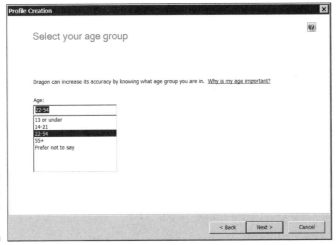

Figure 2-6:
Choose your
age group.

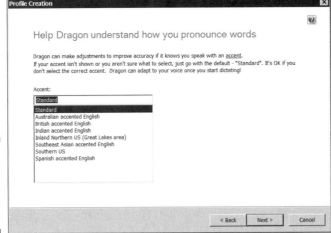

Figure 2-7:
Choose
how you
pronounce
your words.

Figure 2-8:
Choose
how you
talk to your
computer.

2. **Click Next. A screen with all your choices appears. If you agree with them, click the Create button.**

   NaturallySpeaking will create your profile. You will see the progress on the screen, and then your User Profile will be created.

3. **You are automatically taken to the next screen (see Figure 2-9), which will help you properly position your microphone.**

   This is an instructional screen that requires no information from you. It just gives you advice on how to position your microphone, and it shows a picture illustrating the approved technique.

   The main idea is that the microphone needs to be near your mouth, but not in front of it. (In front *seems* natural, but you get interference from your breathing on the microphone.) It should be far enough to the side that you don't bump it with your mouth when you talk. You may need to twist the arm a bit to get the microphone positioned just right.

   Put the distance of two fingers between your mouth and the microphone as the perfect amount. Also, make sure the word *talk* under the boom cushion is pointing toward your mouth; otherwise, you will not be heard.

4. **When your microphone is properly positioned, click Next.**

   It's time to adjust your volume with the Adjust Your Volume screen.

5. **Click the Start Volume Check button and read the text aloud at the volume you plan to use when you dictate.**

   Stop talking when you hear the beep. The important thing is to keep talking until the wizard is done adjusting the volume.

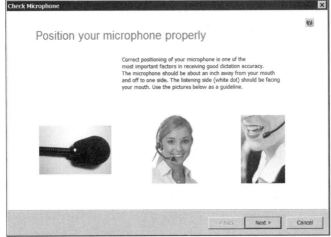

Position your microphone properly

Correct positioning of your microphone is one of the
most important factors in receiving good dictation accuracy.
The microphone should be about an inch away from your mouth
and off to one side. The listening side (white dot) should be facing
your mouth. Use the pictures below as a guideline.

< Back   Next >   Cancel

Figure 2-9:
How to posi-
tion your
microphone.

6. **Click Next to move on to the Test the Quality of Your Sound System screen.**

   This screen is another where you talk to the computer while it analyzes. Earlier, it was only listening to the volume. Now it is analyzing your voice.

7. **When you're ready, click the Start Quality Check button and start talking.**

   Read the text provided on the screen. You should get a Check Microphone: Passed alert, as shown in Figure 2-10. If the test fails, try repositioning your microphone and clicking Start Quality Check to run the test again. You can run it as many times as necessary.

   If you continue to fail this test, you may have a broken headset or the sound card on your computer may not be sufficient. To fix this issue, get a USB adapter for your headset or a new USB headset. The USB adapters or headsets have their own sound card that bypasses the one not working in your computer.

8. **When you're done with the quality check, click Next.**

   You will be presented with the Read Text Aloud message to train Dragon. If you want to stop at this point, click Cancel and exit NaturallySpeaking.

   NaturallySpeaking will remember that you made it through Audio Setup and will start you off reading training text.

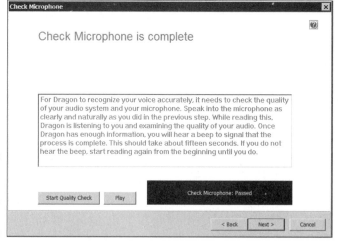

Figure 2-10:
Completed
check of
microphone.

Training Dragon to Recognize Your Voice, Vocabulary, and Writing Style

After NaturallySpeaking has tested and adjusted your speakers and microphone, it's ready to listen to you speak. I'm happy to report that this training will take all of 4 minutes. Follow these steps:

1. **To start training, begin at the screen shown in Figure 2-11.**

   You are presented with three training options. Unless you have done this many times before and know what to choose, select Show Text with Prompting. If you have a speech challenge that must be noted by Dragon, choose Show Text without Prompting. If you have no time to train at this time, choose Skip Training. But you must come back to it later.

2. **Choose Show Text with Prompting and click Next.**

   At the Read Training Text screen, click Go and read aloud the sentences as prompted by the arrow. You will read several prompts and then move to general reading. The prompts are "Welcome to general training" and "Training is about to begin."

3. **You are asked to select some text to read, as shown in Figure 2-12.**

   You can choose the text that you find most interesting. But, because you aren't making a major time commitment, I recommend that you choose What to Expect from Speech Recognition. This gives you a head start on training.

Figure 2-11:
Screen
to start
reading
text aloud
to train
Dragon.

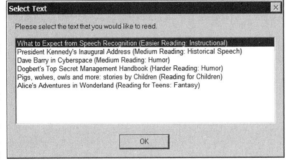

Figure 2-12:
Choose
a Text
selection
to train the
program.

4. **Click OK.**

   Read the text. When you hear a beep and see a screen that says
   Congratulations, You Have Finished Training, yell "YES!" and click the
   OK button.

   Actually, yelling "YES" is optional but quite enjoyable.

Dragon will take a few minutes to adapt your User Profile, so expect a pause
here.

Improving accuracy

When you finish basic training, Dragon recommends that you let it look at
your dictation, corrections, and other files to train itself and improve accuracy. This is a great way for the program to familiarize itself with your voice,

the words you choose, and the type of documents you generate. The more training you allow, the better your results. (You have the option to read the Dragon privacy statement, if that concerns you.)

After Dragon has adapted your User Profile, a screen pops up and asks you if you'd like to let the program scan your documents and e-mails so that it can find unfamiliar words and add them now. This is a one-time scan. Follow these steps:

1. **If you agree, click the Start button. If you choose not to do it now, deselect the document and e-mail check boxes and click Next.**

   The scan may be quick or take up to 30 minutes, depending on the amount of content you have on your hard drive.

2. **After the scan is complete, click Next.**

   You are taken to a screen that deals with improving accuracy. You are asked if you want to run those programs at a scheduled time.

3. **If you agree to run the programs at the scheduled times, then leave the check box that says Automatically Improve Accuracy checked and click Next.**

   If you want to change the default schedule that Dragon has chosen, click the Change Schedule button; otherwise, leave it at Monday at 2:00 AM for Acoustics and 3:00 AM every day for Language Modeling.

   Leave your computer on during the times you selected so Dragon can run the improve accuracy program.

4. **A final screen pops up asking if you want to help Dragon improve the software. Select your choice.**

5. **Click Next to go to the final training screen.**

   You'll be congratulated for completing all the steps required to becoming a more productive individual. Now that wasn't so bad, was it? On that screen, you will also see an Open the Dragon Tutorial button. If you click it, you are taken to the tutorial. (See the "Studying the Dragon Tutorial" section for details.) On that screen, you also have the option to learn about what's new in Dragon NaturallySpeaking 11.0 if you had a previous version.

6. **Click Finish.**

   You will see a message window telling you that the program is initializing and loading your profile. It's complete when the Tip of the Day window pops up.

Now you're ready to open an application and start dictating!

Studying the Dragon Tutorial

If you have the time, I recommend you take the tutorial. If not now, you can always access it later from the Help menu in the upper-right corner of the DragonBar. When you're learning, it's great to use as many different modes as possible: watching, hearing, and, in the case of this book, doing it step by step.

The tutorial is broken into four sections:

- **Getting started:** This section includes information about microphones and the DragonBar.

- **Dictating:** Here you find an overview of dictation and command prompts.

- **Correcting and editing:** This section contains editing topics like correcting and deleting.

- **Using applications:** This section provides information on web basics and desktop searches.

You've jumped over all the hurdles and completed the preliminary training. I'm sure you're already starting to feel confident that you and your new NaturallySpeaking assistant will be great friends. If you're ready, head to Chapter 3 and start mastering the controls.

Chapter 3

Launching and Controlling Dragon

. . . .

In This Chapter

▶ Launching NaturallySpeaking

▶ Choosing or switching users

▶ Using the NaturallySpeaking DragonPad

▶ Customizing options

▶ Understanding the tools and menus

. . . .

*O*kay, you're at the point where you are deciding whether to skip this chapter and jump into dictating or to read this chapter and feel more prepared. Why not take the time to learn how to take control?

In this chapter, I show you the different ways to launch and control NaturallySpeaking. I also tell you what tools you can use to get better performance and behavior, and where to find those tools. I refer you to other chapters in this book for the details. If NaturallySpeaking is already up and running and you simply can't wait any longer, go and dictate! (See Chapter 4.)

Launching NaturallySpeaking

To get started with NaturallySpeaking, launch the product in one of the following ways:

- Double-click the Dragon icon on your desktop.

- Go to the Start menu on the Windows taskbar:

  Choose Start➪Programs➪Dragon NaturallySpeaking 11.0.

- You can also use the QuickStart option in the taskbar tray icon. Right-click the microphone icon and you'll see all the same menu options you have in the DragonBar. (More on the DragonBar later in this chapter.)

By choosing one of these options, you launch the NaturallySpeaking DragonBar, and the Dragon Sidebar from which you can dictate documents and control how NaturallySpeaking works. You can customize this to suit your preferences.

Choosing or Switching Users

When you launch NaturallySpeaking, it may ask you to choose a *user*. If it doesn't ask, don't worry. You probably have only one user: you.

Remember that when you first set up NaturallySpeaking, you created and named a User Profile and then trained NaturallySpeaking on how that user (you) sounded. Now, when you launch NaturallySpeaking, you must choose that user so that NaturallySpeaking can recognize you.

After launching, NaturallySpeaking displays the Open User dialog box. Click the User Profile name you created when you set up NaturallySpeaking, and then click the Open button. You're ready to roll.

If other people use this same copy of NaturallySpeaking (or if you have multiple users for yourself), each person must have his or her own User Profile. If you need to add a user, go to the DragonBar and choose Profile⇨New User Profile. This launches the same New User Wizard you used to set up NaturallySpeaking for yourself. See Chapter 2 for details on that wizard. For more about multiple users and their vocabularies, see Chapter 20.

You can switch users without restarting NaturallySpeaking. Follow these steps:

1. **From the DragonBar, choose Profile⇨Open User Profile.**

   NaturallySpeaking may ask whether you want to save your speech files. Unless for some reason you don't want to save any corrections you have made to NaturallySpeaking's behavior, choose Yes. NaturallySpeaking then displays the Open User dialog box.

2. **Click the username from the User list, then click the Open button.**

If different people have been using NaturallySpeaking, the usernames are listed at the bottom of the Profile menu. Just click a username to choose it.

Meeting the Face of Your NaturallySpeaking Assistant

As anyone who has ever used software knows, its value is most often determined by the design of the user interface. If it's hard to find menus, options, and features, most people give up before they ever find out if the product actually works. If you want simple, think Google Search Box. It doesn't get any easier than that!

Happily, Dragon has given a lot of careful attention to its user interface over the years. With Version 11.0, they've hit it out of the park. They have a DragonBar and a Dragon Sidebar. Both are set by default to open when you launch NaturallySpeaking. You can customize them to suit your needs.

When you first launch NaturallySpeaking, you see the NaturallySpeaking DragonBar and the Dragon Sidebar, as shown in Figure 3-1.

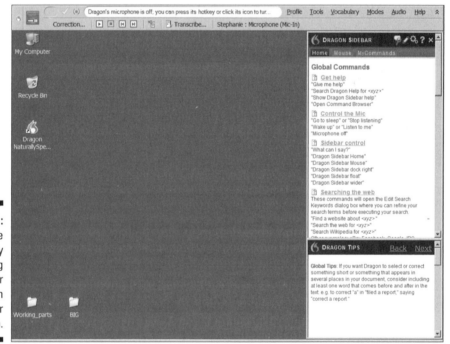

Figure 3-1: The Naturally Speaking DragonBar and Dragon Sidebar open.

✔ **What can you do with the NaturallySpeaking DragonBar?** You can use the menu bar to access various tools for customizing and improving the performance of your NaturallySpeaking assistant. I consider it the base of operations.

✔ **What is the Dragon Sidebar?** It's a nice, controlled environment where you can get to know all the major commands used with NaturallySpeaking. You don't have to wonder about commands. All you have to do is say, **"What can I say?"** The Sidebar pops up if it's closed. The Dragon Sidebar window is context sensitive so it displays commands about the application you are working on at the time. If you're in Microsoft Word, the Sidebar shows you the commands you need to use for Word. This makes learning application-specific commands much easier. It has Global Commands and a tab for Mouse Commands, plus one that allows you to create your own Custom Commands. Customize your commands to make dictating even easier. See Chapters 21 and 22 for more about the Dragon Sidebar.

A closer look at the DragonBar

The DragonBar is docked at the top of the screen. If you prefer, you can change the placement by clicking on the Dragon icon on the left, as shown in Figure 3-2. From here you can also invoke the QuickStart option by choosing Tray Icon Only. This minimizes the DragonBar and places a microphone icon in your system tray. Right-click the icon to see all the same menu options that were available to you when the DragonBar was visible.

To set the option to have QuickStart launch when Windows starts up, go to Tools⇨Options⇨Miscellaneous and select the check box for Launch Dragon in QuickStart mode when Windows starts.

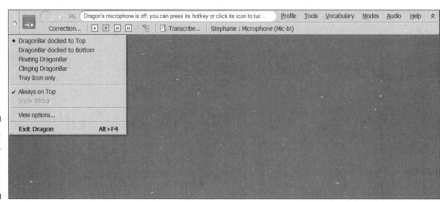

Figure 3-2:
Options for docking the DragonBar.

Here are the items on the toolbar, as shown in Figure 3-3.

Figure 3-3:
Under-
standing the
DragonBar.

Microphone On/Off   Vocabulary Menu

Check Mark Icon   Profile Menu   Audio Menu

Recognition Mode: Normal   Profile Tools Vocabulary Modes Audio Help

Volume Display   Tools Menu   Help Menu

Microphone/Status Window   Modes Menu

- ✔ **The Microphone On/Off Button:** This is the most critical one for obvious reasons. If your microphone is off, you'll be doing nothing more than talking to yourself. Your assistant will be waiting to hear from you. To dictate, click this button so the microphone icon is green and standing up, not red and lying down.

- ✔ **Volume Display:** The volume display is color coded for easy interpretation. It's yellow when it doesn't hear your voice, green when your voice is at a good level, and red if you're too loud. Adjust your voice accordingly.

- ✔ **The Check Mark Icon:** If the check mark is green, you know that all the Full Text Control functions of the application you are in are available and working.

- ✔ **Microphone/Status Window:** This window tells you if your microphone is off and will display tips or information about your dictation.

- ✔ **Profile Menu:** This is where you manage all the functions related to User Profiles, such as adding new users and backing up a User Profile.

- ✔ **Tools Menu:** The tools menu has several important items, including the DragonPad (discussed later in this chapter) and the Administrative settings.

- ✔ **Vocabulary Menu:** This menu contains the all-important vocabulary editor and is the place where you go when you want to have your NaturallySpeaking assistant learn more from your documents and e-mails.

- ✔ **Modes Menu:** You use several modes when dictating, including the dictation mode and the command mode. When you want to move from one to another, you make the switch here.

- ✔ **Audio Menu:** Here you will be able to launch accuracy training along with playback and read.

✔ **Help Menu:** The Help menu is chock-full of helpful resources and tips. It also includes a link to Nuance.com on the web, where you'll find more training.

✔ **Extras Arrow:** This arrow slides out the Extras toolbar extension. When it's extended, it looks like Figure 3-4.

✔ **Correction Button:** Click this button to make corrections and teach your assistant how you say things.

✔ **Transcribe:** Here's where you transcribe an audio file you dictated.

✔ **Start Playback and Stop Playback:** To make this function work, you select text to start or stop hearing your recording of what you dictated. Use the Begin Rewind or Begin Fast Forward button to move to where you want to be in the recording.

When you use these fast movement buttons, your voice will sound high and fast, and you may not be able to find your place. It may be easier to move where you want by either

- Saying **"Insert before xyz"**

- Clicking where you want to start playing from

✔ **Read:** This button enables your NaturallySpeaking assistant to read the text to you in the voice you have chosen.

Figure 3-4:
The
DragonBar
with the
Extras bar
extended.

Extra arrow extended

Choosing options

Now that you're in charge, you can order NaturallySpeaking to work your way. It's time to choose some options! From the DragonBar, choose Tools➪Options to open the Options dialog box. There are seven different category options. Take time to check them out and configure your assistant exactly the way you want it to behave.

Five options you may want to try right off the bat are as follows:

✔ Trade-off speed for accuracy: Miscellaneous tab

✔ Automatically back up User Profile every 5 times: Data tab

✔ Change microphone on/off, correction hotkeys: Hotkeys tab

✔ Double-click to correct in NaturallySpeaking window: Miscellaneous tab

✔ Playback on correction: Miscellaneous tab

Each tab has a Restore Defaults button. Hurray! Click it if you feel you changed something in error and want to put things back the way they were when you first launched NaturallySpeaking.

Following is a brief explanation about what's in each tab:

✔ **Correction tab:** This tab is useful to explore if you want to have things like Spell commands bring up a spelling window. Take your time and go back to these options after you have worked in your documents for a while. As you might guess, corrections are a fact of life. At least they can be dealt with your way.

✔ **Commands:** In this section you have a slider you can configure for the amount of time you want a pause before you dictate a command. It's set on the shorter end. Try this first before you extend it to see what's comfortable. Remember that you'll be dictating both speech and commands, and you want Dragon to understand how you like to do this.

✔ **View:** In this tab, you can set your placement of the DragonBar in addition to the way shown in Figure 3-2. You can also set the DragonBar to display the Extras menu. Additionally, you can set the Results box that was displayed in previous versions of NaturallySpeaking.

✔ **Playback/Text-to-speech:** Text-to-speech is a fun and functional feature of NaturallySpeaking. It uses a computer-synthesized voice to read text aloud. This will be the voice of your assistant, so choose accordingly (several male and female voice choices). It can sound a bit comical until you get used to it. Adjust the up- and down-arrow keys for volume and speed.

✔ **Miscellaneous tab:** This tab includes lots of useful stuff. Most important is the Speed versus Accuracy slider. Move this to the right for fewer recognition errors, or to the left for a quicker, if less accurate, job. The choice is yours.

✔ **Data tab:** Here you can change the amount of disk space reserved for playback. The default is 100 MB. I don't recommend using less than that, but if you need the space you can set it to use less. If you need more space for playback, you can set it to use more. You can also make a choice about whether to "Save recorded dictation with document." If you want to choose each time you dictate, select Ask Me. If you are using Dragon Professional, choose Never so your files don't become large and unwieldy.

✔ **Hotkeys tab:** You're either a devoted hotkey user or you aren't. There's no middle ground. If you like hotkeys, here's where you change them. Why change? You may have trouble pressing the key. Or you may need to use the key for something else (like using the numeric keypad + and – [minus] keys for calculations).

All the buttons on the Hotkeys tab work the same way: Click the button and a Set Hot Key dialog box pops up. When it does, don't try to type the names of the keys, just press them. For instance, press the Ctrl key, and {Ctrl} appears. Click OK when done.

On the Hotkeys tab you see the following options you may want to set:

- **Microphone On/Off:** If you choose a regular keyboard key (like a letter), you must use Ctrl or Alt with it. Otherwise, function keys, arrow keys, and other non-typewriter keys are all fair game either by themselves or in combination with Ctrl or Alt.

- **Correction dialog box:** This key pops up the Correction dialog box to correct the last phrase you spoke. The rules are the same as for Microphone On/Off.

- **Force Command Recognition:** Hold this key down to try to make NaturallySpeaking interpret what you say as a command, not text. It can be only Ctrl, Alt, Shift, or some combination of them.

- **Force Dictation Recognition:** This does the opposite of Force Command Recognition (makes what you say come out as text). Rules for keys are the same as Force Command Recognition.

Previous versions of NaturallySpeaking had a results box that showed what Dragon thought you said as you dictated. In version 11.0, this has been streamlined to a results display. As you dictate, you will notice a little Dragon icon displayed near your text. When you pause dictation, the words show up in your document. Nuance made this change after discovering that users were distracted by following the results box.

I think this is a great improvement and I recommend you do not switch back to the results box option if you are new to NaturallySpeaking. If, however, you are used to seeing the results box and want to display it, do the following:

1. **Go to Tools⇨Options⇨View tab.**

   Look at the section toward the bottom called Results Box.

2. **Click the pull-down arrow under Auto-hide Delay and select Always Hide or some amount of time it will display.**

   You can also choose whether you want it to stay in one place by selecting the anchor check box or whether you want to show preliminary results.

"Okay, so I have familiarized myself with the controls. Now how do I dictate?" you may be asking. Easy: Plug in your microphone, put it on, click the Microphone On/Off button (also duplicated on the Windows taskbar's system tray), and talk! But wait. . . .

Why Use the NaturallySpeaking DragonPad?

Before you start dictating, employing one of the myriad applications you can use with NaturallySpeaking, I want to introduce you to the DragonPad. To open it, go to the DragonBar and choose Tools➪DragonPad.

DragonPad is a simple word processor into which you can dictate or type a document. You then can print the document, copy it to another program window, or save the document as a file that other programs can read.

NaturallySpeaking works with really robust word processors like Word and WordPerfect, so you may be wondering why I mention this simple NaturallySpeaking function.

Here are some of the reasons you may want or need to dictate into the NaturallySpeaking window:

- You don't have Microsoft Word or Corel WordPerfect (or your version of those programs doesn't work with NaturallySpeaking).
- You just need the basic word-processing functions and you're in a hurry.
- Your PC is tight on memory. The NaturallySpeaking window uses less memory than some other applications.
- You see that the check mark on the DragonBar is gray which indicates that you need to open a Dictation Box.
- Your alternative is to use some application in which NaturallySpeaking offers only basic dictation and not other features.

Using the word-processor features of the NaturallySpeaking DragonPad

The NaturallySpeaking window's menu and toolbar may seem familiar to you. They are, with the addition of speech features, the same as the menu and toolbar in WordPad (the small-scale word processor that comes with Windows).

If you're already familiar with WordPad or similar word processors, you can skip this section and move right on to Chapter 4.

Choosing from the menu bar and toolbar

Even if you have never used DragonPad, if you have used any word processor, you'll find all the choices on the NaturallySpeaking menus and toolbars so familiar (except for the speech-related choices) that you'll hardly need this section. But just in case you aren't familiar, following are the details, as show in Figure 3-5.

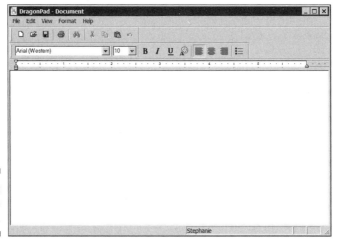

Figure 3-5:
The
DragonPad.

Use the NaturallySpeaking menu bar and toolbar buttons as you would in any Windows program. As with most Windows toolbars, pause your mouse cursor over a button to see the button's name or function.

Because you're running NaturallySpeaking, you can also choose items on the menu bar by using voice commands (as you can in nearly any other application, too). To choose from the menu bar, follow these steps:

1. **Use the verbal command,** "Click <menu text>**."**

   By **<menu text>**, I mean anything listed on the menu bar, such as File, Edit, or Format.

2. **Choose an item from the menu that appears by saying its name.**

   If you want consistency in your commands, you can instead say **"Click"** and then its name. For instance, you can say, **"Click File"** and then say, **"Save."**

Editing: Cut, paste, and the usual suspects

The Edit menu of NaturallySpeaking holds no surprises for anyone who has used a word processor in Windows. It has the usual suspects: Copy, Cut, and Paste using the Windows Clipboard, plus Undo, Select All, Find, and Find and Replace.

If you add the Format bar to the NaturallySpeaking window, you can alternatively use the familiar Cut, Copy, and Paste buttons on that bar. The button with the binoculars icon is a shortcut to the Find dialog box.

Choosing Edit⇨Select All (hotkey: Ctrl+A) is useful when you want to copy all the text in the window in preparation for pasting it into a different program. See Chapter 5 if you want details about copying text from NaturallySpeaking by using voice commands.

Formatting: Fonts, indentations, alignments, bullets, and tabs

The Format menu is where all the formatting stuff hangs out. Like the Edit menu, the Format menu is straightforward if you have used a word processor before. Here are the menu choices that change the format:

- ✔ **Font:** Choose Format⇨Font to get a Font dialog box to make your typeface, style, size, and color choices. Or add the Format bar to your screen by choosing View⇨Format Bar and choose your font on that toolbar. You can set font styles of bold, italic, or underline in alternative ways, just as in many other programs. Click the B, I, or U button on the Format bar; or press Ctrl+B, Ctrl+I, or Ctrl+U, respectively. You can choose font color from the Font dialog box or by clicking the Color button (the palette icon) on the Format bar.

- ✔ **Indents and alignments:** Choose Format⇨Paragraph to get a Paragraph dialog box. Type in an indentation for the left edge, right edge, or just the first line of the paragraph. (For hanging indents, set a left indent, like 0.5 inch, and then an equal but negative indent, like –0.5, for first line.) Click Alignment to choose from Left, Center, and Right alignment. Or if the Format bar is on your screen, click the Align Left, Center, or Align Right button.

- ✔ **Tabs:** To set tab stops (where the cursor stops when you press the Tab key), choose Format⇨Tabs. In the Tabs dialog box that appears, type a position (for example, 0.8 inch) in the Tab Stop Position box, and then click the Set button. Continue until you have set all your tabs, and then click OK. Click Clear All to restore tabs to the normal half-inch defaults.

> ✔ **Bullets:** NaturallySpeaking offers only one style of bullets. To turn bullets on, choose Format⇨Bullet Style (or click the Bullets button on the Format bar). Repeat that choice to turn bulleting off.

You can also set tab stops on the Ruler. (To put the Ruler bar on your screen, choose View⇨Ruler Bar.) Just click wherever you want a tab stop. A tiny L-shaped mark appears; you can drag it to any position you like. To remove it, drag it up or down off the ruler.

Saving and opening documents

You save a NaturallySpeaking document the old-school way: with a menu choice or toolbar button. As in any other application, you can use a voice command to make the menu choice, such as saying, **"Click File,"** and then saying **"Save"** or just saying **"Press Control S."**

The New, Save, Save As, and Open commands in the NaturallySpeaking File menu work as they do in nearly every other Windows application. So do the New, Open, and Save buttons on the toolbar (the first three). In case you forget (or nobody ever told you), here's what they do:

> ✔ To start a new, blank document, choose File⇨New (or click the New button).
>
> ✔ To open an existing document file, choose File⇨Open (or click the Open button).
>
> ✔ To save the document as a file, choose File⇨Save (or click the Save button).
>
> ✔ To save a new copy of the current document under a new name or in a new location, choose File⇨Save As.

NaturallySpeaking enables you to save your work in one of the following ways (file types), so you can pass your work along to others or save it for a fun day of editing later on:

> ✔ **Plain text (.TXT) files:** Text files do not preserve formatting, only the text plus line or paragraph breaks and tabs. (Tab stop *positions* are not saved, however.) Most everything can open a .TXT file.
>
> ✔ **Rich Text Format (.RTF) files:** Rich Text Format files are filled with all the formatting you can do in NaturallySpeaking. Nearly all major word processors can open these files, so your formatting survives the translation if you use .RTF.

When you choose File⇨Save the first time (or anytime you choose File⇨Save As), you have to choose which file type to use. A NaturallySpeaking dialog box appears, warning you that saving a text file will lose formatting.

It presents you with two buttons to choose between: Rich Text Document or Text Document. (If you press the Enter key at this point, NaturallySpeaking will choose RTF.)

Choose Rich Text Format if you want to import your document into a word processor or some other application that enables character formatting (such as bold) and paragraph formatting (such as center-aligned). Choose Text if the application (such as a simple e-mail program) does not support formatting. When you click the button for your choice, NaturallySpeaking presents the typical Save As dialog box you will recognize from other Windows applications. Type a name for the file and choose a folder.

To open an RTF file in your word processor or other application, the usual menu choice is File➪Open. In the Open dialog box that appears, click the box labeled Files of Type (or something like that) and look for Rich Text Format (RTF).

If you want to verbally edit documents, you need to load them into the NaturallySpeaking window. In addition to being able to open the RTF and TXT files it writes, NaturallySpeaking can read some Microsoft Word (.doc files). Using your word processor, check the dialog box that appears when you use the File➪Save As command. Click the Save As Type box there and choose a Word version (.doc), Text (.txt), or Rich Text (.rtf).

You don't have to rely on DragonPad to edit your text. If your first choice is to edit in your favorite word processor or other supported application, choose that.

Customizing the Window

In case you were wondering, you can change the appearance through the View menu in DragonPad. By "appearance," I mean stuff like toolbars, text wrapping in the window, and units of measure on the ruler (metric, English, or typesetting).

To view all the toolbars in the DragonPad, click View to get a list of available toolbars. Click next to a toolbar in that list to put a check mark beside it to turn on whatever toolbar you check. Click again to clear any check mark.

To control how text wraps (continues onto the next line) on your screen, how your mouse selects text, or what units of measure you use, choose View➪Settings. The Settings dialog box springs into action, where you can customize any of the following:

✔ NaturallySpeaking normally uses inches for measurement units (used on the ruler and in paragraph formatting). To change measurement units, click the Options tab of the Settings dialog box. You can then choose Inches, Centimeters, Points, or Picas.

✔ When you select with your mouse, NaturallySpeaking (like many Windows programs) normally selects entire words when you stretch the selection highlight to more than one word. If, instead, you want to be able to set the end point of your selections in midword, click the Options tab, then click to clear the check box labeled Automatic Word Selection.

✔ To control how text wraps on your screen, click Rich Text. (Click Text, instead, if you intend to save your file as plain text.) Then click either Wrap to Window (to fill your window with text) or Wrap to Ruler (to force lines to break at the right margin on the ruler). No Wrap makes your text hard to read. Choose Wrap to Ruler if you intend to print from the NaturallySpeaking window and want to see exactly how your printed lines of text will break while you type.

None of the wrap settings affects how lines of text break when you print, copy, or save a document as a file. The DragonPad always prints according to the page margins you set up, regardless of wrap settings. It never puts line breaks in text that is saved as a file or copied to another program's window. It always leaves the line breaks to that other program, and so avoids any ragged-right margin problems.

Tools and When to Use Them

I know you're saying, "Let's dictate, already!" (See Chapter 4.) But NaturallySpeaking will never get any better at its job if you don't use the tools found in the menus of the DragonBar. They help you get the most accuracy from your NaturallySpeaking assistant. I give you the details of these tools throughout the book, but here's the big picture.

Following are some of the tools that you most likely need:

✔ **Correction menu box:** Use this to educate NaturallySpeaking whenever it makes a recognition error. You may have to use it several times for the same error, but NaturallySpeaking will make the error less often. The Correction dialog box also appears in response to the Correct That voice command, the – (minus) key on the numeric keypad, and the Correct That icon on the toolbar. (See Chapters 4 and 5 for details.) You can also say, **"Correct <xyz>,"** where "xyz" refers to the words you want to select for correction.

✔ **Audio Setup Wizard:** Run this wizard if NaturallySpeaking seems to be making more errors than it did previously. It adjusts the volume of the microphone input. (See Chapters 2 and 19.)

✔ **Vocabulary Editor:** Use this tool to add specific words to your vocabulary or to train NaturallySpeaking in your pronunciation. It's also useful for creating shortcuts in which a single spoken phrase like **"my address"** causes NaturallySpeaking to type some complex text. (See Chapter 18.)

✔ **Audio training:** Use audio tools to tell NaturallySpeaking how you pronounce a particular word or command. (See Chapter 18.)

Table 3-1 lists the Dragon tools or technologies to use in specific circumstances and where to read the full details about them.

If you are running NaturallySpeaking but can't see its window, click the NaturallySpeaking microphone button on your Windows taskbar. Then you can access the tools from the NaturallySpeaking QuickStart menu bar.

Table 3-1	When to Use Tools, and Where They Are		
What You Need to Do	**What Dragon Technology to Use**	**Menu/Toolbar Choice**	**Where to Read More**
Correct a NaturallySpeaking error	Correction dialog box	Correction button on extended DragonBar or – (minus) on keypad	Chapters 4, 5
Adjust for changes in microphone	Audio Setup Wizard	Audio⇨Check Microphone	Chapter 20
Improve recognition of individual words	Audio Tool	Audio⇨Improve Recognition of Word or Phrase	Chapter 20
Expand vocabulary, improve recognition	Vocabulary Tool	Vocabulary⇨Add New Word or Phrase	Chapter 18
Add words in this document to vocabulary	Vocabulary Tool	Vocabulary⇨Learn from Specific Documents	Chapter 18
Add a specific word to your vocabulary	Vocabulary Editor	Vocabulary⇨Open Vocabulary Editor	Chapter 18
Create a shortcut phrase for long text	Vocabulary Editor	Vocabulary⇨ Vocabulary Editor	Chapter 18

(continued)

Table 3-1 *(continued)*

What You Need to Do	What Dragon Technology to Use	Menu/Toolbar Choice	Where to Read More
Add a new user	Profile Tool	Profile➪New User Profile	Chapters 2, 20
Switch to a different user	Profile Tool	Profile➪Open a User Profile	Chapter 20
Transcribe recorded speech	Transcription Tool	Transcribe button on extended DragonBar or Tools➪Transcribe Recording	Chapter 11
Create custom commands	Commands Editor	Tools➪Add New Command	Chapter 21
Modify commands	Commands Editor	Tools➪Edit Command Wizard	Chapter 21

If you often find yourself doing a specific type of function, such as only input-ting numbers, consider using one of the Recognition Modes that are available in NaturallySpeaking. To access them, go to the DragonBar and choose Modes from the menu. Then select the one you need. The five available modes are as follows:

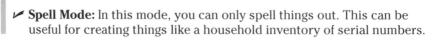

- **Normal Mode:** This is the default mode. In this mode, the program can discern the difference between commands, words, and numbers.

- **Dictation Mode:** In this mode, most of what you say is interpreted as dictation, except for a few standard commands like **"New line."**

- **Command Mode:** Not surprisingly, this mode will only recognize com-mands. Use this one if you only want to move around in a document.

- **Numbers Mode:** Can you guess this mode's function? Yep, this one only recognizes numbers. This may be helpful when you are doing your monthly tally of something.

- **Spell Mode:** In this mode, you can only spell things out. This can be useful for creating things like a household inventory of serial numbers.

Part II
Creating Documents and Spreadsheets

The 5th Wave   By Rich Tennant

"Maybe a better microphone would help."

In this part . . .

When your new NaturallySpeaking assistant is installed and trained, it's time to breathe a little life into your boring old PC. That's not to say you should incinerate your keyboard quite yet, but in this part, you start setting your fingers free from the tedium of typing.

NaturallySpeaking is a bit like the secretary of old movies who quietly takes dictation and then types it up without a single spelling error. Or is it a bit like today's real-life assistant who not only types and spells perfectly, but edits and formats your documents, helps you proofread, and transcribes dictation from your portable recorder @@ md oh, that's you! As with a human assistant, you do need to give clear instructions to NaturallySpeaking; and in this part, we'll show you exactly what to do, what to say, and how to say it to get the results you want in the NaturallySpeaking DragonPad.

NaturallySpeaking is also a good team player that can lend its voice to lots of different applications. When you team NaturallySpeaking with Word, the application gets special voice commands for its word-processing features, like fonts, paragraph alignments, or tables. And Excel gets some special treatment, too.

And don't forget that you need to instruct your NaturallySpeaking assistant to talk back — or at least read back.

Chapter 4

Simply Dictating

*I*t seems to me that dictating should be a far easier way to communicate than by tapping your fingers across a keyboard. And the basics of dictating are, in fact, pretty easy. You just need to know a few tricks that I tell you about in this chapter.

The "basics" of NaturallySpeaking are its keyboardlike capabilities to turn voice into text. NaturallySpeaking can do lots of other things (edit, format, make tables, launch programs, and more) too, but those tasks are covered in later chapters. The keyboardlike features are the ones you find in all versions of NaturallySpeaking.

This basic keyboard capability works not only in NaturallySpeaking DragonPad but in any (well, nearly any) Windows application. See Part III for using NaturallySpeaking with Internet applications.

Chapter 5 goes into detail about correcting errors, moving your cursor around verbally, and other fine points of editing using NaturallySpeaking. Chapter 5 also discusses some of the more advanced editing features NaturallySpeaking offers for certain applications.

Dictating 101: How to Dictate

After you have installed NaturallySpeaking on a computer with all the necessary system requirements and performed the initial training (see Chapter 2), you're on the road to a beautiful friendship with your assistant. Take the following steps:

1. **Launch NaturallySpeaking. Choose Start⇨Programs⇨Dragon NaturallySpeaking11.**

   You can use Dragon NaturallySpeaking with a large number of applications. If you intend to use NaturallySpeaking with another application, launch that application at this point, too.

2. **Put on your headset, and make sure the microphone is positioned as it was during initial training.**

   The microphone should be positioned about a half-inch away from one corner of your mouth, off to the side. It should never be directly in front of your mouth.

3. **Turn the microphone on.**

   The microphone icon in the system tray needs to be pointing up at attention, not lying down relaxing, in order for you to dictate. If the icon is lying down, click it or press the + key on your keyboard's numeric keypad. You can also click it in the upper-left corner of the DragonBar, as shown in Figure 4-1.

   The microphone icon in the toolbar of the NaturallySpeaking DragonBar works exactly the same way as the icon in the system tray. Make sure one of these is open and ready for you to dictate.

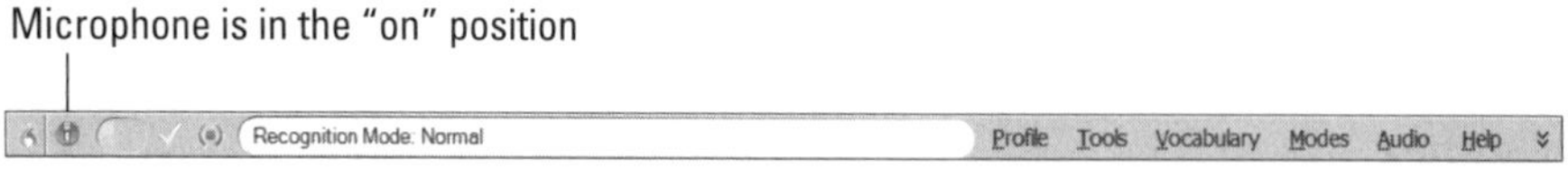

Figure 4-1:
Click the
microphone
in the
DragonBar
to turn it on.

Microphone is in the "on" position

| ⟨ ⊕ ⟨ ⟩ ✓ (•) Recognition Mode: Normal | Profile Tools Vocabulary Modes Audio Help ≫ |

4. **Click where you want the text to go if the cursor isn't already there.**

   Or select (highlight) text that you want to replace with dictated text.

5. **Speak carefully, just as you did when you read the text aloud to NaturallySpeaking during the initial training. Don't rush, and don't speak the words with . . . spaces . . . between . . . them.**

   As you speak, NaturallySpeaking shows you what it thinks you said.

6. **Speak your punctuation, such as** "Period" or "Comma," **as you go, and if you want a word capitalized, say the word** "Cap" **beforehand.**

   See the later section, "Punctuating and Capitalizing," for details.

If NaturallySpeaking makes errors (remember, it's only 99+ percent accurate), correct them rather than edit them. For basic instructions, see "Making Quick Corrections," later in this chapter. See Chapter 5 for additional details on correcting and for instructions for editing by voice.

Figure 4-2 is an example of how dictation works in NaturallySpeaking. These paragraphs show the basic keyboard style input we discuss in this chapter.

Figure 4-2:
The callouts in this example show what to say to get punctuation, capitalization, and numbers.

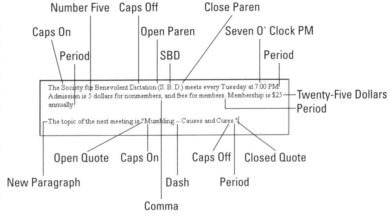

Speak continuously. Don't pause between your words (until you come to the end of a phrase)! Dragon NaturallySpeaking is designed to recognize continuous speech. If you deliberately put pauses between your words, Dragon NaturallySpeaking will make more errors, not fewer. (Pausing between phrases is okay, however.)

Use your keyboard and your mouse just as you would normally — to type, make menu selections, or use command keys (like Ctrl+Z). Or you can use Dragon NaturallySpeaking to perform keyboard and menu commands. See Chapter 16 for details.

Distinguishing between Text and Commands

As you can see in Figure 4-2, NaturallySpeaking lets you mix dictation (words that get converted into text) and commands (instructions to the computer). You don't have to press or click anything to tell NaturallySpeaking, "Here comes a command; don't write this." You just say the command.

Sometimes, however, you may not get what you expect. For instance, **"Cap"** is a command to capitalize the upcoming word. You may, however, dictate a sentence like, "We want to cap expenditures for this year" and see it come out like this: "We want to Expenditures for this year."

Use pauses to control the interpretation. Most commands involve two or more words. NaturallySpeaking must hear them together, as a phrase, to interpret them as a command. To make sure NaturallySpeaking interprets a phrase as text instead of a command, pause between two or more of the words.

To have NaturallySpeaking interpret "cap" as text, for instance, pause between "cap" and the word it operates on, like "expenditure." For a two- or three-word phrase that sounds like a command (like **"Caps On"**), pause between the words to break up the phrase. ("They put their caps . . . on their heads.") You also need to pause before commands that affect what you just said, as **"Scratch That"** does. If you don't pause, NaturallySpeaking will lump **Scratch** with the preceding word and consider it all as text. Fortunately, such a pause is natural.

Most people aren't that careful. They speak the phrase and then say, "Oh, rats" (silently, to themselves, or else NaturallySpeaking will dutifully type *that* out). Instead of "Oh, rats," when you see the error, say, **"Scratch That"** to remove the blooper. Then repeat the phrase with the pauses adjusted. Don't worry, this isn't as complicated as it sounds. It becomes quite natural.

You can adjust the amount of time that NaturallySpeaking considers to be a sufficient pause. (See Chapter 3.)

Pausing doesn't help with punctuation and numbers that you want spelled out. For instance, you can't dictate, **"He typed a comma and continued."** You get the comma symbol, not the word. For those problems, use the Vocabulary Editor (described in Chapter 18) to add the written word *comma* with a new spoken form (for example, "word comma"). Then you can say, **"He typed a word comma and continued."**

Although using pauses is the most reliable way to distinguish between text and command, NaturallySpeaking offers an alternative solution. This alternative doesn't work for so-called "dictation commands" that have to do with capitalization, tabs, and line or paragraph breaks, but it does work for many other commands, such as formatting commands. To force your utterance to be taken as text, hold down the Shift key while you speak. To force it to be taken as a command, hold down the Ctrl key.

Controlling Your (Cough! Sneeze!) Microphone

Some people switch the microphone off and on to avoid inserting the garbage text that comes from coughing, sneezing, or answering the phone. Dragon NaturallySpeaking gives you several ways to control the microphone:

- ✔ Press the + key on the numeric keypad to switch the microphone between "on" and "off." I find this switch to be the most convenient one.

- ✔ Click the microphone icon that appears either on the DragonBar or in the system tray of your Windows taskbar.

- ✔ Say, **"Go to Sleep"** or **"Stop Listening"** to disable the microphone. The microphone icon lies down and a string of *z*'s appears next to the microphone icon. To wake up the microphone again, say, **"Wake Up"** or **"Listen To Me."** (Or click the sleeping microphone icon twice, or press the + key on the numeric keypad twice.) This sleeping and waking stuff is not the same as "off" and "on." What's the difference? When the microphone is asleep, it's still listening for the command, **"Wake Up."** If you turn the microphone off, it isn't listening at all.

You can change the microphone hotkey (normally the + key on the numeric keypad) by choosing Tools➪Options and clicking the Hotkeys tab in the Options dialog box that appears. Then click the Microphone On/Off button in the dialog box; a tiny Set Hot Key dialog box appears. Now press the key or key combination you would prefer for the hotkey, and then click OK.

Tips for Talking

Dictating text, especially if you're used to typing on a keyboard, can seem a little clumsy at first. You need to do things a bit differently than when you type. Following are eight tips to make your dictating easier:

✔ **Try not to watch the screen as you talk.** The two activities are somehow not very compatible. I find I lose my train of thought if I look at what's being typed. Instead, look out the window or gaze off into the distance to compose and speak. Nuance removed the Results Box because people found it distracting.

✔ **Dictate in phrases.** You don't have to dictate the entire sentence, with all its punctuation, all at once (although using longer phrases improves accuracy). For instance, as I dictated the preceding sentence, I paused after "the entire sentence" and paced a while in thought. I also paused before and after the commas.

✔ **Punctuate and capitalize as you speak.** Although you can certainly go back and punctuate and capitalize text after you dictate, punctuating as you speak is often easier, after you become used to it.

✔ **Proofread what you have dictated.** Dragon NaturallySpeaking will make some mistakes, particularly when you first get started. Sometimes those mistakes are both potentially embarrassing and so plausible-sounding that they are hard to detect! NaturallySpeaking provides two tools that address this problem: the Playback feature (directly accessible from the DragonBar Extras menu), which plays back a recording of your own voice (not available in the Home edition), and the Read That feature, which actually synthesizes a voice from your text. See Chapter 7 for more information on these features.

✔ **Avoid the temptation to use unusual or classic texts, such as the Gettysburg Address, when trying out NaturallySpeaking.** Instead, use normal, day-to-day language. See the last chapter of this book if you want to play around with NaturallySpeaking. If you really intend to regularly dictate poetry or something other than contemporary English, use multiple users (see Chapter 20). As it comes out of the box, NaturallySpeaking is designed for conventional and contemporary English; using it otherwise can cause errors.

✔ **Expect dictating to be a bit awkward at first.** If, like me, you are used to typing, you may find that composing your thoughts verbally is disconcerting at first.

✔ **Compromise between using your voice and the keyboard if you can.** Keep your hands on the mouse and keyboard for cursor and menu control, and then use Dragon NaturallySpeaking as a fast way to type and format text. For example, you might highlight some text with your mouse and then say, **"Cap That,"** or move your cursor somewhere and dictate.

✔ **To get used to NaturallySpeaking gradually, try typing normally using the keyboard; then, every so often, dictate a bit of text that you find awkward to type.**

If you're stumped about what command to say, you can always call on your Dragon Sidebar with, **"What can I say?"** and you'll see the appropriate commands.

Punctuating and Capitalizing

Dictating isn't quite like speaking. Unlike human listeners, NaturallySpeaking can't interpret the inflections and pauses in our voices as punctuation. When you dictate, you have to make an effort to help NaturallySpeaking out, although NaturallySpeaking does do some punctuating and capitalizing automatically. Here's how to work with NaturallySpeaking to get your words correctly capitalized and your apostrophizing properly punctuated.

Punctuating your remarks

Speaking punctuation marks as you dictate is annoying but necessary if you want to avoid the tedious process of going back and inserting punctuation. Tables 4-1, 4-2, and 4-3 show you what words to say to insert punctuation marks as you speak.

Table 4-1	Single Punctuation Marks
Punctuation Mark	*Spoken Form*
.	**Period** (or **Dot,** or **Point**)
!	**Exclamation Mark** (or **Exclamation Point**)
?	**Question Mark**
,	**Comma**
'	**Apostrophe**
's	**Apostrophe Ess**
&	**Ampersand**
:	**Colon**
;	**Semicolon**
'	**Open Single Quote**
'	**Close Single Quote**
. . .	**Ellipsis**
$	**Dollar Sign**
-	**Hyphen**
—	**Dash**

Table 4-2	Paired Punctuation Marks
Punctuation Mark	*Spoken Form*
"	**Open Quote**
"	**Close Quote**
(	**Open** (or **Left**) **Parenthesis** (or **Paren**)
)	**Close** (or **Right**) **Parenthesis** (or **Paren**)
[	**Open Bracket**
]	**Close Bracket**

Table 4-3	Math and Computer Symbols
Punctuation Mark	*Spoken Form*
{	**Open Brace**
}	**Close Brace**
/	**Slash**
\	**Backslash**
@	**At Sign**
~	**Tilde**
_	**Underscore**
*	**Asterisk**
>	**Greater Than** (or **Open Angle Bracket**)
<	**Less Than** (or **Close Angle Bracket**)
|	**Vertical Bar**
#	**Pound Sign** (or **Number Sign**)
-	**Minus Sign**
+	**Plus Sign**
.	**Point**
%	**Percent Sign**
`	**Backquote**
,	**Numeric Comma**
^	**Caret**

NaturallySpeaking puts no space before an apostrophe, so you can easily make a noun possessive (such as in "Tom's bicycle") by speaking the word (**"Tom"**) and then saying, **"Apostrophe Ess."** Dragon NaturallySpeaking may supply an apostrophe automatically if, from the context, it thinks you are describing a possessive noun or contraction. But it can't always do that accurately. It's more reliable, if more awkward, to speak the word and then add **"Apostrophe Ess."**

NaturallySpeaking uses a double dash character when you say the word **"Dash."** If you would rather use a different character, you can paste that character into your vocabulary list using Dragon's Vocabulary Editor (described in Chapter 18), and create your own spoken phrase for that character, such as **"Em Dash."**

You can hyphenate any multi-word utterance (such as the phrase, "all-encompassing") by saying, **"Hyphenate That"** immediately after speaking the phrase.

If you meant to use a word as text, such as the word *period* and NaturallySpeaking used that word as punctuation instead, say, **"Correct That"** and choose the interpretation you prefer. See "Making Quick Corrections" later in this chapter for instructions.

Discovering Natural Punctuation

If you'd like to slowly wade into the process of speaking punctuation, you'll be happy to know that NaturallySpeaking provides a function called Natural Punctuation. Natural Punctuation automatically adds periods and commas where Dragon thinks they should go. If you start a new line or a new paragraph or come to what NaturallySpeaking thinks is the end of a sentence based on your pause, it will add a period.

Choose DragonBar⇨Auto-Formatting Options and select the check box that says Automatically Add Commas and Periods.

This doesn't prevent you from saying **"period"** or **"comma,"** but if you forget or are new to the process, you have a backup. Remember that it won't add any punctuation other than periods and commas. You still need to say them. (See preceding tables for punctuation you can use.)

Capitalizing on your text

NaturallySpeaking does some capitalization for you, as you dictate. For example, it generally capitalizes the first letter of a sentence. (Its cue to capitalize is that you have started a new paragraph or punctuated the end of a sentence.) It also capitalizes words that it thinks are proper nouns or that it has been taught to capitalize in its vocabulary training or editing. In general, as long as you don't do any manual typing between finishing one sentence and starting the next, NaturallySpeaking automatically takes care of the initial capitalization.

When NaturallySpeaking doesn't capitalize for you, you have several ways to capitalize words yourself. The two best and easiest ways to capitalize are either *before* you speak a word or phrase or *immediately afterward.*

You can also select any text with your mouse or by voice and then apply capitalization and other formatting. See Chapter 5 for more about that technique.

Here are the basics of capitalizing the initial letters of words:

- ✔ To capitalize the first letter of any word, before speaking it say, **"Cap"** followed immediately by your word. Don't pause between **Cap** and whatever the word is, or Dragon NaturallySpeaking will type *cap* instead of doing it!

- ✔ After you say some words and NaturallySpeaking types them in your program window, say, **"Cap That"** or **"All Cap That."** **Cap** means the initial letters are capitalized. **All Cap** means all the letters of a word are capitalized.

- ✔ If you are about to speak a series of words that must be capitalized, say, **"Caps On."** Speak those words (pausing for as long as you like anywhere in this process), and then say, **"Caps Off."** To capitalize *all* the letters in a series of words (LIKE THIS) use the phrases **"*All* Caps On"** and **"*All* Caps Off"** instead.

Table 4-4 lists all the various ways to capitalize.

Table 4-4	Capital Ideas	
To Do This	*Example*	*Say This*
First letter capital	Like This	**"Cap <word>,"** or **"<phrase> Cap That,"** or **"Caps On <one or more phrases> Caps Off"**
All letters capital	LIKE THIS	Use any of the same three preceding approaches for first-letter capitals, but say, **"All Caps"** in place of **"Caps."**
All letters lowercase	like this	Use any of the same three approaches, but say, **"No Caps"** in place of **"Caps."**
Capitalize something already dictated	Like This	**"Capitalize <xyz>"**

"**Caps On**" and "**Cap That**" don't really mean, "Capitalize the first letter of *every* word." A more accurate interpretation would be, "Capitalize the first letter of every *important* word." NaturallySpeaking tends to omit initial capitals for prepositions, articles, and all those other little words whose correct names I (and probably you) forget. Even though NaturallySpeaking is probably being editorially correct according to the *Chicago Manual of Style* or other such authority, such selective capitalization may not be what you have in mind. If you want NaturallySpeaking to capitalize absolutely all the words, you have to say the command "**Caps**" before each word.

Taking Up Space

Understanding a letter or other document depends not only on the words but on the spaces between the words as well. Getting your document spaced out is relatively easy. NaturallySpeaking automatically does some word, sentence, and paragraph spacing. You can control that spacing, or add space of your own.

Controlling paragraph spacing

NaturallySpeaking has two commands that you can say to create the space that divides paragraphs: "**New Paragraph**" and "**New Line.**" What's the difference?

- ✔ "**New Paragraph**" puts a blank line between paragraphs. It is like pressing the Enter key twice: It inserts two paragraph marks (invisible) into your text. It also makes sure that the first word of the next sentence is capitalized.

- ✔ "**New Line**" does not put a blank line between paragraphs. It is like pressing the Enter key once. The next line isn't capitalized unless you ended the last line with a period, question mark, or exclamation point.

Dragon's way of doing the "**New Paragraph**" command might cause a problem for you if you are going to use any kind of paragraph formatting (such as bullets or, in Word, paragraph spacing). It's better to use the "**New Line**" command instead. Otherwise, in many instances, you double the effect of the paragraph formatting: You get two bullets or twice the spacing you intended, for example.

What if you want to actually type the words "new paragraph" instead of creating a new paragraph? Put a pause between the two words: "**new**" [pause] "**paragraph.**"

Controlling spaces and tabs

Dragon NaturallySpeaking does a pretty good job of automatic spacing. It usually deals with spaces around punctuation in the way that you want it to. Occasionally, however, you will want to add a few spaces or a Tab character in your text.

Automatic spaces

NaturallySpeaking automatically puts spaces between your words. It looks at your punctuation to figure out the rest of the spacing. If, for some reason, you don't want spaces between your words, speak the command **"No-Space On,"** speak your words, and then say, **"No-Space Off."** Or if you anticipate that NaturallySpeaking is about to precede your next word with a space that you don't want, say, **"No-Space"** and then your next word, with no pauses between.

NaturallySpeaking does different amounts of spacing after other punctuation marks. It is done in a way that usually works. For instance, NaturallySpeaking puts one space after a comma, unless that comma is part of a number, such as 12,000 (whether spoken as **"twelve thousand"** or **"twelve comma zero zero zero"**). NaturallySpeaking also offers a so-called "numeric comma" that's never followed by a space. You can find these choices by going to Tools⇨Auto-Formatting Options.

Adding spaces and tabs

The quickest way to add a space is to say the word **"Spacebar."** For a tab character, say, **"Tab Key."** Just as NaturallySpeaking does for **"Comma"** or **"Period,"** it accepts these words or phrases as a character that it should type.

Another way to do the same thing is to say, **"Press Spacebar"** or **"Press Tab."** In fact, you can tell NaturallySpeaking to press any key on the keyboard by saying the word **"Press"** and then the name of the key. So, to press the spacebar, you can say, **"Press Spacebar."** Or to press the F1 key, you say, **"Press F1."**

When should you use **"Press Spacebar"** or **"Press Tab"**? If you sometimes write about the keyboard, you may end up training NaturallySpeaking to type out the word *spacebar* or *tab* when you speak it, instead of inserting a space character. Sometimes, you may need to use the word *tab* in other contexts. (For example, "Run me a tab.") In that event, the **"Press"** command will be the more reliable way to get a space or tab character.

Entering Different Numbers and Dates

When people speak about numbers and dates, they use so many different forms that it's remarkable that a software program can actually figure them out. And yet, NaturallySpeaking can do it. You can say, **"eight o'clock AM"** and Dragon NaturallySpeaking types 8:00 AM. Or you can say, **"forty-five dollars"** and NaturallySpeaking types $45.

Most of the time, NaturallySpeaking types numbers and dates just the way you want it to, without doing anything special. The most common correction that you'll have to do is tell NaturallySpeaking to use numerals rather than words for digits zero through nine. To do so, say, **"numeral"** before speaking the digit. Table 4-5 lists some of the ways you can say numbers and dates.

If a number, date, or time doesn't come out in the form that you want, you may be able to choose the form you want by saying, **"Correct That,"** and then choosing from the list in the Correct That dialog box. For instance, when speaking the words **"seven o'clock,"** NaturallySpeaking initially typed *seven o'clock*. But, by saying, **"Correct That"** and choosing 7:00 from the pop-up window choices displayed as shown in Figure 4-3, NaturallySpeaking learned that I wanted the numerical form. See Chapter 5 for more about the **"Correct That"** command.

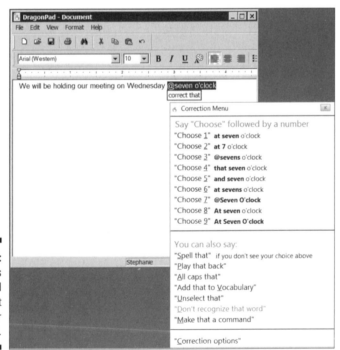

Figure 4-3:
The choices
displayed
to correct
a number
format.

Table 4-5	Numbers and Dates
To Get	*Say*
.5	**Point** (or **Period** or **Dot**) **five**
0.45	**Zero point four five** or **oh point four five**
One	**One**
1	**Numeral one**
42	**Forty two** or **four two**
192	**One ninety two, one nine two,** or **one hundred (and) ninety-two**
4627	**Four thousand six hundred (and) twenty seven, forty-six hundred twenty-seven,** or **four six two seven**
4,627	**Four comma six hundred (and) twenty seven** or **four comma six two seven**
$152.07	**One hundred fifty-two dollars and seven cents** or **dollar sign one five two point zero seven**
Aug. 28, 1945	**August twenty-eight comma nineteen forty-five**
May 11, 2010	**May eleven comma two thousand (and) ten**
2:12 p.m.	**Two twelve pee em**
7:00	**Seven o'clock ay em**
V	**Roman five**
XLV	**Roman forty roman five**
842-8996	**Eight four two hyphen eight nine nine six**

Making Quick Corrections

Although making corrections technically falls into the editing category, and editing is discussed in Chapter 5, you usually want to make a few corrections the instant you see an error. Errors fall into two categories:

- ✔ Errors that you make — which I call "bloopers"
- ✔ Errors that NaturallySpeaking makes in interpreting your speech

You deal with those errors in two different ways: *scratching* and *correcting*. Read on!

Scratching your bloopers

Making a verbal "blooper" is easy to do with speech input. You call across the office to someone or mutter something sarcastic, and NaturallySpeaking dutifully types it. If you make a mistake verbally, however, you can also undo it verbally. (On the other hand, if NaturallySpeaking, not you, makes the mistake, you should "correct" NaturallySpeaking, not undo the mistake. See the following section for details.) The two verbal commands that are most useful for undoing your bloopers are these:

- ✔ **"Scratch That"**
- ✔ **"Undo That"**

The NaturallySpeaking command for undoing your bloopers is **"Scratch That."** To use the command, you must not have edited anything with your mouse and keyboard since you last spoke. The command will undo up to ten consecutive utterances, up to the last break in your dictation (where you did some keyboard work).

Alternatively, you can say, **"Undo That"** (or **"Undo Last Action"**). That verbal command is the equivalent to the undo command, so it works not only on dictated text, but also on anything that you could normally undo. For example, if you had just applied bullet-style formatting, you could undo that formatting.

Of course, nothing says that you have to use NaturallySpeaking to undo your bloopers. You can use your keyboard or mouse (press Ctrl+Z, for example, press the Backspace key, or select the text and press the Delete key) just as you would if you had typed the mistake.

If physically pressing the Backspace or Delete key is not an option for you, here are two verbal commands you can use for the same purpose:

- ✔ **"Backspace"** (or **"Press Backspace"**)
- ✔ **"Delete"** (or **"Press Delete"**)

You can backspace or delete several characters by saying, **"Backspace 7"** to backspace seven characters, for example, or **"Delete 8 characters"** to delete eight characters to the right of the typing cursor. The **Backspace** command can be more reliable. (Because the word *delete* is more commonly written out in text than the word *backspace*, NaturallySpeaking sometimes errs on the side of writing out *delete* rather than doing the **"Delete"** command.)

Resuming dictation with an earlier word

Tripping over your tongue is easy when dictating. Also, composing sentences on the fly isn't easy, and sometimes you want to change your mind about the phrase you just used.

You can solve both problems (misspeaking and changing your mind) with the **"Resume With <*word*>"** command. For **<*word*>**, substitute the word you want NaturallySpeaking to back up to. That word must be within the last 100 characters you have dictated, and you must have dictated continuously (typed or edited nothing by hand) since that word.

For instance, following is dictation where someone makes an error in the first line, gives a correction using **"Resume With,"** and completes the phrase correctly:

1. Speaking the original error: **"I keep on getting my tang tungled up."**

2. (Brief pause, as the user realizes the error)

3. Backing up: **"Resume With *my*."**

4. Correcting from that point: **"tongue tangled up"**

The resulting text is: Getting my tongue tangled up.

This command is particularly useful when you dictate into a portable recorder. See Chapter 11 for more about using commands when you dictate into a recorder.

Correcting a NaturallySpeaking error

If NaturallySpeaking has misinterpreted something that you said, you can fix that mistake and also help train your NaturallySpeaking assistant. To accomplish this, you have to correct the error rather than just typing in the correct text, scratching the error, or undoing it. What's the difference?

In Dragon terms, correcting something means to tell NaturallySpeaking what you actually said rather than merely editing the text in the document. When you correct an error, you not only fix the resulting text, but you also educate your NaturallySpeaking assistant to understand your individual speech habits. Correction is one of the main ways in which NaturallySpeaking gets better over time. Don't shortchange your assistant by not correcting it.

I describe all the different ways of correcting NaturallySpeaking in Chapter 5, but here are two easily remembered ways using the command **"Correct That":**

✔ If NaturallySpeaking just made the error, say, **"Correct That"** or **"Spell That."** Either the Correction menu box or the Spell Window appears. (You can also spell from the Corrections menu box.)

✔ If NaturallySpeaking made the error a while back, select the erroneous text and say, **"Correct That"** to get the Correction dialog box.

Another quick way to make the correction would be to say, **"correct \<xyz>"** (where **\<xyz>** is the word that Dragon didn't recognize).

This second way of correction works only in the NaturallySpeaking window and in what are called "Full text control" applications. In other applications, you select the text, and then you must speak replacement text. If the new text is also erroneous, say **"Correct That."** See Chapter 8 for more tips on using NaturallySpeaking with other applications.

When the Correction dialog box appears, it lists numbered alternatives. Verbally choose one of the alternatives by saying, **"Choose \<*number*>."** For instance, say, **"Choose five."** This approach is my favorite. If none of the alternatives are correct, you may verbally spell out the replacement text.

Another way to handle it if none of the options are correct is to redictate what you meant to say. If you get that wrong, say "spell that" and you can spell it out. When you use the "Spell window," the word is added to the vocabulary for future use.

Tackling Common Dictation Problems

Following are some common problems users experience with dictation. You can fix many of them by using the Correction menu box, described earlier in this chapter, or by word or vocabulary training (see Part V for the details of vocabulary and word training):

✔ **Sound-alike words:** When two words normally sound exactly alike, even human speakers make mistakes. The way that humans distinguish one word from the other is by the context. That's how NaturallySpeaking works, too. If it didn't work that way, you couldn't say a sentence like "It was too far for two people to go to purchase two tickets" and have any hope that NaturallySpeaking would get it correct. Vocabulary training and using the Correction menu box will alleviate this problem to some degree.

- **Commands as text:** Sometimes, if you say, **"Go To End of Line,"** NaturallySpeaking will type those words instead of performing the command. One solution that may work is to pause very slightly before speaking those words. Another solution is word training, as described in Part V. A quick fix is to hold down the Ctrl key while speaking a command, which forces NaturallySpeaking to interpret your utterance as a command.

- **Text as commands:** Sometimes you want to actually type something like "go to end of line," but NaturallySpeaking instead interprets your utterance as a command. Avoid pausing before and after that phrase, if you can. A quick fix is to hold down the Shift key while dictating, which forces NaturallySpeaking to interpret speech as text.

- **Extra words:** If NaturallySpeaking gives you small, extra words in your text, it may be interpreting microphone noises as words. Make sure the microphone isn't in front of your mouth, or else it will pick up tiny puffs of breath and interpret them as words. (Also, if applicable, make sure the microphone cover isn't brushing against your beard or moustache.)

- **Acronyms and other non-words:** Contemporary English uses a lot of acronyms, abbreviations, initials, and other unconventional words. You can add these terms to NaturallySpeaking by using the Vocabulary Editor, described in Chapter 18. You can also add them by speaking them and then correcting the NaturallySpeaking interpretation with the "spell window." The NaturallySpeaking vocabulary already includes many common abbreviations. If NaturallySpeaking thinks it hears initials, and those initials aren't otherwise in its vocabulary, it capitalizes them and puts a period after each letter.

- **E-mail addresses:** If you use a particular e-mail or web address a lot, you can add it to your vocabulary like other "non-words," as the preceding bullet describes. Otherwise, you can say an e-mail address, such as <person>@company.com, much like you would in conversation. To make sure everything is lowercase, say, **"No Caps On,"** then say the e-mail address, and then say, **"No Caps Off."** For the address itself (person@ company.com, for instance), say, **"<person> at company dot com."** If you are getting spaces within the name in the e-mail address, you can also bring up the Spell window and add it there.

- **Web addresses:** Use the **"No Caps On"** and **"No Caps Off"** commands as suggested in the preceding bullet to prevent capitalization. Speak a web address in the form, **"w w w dot <company> dot com."** For a full address (such as http://www.company.com) say, **"h t t p w w w dot <company> dot com,"** saying nothing about the colon or slashes. NaturallySpeaking adds the colon and slashes and recognizes the terms *com, gov, mil, net, org,* and *sys* just as you would normally say them. If you prefer, you can verbally spell out the letters in those terms.

Chapter 5

Selecting, Editing, and Correcting in DragonPad

In This Chapter

▶ Using voice commands to move the cursor

▶ Selecting text

▶ Inserting and deleting text

▶ Undoing actions after you change your mind

▶ Correcting NaturallySpeaking mistakes and training it to do better

*I*n my most optimistic moments, I like to imagine that I will write a document (like this chapter) by starting at the beginning and continuing flawlessly to the end. I've heard of such miracles, but unfortunately have never experienced one myself. Whether you write your documents by hand, use a keyboard to enter them into a computer, or dictate them to an assistant, from time to time you're probably going to want to insert new text into the middle of the document, delete some text, rearrange a few paragraphs, and rewrite a sentence here and there.

If you prefer, you can continue using the mouse and keyboard to do this editing, just as if you had never heard of NaturallySpeaking. In fact, dictating your first drafts and editing by keyboard is not a bad way to get your feet wet with NaturallySpeaking. And you can add the editing voice commands to your repertoire as you get more experienced.

Or you can plunge right in and do all your editing by voice, just as if you were dictating your changes to a real person instead of your virtual NaturallySpeaking assistant. But, unlike a real person, your assistant works nights and holidays without complaining and never rolls its eyes when you rewrite a sentence for the tenth time. (Yeah, I've done that too.)

In addition to making changes that are a normal part of your creative process, you also want to correct the errors that get into your documents whenever your NaturallySpeaking assistant thinks that you said something different from what you actually said. Occasional mistakes of this sort (known as *recognition errors*) are inevitable, just as occasional typographical errors always manage to sneak into typed documents. The NaturallySpeaking mistakes tend to be funnier than typos, because they are correct English words that sometimes give your sentences entirely new and unintended meanings (for example, "Quoth the raven, 'Never bore.'").

Although you can just write (or dictate) over these mistakes, NaturallySpeaking has a special correction procedure that teaches it to not make similar mistakes in the future. Just as you teach your children to perfect their language skills by correcting their errors, you teach your NaturallySpeaking assistant to understand you better by using the correction procedure.

Moving Around in a Document

When you're in a cab, you can tell the driver where to go in three ways (excluding the ever-popular "Follow that car").

- ✔ You can give directions, as in "Turn left and go three blocks."
- ✔ You can specify a location without saying what's there, as in "Go to 49th and Madison."
- ✔ You can name a destination without saying where it is and count on the driver to find it, as in "Take me to the airport."

The same basic ideas work when you tell NaturallySpeaking where to move the cursor in its document window. You have three options:

- ✔ You can give a directional command like **"Move Up Five Lines."**
- ✔ You can specify a location in the document by saying, **"Go to End of Paragraph."**
- ✔ You can say some text and count on NaturallySpeaking to find it by saying, **"Insert After wish you were here."**

These commands are summarized in Table 5-1, as well as in the "What Can I Say?" topic of NaturallySpeaking Help. To display this topic, speak the command **"What Can I Say"** and the Dragon Sidebar will pop up with suggestions (if it isn't open already). The following sections of this chapter provide more detailed instructions for using these commands and their various synonyms.

You don't have to use the voice commands if you'd rather not. The mouse and the arrow keys on the keyboard can also move the cursor. It's your choice.

Table 5-1	**Commands for Moving Around in a Document**		
First Word	*Second Word*	*Third Word*	*Fourth Word*
Go To	Top, Bottom		
Go To	Top, Bottom	of	Selection, Line, Paragraph
Move	Up, Down, Left, Right	1 – 20	
Move	Back, Forward	1 – 20	Words, Paragraphs
Insert	Before, After		

Giving the cursor directions and distances

You can use the **Move** command to move the cursor in different directions: forward or backward a certain number of characters, words, lines, or paragraphs. The short form of the **Move** command uses just three words (as in **"Move Down Three"**). You can also add a word to specify units (as in **"Move Back Two Paragraphs"**).

The short, three-word version of the **Move** command imitates the cursor keys on the keyboard. The three words are **Move**, a direction (**Up, Down, Left,** or **Right**), and finally a number from **1** to **20.** You don't specify any units. So, for example:

- ✔ **"Move Down 12"** gives you the same result as if you press the down-arrow key 12 times. In other words, the cursor goes down 12 lines.

- ✔ **"Move Right 2"** moves the cursor two characters to the right, the same result you get from pressing the right-arrow key twice.

When you want to move a certain number of words or paragraphs, just add **Words** or **Paragraphs** to the command. Use the four-word **Move** command. First you say **Move;** then say a direction (**Back** or **Forward**); then say a number (**1 – 20**); and finally, say a unit (**Words** or **Paragraphs**). For example:

- ✔ **"Move Back Six Words"**
- ✔ **"Move Forward Two Paragraphs"**

You can also use the units **Characters** or **Lines** instead of **Words** or **Paragraphs.** When the units are **Words** or **Characters,** you can use **Left/Right** instead of **Back/Forward.** When the units are **Lines** or **Paragraphs,** you can use **Up/Down** instead of **Back/Forward.** For example:

- ✓ **"Move Left Three Characters"** means the same as **"Move Back Three Characters"** or **"Move Left Three."**
- ✓ **"Move Down Eight Paragraphs"** gives the same result as **"Move Forward Eight Paragraphs."**

Finally, the word "a" can be used as a synonym for the number 1. **"Move Back a Word"** is the same as **"Move Back One Word."**

If you just want to scroll the text up or down, and you don't care about moving the cursor, say **"Press Page Up"** or **"Press Page Down."**

Going to the head of the line (or paragraph, or . . .)

Like telling your cab driver to go to the end of a street, you can tell NaturallySpeaking to go the beginning or end of various chunks of a document: the beginning or end of the document, current paragraph, current line, or whatever block of text is selected. (The current line or paragraph is the line or paragraph where the cursor is now.)

The simplest destination commands are

- ✓ **"Go To Bottom,"** which moves the cursor to the end of the document
- ✓ **"Go To Top,"** which moves the cursor to the beginning of the document
- ✓ **"Go To Top (or Bottom) of Paragraph (or Line or Selection)"**

NaturallySpeaking understands a number of synonyms for these commands. In particular, you can use **Move To** instead of **Go To** as long as you specify the chunk of text you're moving within. Begin with **Move To** and then use **Start, Beginning,** or **End,** and then specify a **Line, Paragraph, Selection,** or **Document.**

Sometimes NaturallySpeaking understands one form of a command more consistently than another. For example, when I say, **"Go To,"** it often gets interpreted as "due to," "do to," or "good." I'm sure I could eventually train NaturallySpeaking to recognize my slurring pronunciation of **"Go To,"** but I find it easier just to say, **"Move To"** instead.

Specifying a destination by quoting text

Sometimes you want to put the cursor right smack in the middle of a block of text on your screen, not near the beginning or end of anything. And you'd rather not count lines or words or characters. You'd like to tell NaturallySpeaking to put the cursor after this phrase or before that one.

You want the **Insert** command. Suppose you dictated, "She sells seashells by the sea shore," and you want to put the cursor between "sells" and "seashells." You can say,

- ✔ **"Insert After *sells*"** or
- ✔ **"Insert Before *seashells*"**

Each of these commands accomplishes the same result.

If the words "sells" and "seashells" appear in several locations, you will see all the instances numbered. You can choose the one you want.

If text is already selected, you can move the cursor to the beginning or the end of the selected text by using the commands **Insert Before That** or **Insert After That.** These commands are equivalent to **Go To Beginning of Selection** and **Go To End of Selection,** respectively.

Editing by Voice

Editing a document involves several activities: inserting new text, deleting text, replacing text by dictating over it, and rearranging the document by cutting text from one place and pasting it into another. All these topics are covered in this section. I discuss reformatting text in Chapter 6.

You can use these techniques to fix the NaturallySpeaking mistakes as well as your own. But in the long run, you'll be happier with your NaturallySpeaking assistant's performance if you teach it to do better by using the Correction commands. See "Fixing NaturallySpeaking's Mistakes," later in this chapter.

Because NaturallySpeaking can only transcribe the words in its vocabulary, both your errors and its own are cleverly disguised as actual English words. They're even correctly spelled. In these circumstances, proofreading becomes an art. Be sure to check out the proofreading tricks in Chapter 7.

Selecting text

You can select text in three ways:

- Select text near the cursor by using commands like **"Select Next Two Characters."**

- Select text by saying it, as in **"Select *we'll always have Paris.*"**

- Select a large block of text by saying the beginning and the end, as in **"Select *once upon a time* through *lived happily ever after.*"**

Table 5-2 summarizes these commands.

Table 5-2	Commands for Selecting Text		
First Word	*Second Word*	*Third Word*	*Fourth Word*
Select	Next, Previous	1 – 20	Characters, Words, Paragraphs
Select	*<text>*		
Select	Again		
Select	*<text>*	Through	*<text>*

Selecting text near the cursor

To select text immediately before or after the current location of the cursor, use the **Select** command in a four-word sentence of this form: **Select,** followed by a direction (**Next** or **Previous**), followed by a number (**1 – 20**), followed by a unit (**Characters, Words,** or **Paragraphs**). For example:

- **"Select Next Seven Words"**
- **"Select Previous Three Paragraphs"**

If you want to select only one character, word, or paragraph, leave the number out of the sentence, as in **"Select Next Character"** or **"Select Previous Word.**

You can use **Back** or **Last** as synonyms for **Previous,** and **Forward** as a synonym for **Next.**

Selecting text by saying it

If text is visible on your screen, you can select it by saying, **"Select"** and then saying the text you want to select. For example, suppose Shakespeare is editing the file Hamlet.doc, and the phrase "To be or not to be" is visible. He can select the phrase by saying, **"Select to be or not to be."**

Sometimes, the phrase you select occurs several times in the current window. Which occurrence gets selected? NaturallySpeaking will display numbers next to the text and you can say, **"Choose <number>"** if you want to remove all the offending occurrences.

Selecting more text than you want to say

When you want to select a large block of text, you don't want to have to repeat all of it just to tell NaturallySpeaking where it is. NaturallySpeaking provides a special command for this purpose: **Select . . . Through.** Pick a word or two at the beginning of the selection and a word or two at the end, and then tell NaturallySpeaking to select everything in between by saying, **"Select <beginning text> Through <end text>."** For example, if your NaturallySpeaking window contains the Pledge of Allegiance, you can select it all by saying, **"Select I pledge allegiance Through justice for all."**

Deleting text

The simplest way to delete text is to use the **Scratch That** command to delete recently dictated text, as I explain in the preceding chapter. You can use **Scratch That** up to ten consecutive times. Another way to delete recently dictated text is the **Resume With** command, also covered in Chapter 4.

Table 5-3	**How to Make a Deleterious Statement**		
First Word	*Second Word*	*Third Word*	*Fourth Word*
Delete	**That**		
Delete	**Next, Previous**	**Character, Word, Paragraph**	
Delete	**Next, Previous**	**1 – 20**	**Characters, Words, Paragraphs**
Backspace			
Backspace	**1 – 20**		

To delete text immediately before or after the current location of the cursor, begin with **Delete** and then give a direction (**Next** or **Previous**), a number (**1 – 20**), and finally a unit (**Characters, Words,** or **Paragraphs**). For example:

- ✔ **"Delete Next Seven Words"**
- ✔ **"Delete Previous Three Paragraphs"**

If you want to delete only one character, word, or paragraph, you can leave the number out of the sentence, as in the following:

- ✔ **"Delete Next Character"**
- ✔ **"Delete Previous Word"**

You can use **Back** or **Last** as synonyms for **Previous,** and you can use **Forward** as a synonym for **Next.**

Saying **"Backspace"** gives the same result as pressing the Backspace key on the keyboard: The character immediately behind the cursor is deleted. To backspace up to 20 characters, say, **"Backspace,"** followed by a number between 1 and 20. **Backspace** is a simpler version of the **Delete Previous Character** command. For example, saying, **"Backspace Five"** produces the same results as saying, **"Delete Previous Five Characters."**

Sharp tongues: Cutting and pasting by voice

To cut or copy text from a document, select it (using the techniques from the "Selecting text" section earlier in this chapter) and then say either **"Cut That"** or **"Copy That."** To copy the entire document (which is useful if you like to compose in the NaturallySpeaking DragonPad or Dictation Box and then paste the results into an application), say, **"Copy All to Clipboard."**

If something is on the clipboard, you can paste it into your document by saying **"Paste That."**

Just undo it

Sometimes the result of editing or dictating something isn't what you pictured. All is not lost; you can still undo it. Just say, **"Undo That"** or **"Undo Last Action."** These two commands are equivalent.

In the NaturallySpeaking window, **Undo That** is like flipping a switch: If you say it twice, you wind up back where you started. In other words, the second **Undo That** undoes the first **Undo That.** When you use NaturallySpeaking with other applications, what you get varies from one application to another. In some applications, saying **Undo That** twice undoes the application's last two actions.

What **Undo That** actually does is type a Ctrl+Z. Different applications handle a Ctrl+Z in different ways, which is why they respond to **Undo That** differently.

Fixing NaturallySpeaking's Mistakes

Even though NaturallySpeaking 11.0 is 99 percent accurate out of the box, it will occasionally make a hilarious error. That's because NaturallySpeaking is incapable of a simple typo or misspelling. All its mistakes are still correct English words — just not the words you said or meant to say. But as funny as some mistakes might be, you don't want to create documents that amuse your readers because of unintentional errors. You want those mistakes fixed, preferably in a way that keeps them from happening again the next time you dictate. That's what NaturallySpeaking's **Correct That** and related correction commands are for.

If you don't care about correcting NaturallySpeaking, and all you want to do is get an error out of the document you're working on, just select the offending text and dictate something else over it. Or, if you catch the error immediately, you can get rid of it by saying **"Scratch That"** or **"Undo That,"** as described in "Editing by Voice," earlier in this chapter.

If you have made any corrections during a session, NaturallySpeaking reminds you to save your speech files before exiting. Be sure to choose Yes. Otherwise, all the lessons NaturallySpeaking learned from these corrections are lost.

Correcting a NaturallySpeaking recognition error

Depending on how quickly you catch the error, you can correct it in one of the following two ways:

- If you catch the error as soon as NaturallySpeaking makes it, say, **"Correct That"** or **"Spell That."** See "Casting a spell," later in this chapter for more about **Spell That.**

- If you don't catch the error immediately, say, **"Correct *<incorrect text>*."** (You can also select the erroneous text verbally or with your voice and then say, **"Correct That."**)

Table 5-4 summarizes these ways of making a correction. If you would rather not use voice commands at all, select the text and then press the – (minus) key on the numeric keypad of your keyboard or click the Correct button on the NaturallySpeaking DragonBar Extras section. (You can substitute a different key for the – (minus) key; see the discussion of NaturallySpeaking options in Chapter 3.)

Table 5-4	Making Your Corrections		
First Word	*Second Word*	*Third Word*	*Fourth Word*
Correct	That		
Spell	That		
Correct	*<text>*		
Correct	*<text>*	Through	*<text>*

No matter how you do it, the Correction menu box appears, as shown in Figure 5-1.

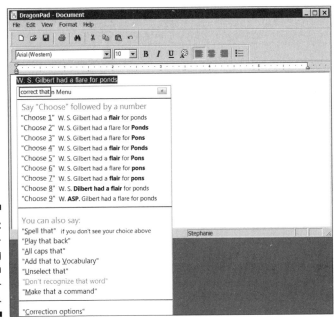

Figure 5-1:
Naturally-
Speaking
generates a
list of alter-
natives.

The dictation error that Figure 5-1 illustrates occurred when I said, "W. S. Gilbert had a flair for puns." What NaturallySpeaking thought I said was, "W. S. Gilbert had a flair for ponds." When I said **"Correct That,"** the Correction menu box shown in Figure 5-1 appeared.

NaturallySpeaking chose some alternative interpretations of what I said, listed in the box, up to a maximum of nine. Figure 5-1 shows NaturallySpeaking got most of the phrase right.

If the correct phrase is listed in the Correction menu box, you need only tell NaturallySpeaking which number it is. If I had said, "W. S. Gilbert had a flair for ponds," then I could make the correction in Figure 5-1 by saying **"Choose 1."** You can also click the correct version with the mouse. When you indicate your choice, the Correction dialog box closes and the correction is made in the text.

Sometimes, none of the options offered is correct, as is the case in Figure 5-1. In those instances you should try to re-dictate over the highlighted text. If Dragon gets it wrong again, say, **"Spell that."** The Spelling Window will open. Start spelling the correct version out loud. (See "Casting a spell," later in this chapter.) With each new letter, more alternatives appear in the box as NaturallySpeaking continues trying to guess what the correct version is. If the correct version appears, you can stop typing or spelling and choose it by number. The Correction menu box closes and the correction is made in the text.

Here are a few additional reminders and tips:

✔ Don't attempt to dictate replacement text in the Spell window. NaturallySpeaking tries to interpret your utterances as letters!

✔ If you are correcting a large block of text, you can say, **"Correct <*begin-ning of incorrect text*> Through <*end of incorrect text*>."**

Casting a spell

One way to correct a simple mistake is to select the mistaken word and spell the correct one. You can do this from the Corrections Menu by choosing Spell That if you don't see the choice you want.

Suppose you dictated "New York" and NaturallySpeaking interpreted it as "Newark." You could correct it as follows:

1. **Find the mistaken word, "Newark," in the active window.**

2. **Say,** "Select Newark."

   If NaturallySpeaking hears you correctly this time, the mistaken word is selected. If "Newark" occurs several times in the active window, you may need to say, **"Select Again"** to select the occurrence that you want to correct. See "Selecting text by saying it," earlier in this chapter.

3. **Say the correction:** "New York."

4. **Say,** "Spell That" **and the Spelling window opens. Say** "cap N-e-w space bar cap Y-o-r-k." **Or you can use the International Communications Alphabet by saying,** "Spell That cap November Echo Whiskey space bar cap Yankee Oscar Romeo Kilo."

   The Correction dialog box appears with the correctly spelled "New York" selected. You will also see the choices to say "Play that back," and "Train or Tell me more about this window" (for help). These are described below.

5. **Say** "Click OK" **or** "Press Enter." **Or you can click the OK button or press the Enter key.**

   NaturallySpeaking replaces the incorrect "Newark" in the text with the correct "New York." Also, NaturallySpeaking makes an invisible little note to remind itself not to be so quick to hear "Newark" instead of "New York." (See the later sidebar "Bravo! Charlie Tangos with Juliet in November," for more about the International Communications Alphabet, or ICA.)

But what if you didn't see the choice you wanted? You could choose the option **"Spell That"** from the Correction menu and bring up the Spelling Window, shown in Figure 5-2. Follow these steps:

1. **Choose "Spell That" from within the Correction menu.**

   The Spelling Window appears with several choices. One of the choices is in the typing window.

2. **Click in the typing window if you want to type your correction, or start spelling it if you want to use a verbal command.**

3. **Say** "Click OK" **or** "Press Enter." **Or you can click the OK button or press the Enter key.**

If you use a lot of proper nouns (names of people, places, and things), learning the ICA might be worthwhile. You can use the ICA to spell a word even during dictation, not just in the Correction menu box.

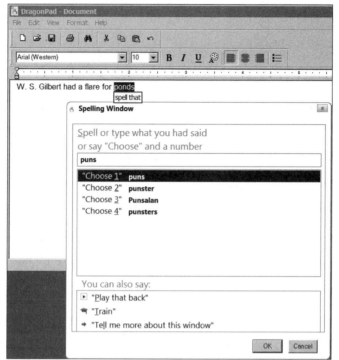

Figure 5-2:
Using the
Spelling
Window for
correction.

Recurring errors

The correction process is supposed to prevent the same errors from happening in the future, but sometimes NaturallySpeaking makes a particular error a couple of times. In these cases, you need something stronger than just correction; you need to train NaturallySpeaking (otherwise known as boot camp for assistants).

Begin by identifying the error and typing or dictating the correct version into the Correction menu box. Then say, **"Spell That"** and the Spelling Window opens. But instead of clicking the OK button in the Spelling Window, click Train instead. This opens the Train Words dialog box, where you record the correct word. See Chapter 18 for detailed instructions.

Playing back an error

NaturallySpeaking includes a Play Back feature that you can use to listen to your dictation. In particular, when you are correcting a mistake, you can click the Play Back button in the Correction dialog box to hear what you said. You may discover that you aren't dealing with a recognition error at all and that you didn't say what you think you said. See Chapter 7 for more about the playback feature.

Bravo! Charlie tangos with Juliet in November

The problem with dictating letters is that they all sound alike. If you've ever had to spell your name to someone over the telephone, you know how easily *d*'s become *t*'s or *m*'s turn into *n*'s.

This is an old problem, so it isn't surprising that someone solved it a long time ago by creating the International Communications Alphabet. In the ICA, the names of the letters all sound different, so you can spell aloud with confidence if you know the ICA vocabulary:

a alpha

b bravo

c charlie

d delta

e echo

f foxtrot

g golf

h hotel

i india

j juliet

k kilo

l lima

m mike

n november

o oscar

p papa

q quebec

r romeo

s sierra

t tango

u uniform

v victor

w whiskey

x xray

y yankee

z zulu

Chapter 6

Basic Formatting in Text-Editing Applications

. . . .

In This Chapter

▶ Using left and right alignment

▶ Centering a paragraph

▶ Creating numbered or bulleted lists

▶ Using italic, bold, and underlined text

▶ Changing font size and style

. . . .

*T*ext that is all the same font, size, and style can be pretty boring. Because of advances in web design, everyone's expectations for design are higher. Formatting puts some zing into your content and makes it exciting. Your favorite applications are all loaded with formatting buttons and icons. You can, of course, continue to use them. But NaturallySpeaking lets you produce many of the same results with voice commands.

In this chapter, we're talking about voice commands especially for formatting, like **Bold That.** As Chapter 21 discusses, you can also choose formatting commands from the Sidebar by using general-purpose voice commands, but those take longer. Save those for other applications. In the NaturallySpeaking DragonPad (and specific other applications), you can get the job done quickly with formatting commands.

NaturallySpeaking provides several different commands for most actions. These commands fall into two basic types. On one hand, you can use short, very specific commands for most actions, such as **Underline That** for underlining text or **Center That** for centering a paragraph. Table 6-1 shows the short formatting commands.

Table 6-1	The Short Formatting Commands	
To Do This	*Example*	*Say This*
Make selected text bold	**Like This**	"Bold That"
Italicize selected text	*Like This*	"Italicize That"
Underline selected text	<u>Like This</u>	"Underline That"
Make selected text normal	Like This	"Restore That"
Center current paragraph	Like This	"Center That"
Right-align current paragraph	Like This	"Right-Align That"
Left-align current paragraph	Like This	"Left-Align That"

On the other hand, you can use the slightly longer but more general commands **Format** and **Set** to do almost anything if you know the right syntax. For example, **Format That Bold** and **Format That Centered** bolds or centers text, respectively, whereas **Format That Courier 18** changes the font to 18-point Courier. Whether you find it easier to remember a lot of short commands or a general family of longer commands that follow predictable patterns is largely a matter of taste.

Left, Right, and Center: Getting into Alignment

To change the alignment of a paragraph, move the cursor into the paragraph and use one of the following commands:

- **Center That**
- **Left-Align That**
- **Right-Align That**

(If you're currently dictating a paragraph, you don't have to move the cursor; it is already in the right paragraph. Just speak the command.)

To change the alignment of up to 20 consecutive paragraphs, follow these steps:

1. **Move the cursor to the beginning of the first paragraph.**

2. **Say, "Select Next** *<number>* **Paragraphs," where** *<number>* **is the number of paragraphs you want to realign.**

   For example, say, **"Select Next Two Paragraphs."**

3. **Say,** "Center That," "Left-Align That," **or** "Right-Align That."

   In Figure 6-1 you see what happens when you select two paragraphs and say, **"Right-Align That."**

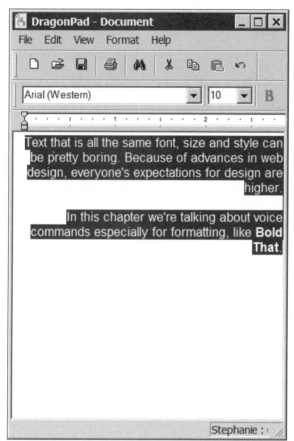

Figure 6-1:
Right aligning two paragraphs.

To change the alignment of the entire document, follow these steps:

1. **Say,** "Select Document."

2. **Say,** "Center That," "Left-Align That," **or** "Right-Align That."

You can use the **Format** command to substitute for any of the alignment commands.

- ✔ **Format That Centered** gives the same result as **Center That.**
- ✔ **Format That Left Aligned** gives the same result as **Left-Align That.**
- ✔ **Format That Right Aligned** gives the same result as **Right-Align That.**

Using Bullets and Numbered Lists

Clear, concise writing requires more than just simple paragraphs. For example, *For Dummies* books just couldn't exist without

- ✔ Bullets
- ✔ Numbered lists

Or perhaps I should say that these books couldn't get by without

1. Numbered lists
2. Bullets

How can you create bulleted and numbered lists with voice commands? In Natural Language and Full Text Control applications, dictate the text that you want a bullet next to and then say, **"Format That Bullet Style."** To get a second bullet, say, **"New Line."**

In this chapter, I give commands for dictating in the NaturallySpeaking window. (The same commands also work in Full Text Control applications, including Natural Language Commands in Word or WordPerfect, for example.) This command doesn't work in all applications. If your document is in an application that doesn't support Full Text Control, make the bulleted list in the DragonPad and then copy and paste it into your document.

Like **Bold That** and **Italicize That,** the **Format That Bullet Style** command undoes itself. In other words, you can turn a bulleted paragraph back into regular text by moving the cursor to that paragraph and saying, **"Format That Bullet Style."** You may not think this makes sense — but that's the way it works. (See the "Commands that undo themselves" sidebar, later in this chapter.) Use this technique to end the bulleted list: After the last bulleted paragraph is done, say, **"New Paragraph"** and then, **"Format That Bullet Style."** The new paragraph is now in regular style.

The NaturallySpeaking Dictation Box doesn't provide a means for generating numbered lists automatically. You have to construct them yourself. For example, say, **"New Line. One period. Cap *this is the first entry on my numbered list*. Period. New Line. Two period. Cap *this is the second entry*. Period."** The result is

1. This is the first entry on my numbered list.
2. This is the second entry.

Formatting in applications other than NaturallySpeaking

The NaturallySpeaking formatting commands in this chapter work only with the NaturallySpeaking word processor and specific other applications: the Natural Language applications (for example, Word, WordPerfect, and OpenOffice.org) and the Full Text Control applications (for example, DragonPad, WordPad, and Microsoft Outlook).

In general, if you want to create or edit a formatted document in an application that is not compatible, you have two choices:

✔ Work in the NaturallySpeaking window, and then paste the result into the other application.

✔ Work in the application's own window and get all your formatting commands from the menus.

Choosing formatting commands from the menus means you can use voice control for *anything* the application can do, not just formatting. For example, if you want to make some selected text bold in an unsupported application, you couldn't use the NaturallySpeaking **Bold That** command, but you could access the Bold command on the application's own Style menu by saying, **"Click Style, Bold."** Specially supported word processors such as Word and WordPerfect have more formatting features than NaturallySpeaking gives you direct commands for. In these cases, you can access the word processor's own menus by voice as well as by mouse or keyboard. For example, NaturallySpeaking provides no **Footnote That** command for inserting footnotes into Word documents, but you can use the Footnote command on Word's insert menu by saying, **"Click Insert, Footnote."**

Changing Font

NaturallySpeaking provides commands like **Bold That** to change the style of a font. You can use the **Set** or **Format** commands to change the size or style of a font, to choose a new font family, or to change everything at the same time.

Changing your style: Bold, italic, and underlined text

One way to create bold, italic, or underlined text is to select the text and then say, **"Bold That," "Italicize That,"** or **"Underline That."**

These three commands are equivalent to clicking the corresponding buttons (**B**, *I*, or <u>U</u>) on the toolbar. An unusual effect of making them work like the buttons is that these commands undo themselves. For example, if you select some underlined text and say **"Underline That,"** the underlining is removed. See the "Commands that undo themselves" sidebar, later in this chapter.

To dictate bold, italic, or underlined text, follow these steps:

1. **Move the cursor to the place in the document where you want the text to be.**

2. **Say,** "Bold That," "Italicize That," or "Underline That," **depending on what kind of text you want to produce.**

3. **Dictate your text.**

When text is already bold, italic, underlined, or some combination of all three, you can change it back to plain Roman text by selecting it and saying, **"Restore That."**

The **Format** and **Set** commands can substitute for any of these commands. For example, the following three commands have the same effect:

- ✔ **Bold That**
- ✔ **Format That Bold**
- ✔ **Set Font Bold**

You can also use **Format That** or **Set Font** with **Italics, Underline,** or **Regular.** For example,

- ✔ **Set Font Regular** and **Format That Regular** are equivalent to **Restore That.**
- ✔ **Set Font Bold** and **Format That Bold** are equivalent to **Bold That.**

 In version 11.0, you can also use Quick Voice Formatting commands for Bold, Underline, Italicize, Capitalize, Copy, Delete, and Cut by saying, **"Select <*text*>"** or **"Select <*start*> through <*end*>,"** saying the command (for example, **"Bold"**), and then saying the words to which you want to apply the command.

Changing font size

To change the size of a font, you must know the point size that you want. If, for example, you want to change some text to 18 point, you can select it and say,

- ✔ "Set Size 18"
- ✔ "Format That Size 18"

Commands that undo themselves

The commands **Bold That, Underline That, Italicize That,** and **Format That Bullet Style** all share a quirky property: They undo themselves. For example, if you select some regular text and say, **"Bold That,"** the text becomes bold. But if you select some bold text and say, **"Bold That,"** it becomes regular. If you say, **"Bold That"** twice, you wind up back where you started.

Huh? In real life, voice commands almost never undo themselves. If I tell my dog to sit when I am not looking at him, and he's already sitting, I don't expect him to stand back up again. What's special about these four voice commands that they should undo themselves?

These commands have something in common: In most word processors, you perform these actions by clicking buttons on a toolbar. The Bold, Italic, Underline, and Bullet buttons on a word processor's toolbar typically work like the power button on a TV: You push it again to turn the power off.

So the designers at Dragon had a decision to make: Should bold, italic, underline, and bullet commands work like typical voice commands or should they work like the toolbar buttons that people are used to using? The designers decided to model the commands after the buttons, and that's why they undo themselves.

In Figure 6-2, the **"Format That Size 18"** command is given.

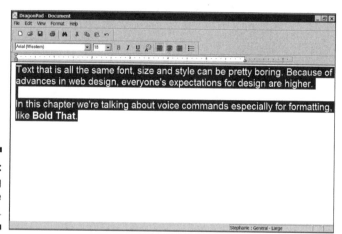

Figure 6-2:
Changing
the font size
to 18.

Not all point sizes exist for all font families. If you request a nonexistent point size, your command is ignored.

If you want to start dictating in a new font size, move the cursor to the place where you want to begin dictating and give a **Set Size** or **Format That Size** command. For example,

  ✔ **Set Size 10**

  ✔ **Format That Size 24**

When you begin to dictate, the text appears in the size type that you requested, if that size exists in the current font family.

Changing font family

Who said you can't choose your family? NaturallySpeaking recognizes most font families. You can use the **Set** or **Format** commands to change from one of these font families to another. For example,

  ✔ **Set Font Times**

  ✔ **Format That Times**

Both change the current font to Times New Roman on any text that was selected when you issued this command. If you did not select any text, any new text you dictate at the insertion point will be in Times New Roman font.

If you want to use a font whose name NaturallySpeaking doesn't recognize, you must choose it from the menu, either by voice or using the mouse. See Chapter 16 for a discussion of controlling the menus by voice.

Changing everything at once

The **Format** and **Set** commands demonstrate their full power when you want to change font, size, and style all with one command. For example,

  ✔ **Format That Courier 14 Italic**

  ✔ **Set Font Courier 14 Italic**

These are equivalent commands that change the font to Courier, the font size to 14, and the style to italic. Tables 6-2 and 6-3 tell you how to speak a Format or Set command.

When I put something in angle brackets and italics, like *<style>,* it is a place-holder. You don't literally say that word; instead, you replace it with your own particular choice of word from a list of styles that I give you.

What does "That" mean now?

When you use capitalization, spacing, and hyphenation commands (what Dragon refers to as dictation commands), such as **Cap That**, the word *that* refers to what you just spoke — text that's still being worked on by the NaturallySpeaking engine. When you use formatting commands, however, the word *that* no longer refers to the text you just spoke. It refers only to whatever you have selected! Or if you haven't selected anything, the command affects the formatting for whatever you dictate next.

So, for instance, if you dictate, **"Haste makes waste"** and then (not stopping to select anything) say, **"Bold That,"** nothing happens to the text you dictated. However, if you continue,

saying, **"but a stitch in time saves nine,"** that text appears bold. The command simply turned on bold style. The result looks like this:

Haste makes waste **but a stitch in time saves nine.**

The difference in the meaning of *that* sounds like a complicated distinction to remember, but the truth is actually simple. When you say **"Bold That," "Italicize That," "Underline That,"** or any of the paragraph alignment commands, NaturallySpeaking presses the command key (for example, Ctrl+B for Bold) assigned to that format.

Table 6-2	The Syntax of Format		
Command	*Then Say*	*Then Say*	*Then Say*
Format That	**Capitals**		
	All Caps		
	Bold		
	Italics		
	Underline		
	Regular		
	Left-Aligned		
	Right-Aligned		
	Bullet Style		
	Size	4 – 120	
	<font family>	4 – 120	*<style>*

Plain, Plain Text, and Regular mean the same thing: not bold and not italic. They do not remove underlining. To undo underlining, see the earlier section, "Changing your style: Bold, italic, and underlined text."

Table 6-3		The Syntax of Set		
Command	*Then Say*	*Then Say*	*Then Say*	*Then Say*
Set	Size	4 – 120		
	Font	*<style>*		
		<font family>	4 – 120	
		<font family>	4 – 120	*<style>*

You can change color with the font commands in the NaturallySpeaking DragonPad.

Chapter 7

Proofreading and Listening to Your Text

*O*n one hand, NaturallySpeaking never misspells a word. On the other hand, NaturallySpeaking can make some mistakes by choosing the wrong (if perfectly spelled) word. A person who writes to the bank, "I have trouble paying this year" rather than, "I am double paying this year" is going to have a big problem. No computerized grammar checker or other kind of checker is likely to catch that error. Proofreading is the only answer.

Of course, you don't need to hear your text in order to proofread it. But in NaturallySpeaking, you can hear your dictation in one of two ways:

✔ **Playback of your voice.** NaturallySpeaking records your voice as you dictate and can play it back to help you proofread (not available in the Home edition).

✔ **Read the text.** You can read what NaturallySpeaking has generated from your dictation — or of any other text you bring into the NaturallySpeaking DragonPad or any other supported application. The NaturallySpeaking text-to-speech feature uses a computer-synthesized voice to convert any text into speech.

Why play your own voice back? For one thing, it tends to make the NaturallySpeaking errors stand out. If you read what NaturallySpeaking typed, as you listen to your voice, the discrepancy between, say, the written word *double* and the word you spoke, *trouble* becomes obvious.

Also, playback lets you know what you *actually* said, rather than what you *think* you said. Knowing what you actually said is important when you correct NaturallySpeaking. If NaturallySpeaking has typed *fourth-quarter profits are down,* for instance, and you think you said, "in the fourth quarter, profits are down," you should correct NaturallySpeaking — even if you like its phraseology better! If, on the other hand, you really *did* say, "fourth-quarter profits are down," do *not* correct NaturallySpeaking. Playing back your voice helps you do a better job of correcting NaturallySpeaking.

What about text-to-speech read back? Why listen to synthesized speech, instead of your recorded voice, when you proofread? Text-to-speech, though not a perfect reader, lets you hear what NaturallySpeaking actually typed. The NaturallySpeaking errors (wrong words) are sometimes more obvious when you hear them than when you see them.

Text-to-speech can be useful for other purposes. If you have a visual impairment, for example, you can verbally copy documents or e-mail messages to the NaturallySpeaking window and play them.

A quick way to access the commands to **Read That** or **Play That Back** is by going to the DragonBar⇨Audio and selecting the command from the menu items.

Using Voice Commands for Playback

The simplest form of playing back your voice is to speak the command **Play That** (or **Play That Back**) after you dictate some text. The **Play That** command reads back the last thing you said. **Play That Back** is just another form of the same command.

A more practical use of the **Play That** command is to proofread larger blocks of text than just your most recent utterance. You can select the text you want to proofread and then say, **"Play That."** You can use any means you like to select the text: your mouse, your keyboard, or a NaturallySpeaking voice command such as **Select Document, Select Paragraph,** or **Select Line.** (See Chapter 5 for details of various selections.)

Instead of selecting text first and then giving the **Play** command, you can specify what chunks of text are to be played back, right in the command. Use any of the following commands; you can say either **"Play"** or **"Play Back,"** as you prefer (I only show the **Play** form here):

- ✔ Play Line
- ✔ Play Paragraph
- ✔ Play Document
- ✔ Play Window
- ✔ Play Screen
- ✔ Play To Here
- ✔ Play From Here

The **Play To Here** and **Play From Here** commands let you play everything up to the current typing cursor position ("here") or from that position to the end.

Pressing Ctrl+Shift+S starts the playback from your typing cursor's current position. (It's the same as **Play From Here.**)

NaturallySpeaking stores about a half-hour's worth of dictated text. (Pauses don't count.) Anything you dictated before that point can't be played back.

Proofreading and Correcting with Playback

Voice playback is a nice feature for proofreading and editing your documents. NaturallySpeaking provides convenient buttons on the DragonBar and hotkeys on the keyboard for controlling the playback feature as you proofread.

Note that playback doesn't work for text entered in the following ways:

- ✔ Text that has been typed in
- ✔ Text that you didn't dictate in the first place
- ✔ Text that you dictated, but later moved

To hear such text, use the NaturallySpeaking text-to-speech feature instead.

You can extend the DragonBar to reveal the Extras Bar by saying, **"View Extras Bar"** or **"Hide Extras Bar"** or by clicking on the up arrows.

When you are ready to proofread your document and correct NaturallySpeaking errors, follow these steps:

1. **Select the text you want to proofread.**

   For instance, say, **"Select Document,"** or select text by using your mouse.

   You can select and play in one command by saying a command like **"Play Document"** or **"Play Paragraph"** instead. You can then skip to Step 3.

2. **Say,** "Play That."

   Or press Ctrl+Shift+S or click the Play button on the toolbar shown in Figure 7-1.

Figure 7-1:
Playback
controls.

3. **Scan the text with your eyes as your dictation plays back.**

   At this point, poise your finger over the minus (–) key on the numeric keypad. (The numeric keypad is usually on the far right end of your keyboard.) Strike this key quickly when you hear an error! To help you follow the text, a yellow arrow points as it continues reading.

4. **When you come to a NaturallySpeaking error, press the – (minus) key on the numeric keypad of your keyboard.**

   The playback stops and the Correction menu box pops up, display-ing the last four spoken words. (Clicking the Correction button on the DragonBar does the same thing as the minus key.)

   You must press the minus key within four words or punctuation marks of when you hear the error, or you will overshoot the error.

5. **Choose the correct interpretation from the list in the Correction menu box.**

   (See Chapter 5 if you aren't familiar with the Correction menu box.)

   When you make your choice, the Correction menu box closes and play-back continues immediately. Continue correcting errors as in Steps 4 and 5 until you reach the end of the text to be played.

If you press the minus key too late, you'll overshoot the error. That is, the Correction menu box displays a phrase after the one you want. Here are a few solutions for that issue and other related problems:

✔ If you realize you have overshot the error, but still haven't pressed the minus key, press the left-arrow key (one of the navigation keys on the keyboard). This backs NaturallySpeaking up by about eight to ten words. Press the left-arrow key repeatedly until you catch the phrase you want. Alternatively, you can click the Begin Rewind button on the toolbar.

✔ If you have already pressed the minus key and the Correction menu box pops up with the wrong phrase in it, first click Cancel or press the Esc key on your keyboard to exit the Correction menu box. Then press the left-arrow key to skip backwards.

✔ Keep in mind that when you click the minus key, the Correction menu box displays only the last four words (or punctuation marks). If playback is already more than three words ahead of the error, press the left-arrow key to skip backwards.

✔ A secret (well, undocumented) alternative to the minus key in the DragonPad is the down-arrow key (among the navigation keys on your keyboard). I find this key more convenient, because it's next to the left-arrow key. You can also change the hotkey for corrections to any key you like, using the Tools⊃Options command in NaturallySpeaking. See Chapter 3 for details.

Other playback buttons and hotkeys can help you make corrections more efficiently. Here's what they do:

✔ **To stop the playback:** Click the Stop button (with the square) in the toolbar or press the Esc key (or Ctrl+1).

✔ **To play back at high speed:** Click the Begin Fast Forward button (with the > symbol).

✔ **To skip forward in your text:** Press the right-arrow key until you reach your text.

✔ **To skip backward at high speed:** Click the Begin Rewind button.

✔ **To skip backward in your text:** Press the left-arrow key until you reach your text.

Using the Text-to-Speech Feature

The NaturallySpeaking text-to-speech feature is a great piece of wizardry. While not perfect, it can help your PC do a reasonable job of turning text into speech. It might even be disconcerting if it sounded like a real person. Are you ready for that?

Playback in the Corrections dialog box

A good reason for playing back your dictation is so that you can properly correct NaturallySpeaking. You want to be sure that the text you type in the Correction menu box is what you actually said!

One way to ensure that your correction matches your spoken word is to click the Play That Back selection in the Correction menu box. NaturallySpeaking then plays your original speech for the phrase being corrected.

If you like this feature, you can tell NaturallySpeaking to play the recorded speech whenever you use the Correction menu box. Choose Tools⇨Options from the NaturallySpeaking menu. In the Options dialog box that appears, click the Correction tab and click to place a check mark in the Automatic Playback On Correction check box. Click OK to close the Options dialog box.

Text-to-speech isn't limited to proofreading. It's a general-purpose tool for listening to documents. For instance, you could play a document by copying it into the NaturallySpeaking window. A visually impaired person could do the whole job with the verbal copying and window-switching commands described in Chapter 16.

One reason for using text-to-speech is to help proofread your text. But which is better for proofreading — playback of your own voice or reading it with text-to-speech?

Many people find that playing back their own speech is the best way to find errors. With playback, you hear the correct text and spot errors with your eyes. Because you're comparing the original dictation to the resulting text, playing back tends to be a more accurate way of proofreading.

If you're an auditory learner, however — for instance, if you find you pay better attention to the spoken word than to the written word — you might try text-to-speech read back. With the reading back, you hear the text that NaturallySpeaking wrote and mentally judge whether that was what you intended. You aren't presented with your original dictation, just the NaturallySpeaking interpretation. A second advantage of reading it back is that it works even if you edit text manually; playback can't handle manual edits.

To start Read, select some text in the NaturallySpeaking window (using the mouse, the keyboard, or a voice command). Then click the Read icon in the DragonBar extras section or speak the verbal command, **"Read That."**

Read verbal commands are the same as Playback verbal commands, except instead of saying **"Play,"** you say **"Read."** Here are the verbal commands:

- ✔ **Read That** (referring to text you have selected)
- ✔ **Read That Back** (same as **Read That**)
- ✔ **Read Line**
- ✔ **Read Paragraph**
- ✔ **Read Document**
- ✔ **Read Window**
- ✔ **Read Screen**
- ✔ **Read Up To Here** (where "here" is wherever your typing cursor is)
- ✔ **Read Down From Here**

You can stop reading back in the NaturallySpeaking window by pressing the Esc key. If you hear a NaturallySpeaking error during read-back, first stop the read-back, and then select the erroneous text any way you like (with your mouse and keyboard or a verbal command). With text selected, launch the Correction menu box in any of the usual ways, including pressing the minus key on the numeric keypad, clicking Correction on the DragonBar, or saying, **"Correct That."**

If you hear an error that you (not NaturallySpeaking) made, stop reading back first by pressing the Esc key. Then, select and edit your text any way you like (by speech or by using the keyboard and mouse).

Want to fine-tune the voice to speak as fast or slow as you like? Want to spend some fun time just playing with all the voices available? You can adjust the speed, volume, and pitch attributes of text-to-speech. Choose Tools➪Options, and then click the Playback/Text-To-Speech tab on the Options dialog box that appears. The dialog box sports three sliding adjustments, one for each attribute. Drag the slider to the right for higher speed, volume, or pitch or to the left for lower values. To test the sound at your chosen settings, click the Read Text button. NaturallySpeaking will read the text in the Preview window. To return the values to their original settings, click the Restore Defaults button. Click the OK button when you're done. ("British English Jane" and "American English Jennifer" don't allow pitch adjustments.)

Chapter 8

Dictating into Other Applications

*Y*ou can get quite a bit done just by dictating into the NaturallySpeaking Dictation Box and then using cut-and-paste techniques to move the text into documents belonging to other applications. But you haven't seen the full potential of NaturallySpeaking until you've used it to dictate directly into other applications. At that point, NaturallySpeaking becomes an essential component of your computer, like the keyboard and the mouse.

In this chapter, I focus on general techniques that you can use with many applications, using the Dictation Box and Full Text Control in the NaturallySpeaking terminology. I tell you about the interactions you can expect in different sets of applications, plus the details. When you are not sure why something is working a certain way, you can turn here to at least find out how it should work.

The bottom line in using NaturallySpeaking with other applications is that basic dictation works pretty much the same, but the capabilities to do other tasks vary.

Finding Levels of Control

In addition to entering text into another application's windows, NaturallySpeaking voice commands can also control another application's menus. When you combine these techniques with the desktop control commands and dialog box techniques described in Chapter 16, you get a true no-hands computer experience.

One of the most frequently asked questions about NaturallySpeaking is, "Does it work with *<name of application>*?" The answer is yes. If the application has menus, dialog boxes, or a window into which you can type text, then you can use NaturallySpeaking with it. The more interesting question isn't *whether* NaturallySpeaking voice commands work with some application, but *which* commands work with which applications.

Over the years, I've watched NaturallySpeaking software evolve to the point where it's sometimes hard for me to demonstrate a mistake. The out-of-the-box accuracy is truly stunning. The number of programs and apps available to dictate into has exploded as well. For this reason, I want to present you with a way of thinking about using other applications so that you know what to expect.

NaturallySpeaking has different levels of control with different programs (on the web, as software, or as a mobile app). Commands that work in some applications don't work in others. You'll save yourself a lot of frustration if you understand the level of control you have in a particular type of application.

Table 8-1 summarizes these basic control levels:

✔ **Desktop:** Even if you have no applications other than NaturallySpeaking open at all, you still have a few dictation powers:

- Open files and applications on the desktop or the Start menu.

- Switch from one open window to another.

- Use the mouse commands.

See Chapter 16 for details.

✔ **Nearly Any Windows Application:** You have all the desktop commands plus

- Basic menu control

- Dictation

- Navigation

✔ **The Dictation Box with another application:** You retain all the desktop interactions. You can enter text by dictating. You can use the application's hotkeys and menus. You can move around in a document by using the Move and Go commands. You have a limited amount of selection and correction capabilities.

See "Creating Documents with the Dictation Box," later in this chapter.

✔ **Full Text Control:** You have all the Dictation Box capabilities, plus the capability to create, edit, or format content. In other words, editing and correcting work exactly the way they do in the NaturallySpeaking DragonPad.

You can check if an application has Full Text Control by looking at the DragonBar and seeing if the check mark is green. If it is, you have Full Text Control. For example, if you use OpenOffice.org Writer, version 3.1 or 3.2, you have Full Text Control.

✔ **Natural Language Commands:** These allow you to speak commands in a more natural way. For example, rather than having to say, **"Click File >Click Save As>,"** you can simply say, **"Save Document."** You speak as you normally would. You have the full editing, correcting, and formatting control of the NaturallySpeaking DragonPad, plus a Dragon NaturallySpeaking menu is visible above the other application's menu bar.

Using this menu, you can do virtually anything that you can do with the DragonBar: Create a new User Profile, launch Accuracy Training, check your microphone, and so on.

This level is available in applications such as Microsoft Word, Internet Explorer, and Mozilla Firefox.

Table 8-1   NaturallySpeaking in Different Applications

Application	Windows Desktop	Nearly Any Windows Application	NaturallySpeaking Dictation Box with Another Application	Full Text Control Applications	Natural Language Commands
Launch applications	X	X	X	X	X
Control windows	X	X	X	X	X
Clipboard		X	X	X	X
Basic menu control		X	X	X	X
Dictation		X	X	X	X
Navigation		X	X	X	X
NaturallySpeaking DragonBar			X	X	X
Menus			X	X	X
Full Text Control				x	X
Additional formatting				x	X
Additional natural phrases					X

Getting Started

You may already be comfortable dictating into the NaturallySpeaking DragonPad, and you may have developed confidence that you can create documents there. If so, then you have already mastered the techniques that allow you to dictate to other applications. You just need to know which commands you can use in which situations.

If you aren't already familiar with dictating in the NaturallySpeaking Dictation Box, the next sections tell you what you need to know.

Dictating your first words

The first step in achieving dictation mastery of other applications is to make the words you say appear in a window controlled by the other application. (You can worry later about whether those words are correct or what you should do if they aren't.)

To get those first words to show up in the correct window, do the following:

1. **Open NaturallySpeaking and another application.**

   In the figures, I am dictating into WordPad, but you can use any application you want. It doesn't matter whether you open NaturallySpeaking or the other application first.

2. **Click the microphone icon in the DragonBar to turn the microphone on.**

   If the icon is elevated, the microphone is on; if the icon is lying flat, the microphone is off. Change from one state to the other by clicking the microphone icon. By default, the microphone is off at startup.

3. **Activate the window of the other application.**

   - If the application is already opened but not visible, you can say, **"List open applications."**

     A numbered list of open applications pops up. Choose the application you want.

   - If the application has not been opened, say, **"Open *<application name>*."**

     The application should open and the cursor should be blinking in the text-editing window. If not, click in the text-editing window.

   In the open text window, I dictated, **"Dictating into other applications really works. Period."** The WordPad window then looked like Figure 8-1.

Figure 8-1:
WordPad
takes dicta-
tion from
Naturally-
Speaking.

If you aren't going to use the NaturallySpeaking DragonBar for awhile, minimize it by clicking on the Tray Icon Only choice from the Dragon icon in the
DragonBar. A minimized window uses less of your computer's resources for
display and leaves more for the really important tasks, like figuring out what
you just said. But don't *close* the NaturallySpeaking DragonBar. If you do,
you'll instantly lose your dictating capabilities.

The one NaturallySpeaking element that follows you around

One item from the NaturallySpeaking DragonBar is always available to you
when NaturallySpeaking is running: the microphone. Without it, you're talking to yourself.

The microphone box is in the up position (at a slight angle) when it's on.
Click it to switch between on and off.

You can use the + (plus) key on the numeric keypad (at the far right end of
your keyboard) as a microphone on/off button.

Points to ponder

NaturallySpeaking uses several windows at once. Normally, you launch an application, you get an application window, and you work in that window. End of story. Not so with NaturallySpeaking, and for good reason: You want to be able to use voice input in lots of different places, not just in a single window.

The core of NaturallySpeaking — the basic program that turns your speech into text or actions — actually runs in the background. It is hidden:

✔ This hidden program puts its text into whichever application window you are using at any given moment.

✔ If you give a menu command, such a **Click File**, the command goes to that application's window, too.

To be technically precise, NaturallySpeaking works with whichever application is active at the time. An application is active if its title bar is darkened. Click on an application's title bar, or anywhere in its window, to make it active.

Capabilities you have in any application

No matter what application you find yourself working in, you can do the following (as long as NaturallySpeaking is running):

✔ **Use the Dictation Box:** Once another application is open, you can access it from the DragonBar menu. Choose Tools⇨Dictation Box and say, **"Show Dictation Box,"** or press Ctrl+Shift+D.

✔ **Use menus:** See "Ordering from the Menu," later in this chapter.

✔ **Use hotkeys:** In any application that has hotkeys, you can use them with the **Press** command.

✔ **Dictate text:** In most applications, you have the simple capability to dictate a phrase (including capitalization, punctuation, and hyphenation) and see it appear on the screen.

✔ **Undo your last action:** The **Undo That** command works in all applications.

✔ **Move the cursor around in a document with the Move and Go commands:** The **Move** and **Go** commands work in any application. See Chapter 5.

✔ **Use the mouse commands:** See the section about mice understanding English in Chapter 16.

✔ **Control windows:** You can open and close windows, start applications, and switch from one window to another. See Chapter 16.

Creating Documents with the Dictation Box

Wondering when to use the Dictation Box? Work at the Dictation Box level when you find you don't have all the voice commands you normally use. Pop open the Dictation Box as shown in Figure 8-2 and see what happens.

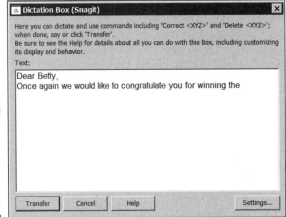

Figure 8-2: The Dictation Box in Naturally-Speaking.

Using the Dictation Box

When you dictate into an application where only the Dictation Box applies, you don't have access to several capabilities that you would have in a Full Text Control application or a Natural Language application. But, fear not, you can:

- Easily move around in a document
- Select and edit text
- Delete text
- Make corrections

Doesn't seem like much of a sacrifice, right? The Dictation Box gives you the option to do things in applications that otherwise don't want to play nicely with NaturallySpeaking.

First, confirm that your application doesn't have Full Text Control (the check mark in the DragonBar is gray instead of green). Put your cursor in the desired application and say, **"Show Dictation Box."** The Dictation Box will open. It's a plaintext application, so there is no advanced formatting; you have Full Text Control.

You can use the application's menus and hotkeys to work around some limitations. For example, you can get italics by saying either

- A menu command (**Click Style, Italic**)
- A hotkey (**Press Control I**)

Moving around in a document

The **Move** and **Go** commands work the same way in the Dictation Box as they do in the NaturallySpeaking DragonPad. The **"Insert before"** and **"Insert after"** commands also work here. See Chapter 5. You can also use the mouse commands to position the cursor.

If you are just reading a document and don't care where the cursor is, use the **Press Page Up** and **Press Page Down** commands.

If an editing job turns out to require more work than you feel like doing in the Dictation Box application, take it back to the shop. Cut the text out of the application window and paste it into the NaturallySpeaking DragonPad, where you have more tools to work with. After you get the text the way you want it, cut and paste it back to the original application.

Making corrections

Your ability to make corrections at the Dictation Box level is affected by how recently you spoke it:

- If you spot a NaturallySpeaking mistake immediately after it happens, you can say, **"Correct That"** to invoke the Correction menu.
- To correct a NaturallySpeaking error that happened a while ago, select the text with your mouse and then dictate new text.

  If the new text is still wrong, say, **"Correct That"** to invoke the Correction menu. You can also say, **"Correct <xyz>"** or **"Select <xyz>"** to highlight and correct the text.

The Correction dialog box itself always works the same way, no matter what application you call it from. See Chapter 5.

You can use all the capitalization, hyphenation, and spacing commands from Chapter 4. You can't, however, say things like **"Bold <xyz>."**

Using Full Text Control Applications

In some applications, NaturallySpeaking gives you the ability to select, correct, or move the cursor to text in a document by saying the text. This capability is called Full Text Control, and the applications in which you have this capability are called Full Text Control applications.

Following are some applications that have the Full Text Control capability:

- ✔ **NotePad**
- ✔ **WordPad**
- ✔ **Outlook.** When you use Word to edit Outlook's e-mail messages, the Word windows are also Full Text Control.
- ✔ **Internet Explorer and Mozilla Firefox.** Internet Explorer's Full Text Control capability only applies to web pages that expect your input, such as online forms or web e-mail interfaces.

The cut-and-paste commands like **Cut That** or **Copy That** work in some, but not all, Full Text Control applications. In the applications where they don't work, you can easily accomplish the same purpose with menu commands. For example, use **Click Edit, Cut** instead of **Cut That.**

The formatting commands described in Chapter 6 all work in WordPad, but not in some of the other Full Text Control applications. (You wouldn't expect them to work in NotePad, for example, because NotePad doesn't allow formatting in any case.)

Dictation only works if NaturallySpeaking is running. You can minimize the NaturallySpeaking window while you dictate into another window, but if you close NaturallySpeaking, you won't be able to dictate.

Ordering from the Menu

The engineers at Nuance can't anticipate every command that any stray application could possibly use, so they've done the next best thing: They made the **Click** command turn an application's own menus into voice commands.

TIP

What if it doesn't work?

So there you are, dictating into an application. You aren't sure whether the command you want (for example, **Set Font Arial**) will work here or not, so you try it once and it doesn't. Does that mean it just doesn't work and you should never try it again? Maybe, maybe not. Here's how to decide:

✔ Maybe NaturallySpeaking didn't understand you properly. So try the command again, and watch to see what NaturallySpeaking thinks you said. If "set phone to aerial" appears, then the jury is still out on whether the command works here or not. Keep trying.

✔ On the other hand, if **Set Font Arial** shows up as text on your screen, but still nothing happens font-wise, then you can reasonably conclude that the command isn't going to work.

Here's how to use it:

1. **Say,** "Click *<menu name>*" **to expand a menu.**

   Any title that appears on an application's menu bar will work: **Click File, Click Edit,** and so on.

2. **After the menu expands, say an entry on the menu.**

   For example, after you say, **"Click Edit,"** you can say, **"Paste"** if Paste appears on the Edit menu. The result is the same as if you had chosen Edit⇨Paste.

Extending Posts to Facebook and Twitter

Generally, you can dictate into an application while running NaturallySpeaking if you have an open text window. Using NaturallySpeaking Version 11.5, you can use a special command that calls up a text window and posts directly into Twitter or Facebook. Following are three versions of a voice command you can use:

✔ **"Post that to <Facebook/Twitter>":** Notice the use of the word *that.* In this version of the command, *that* refers to text you have already dictated and want to post on Facebook or Twitter. So, when you say this command, the text is in the box when the window opens.

✔ **"Post to <Facebook/Twitter> <text>":** In this version of the command the window will open and the text you uttered in the command above will be placed in the text window.

✔ **"Post to <Facebook/Twitter>":** Using the command this way opens a blank text window for either Facebook or Twitter and then you dictate text.

If one of these preceding commands is not recognized, a blank window will open. You'll have to dictate it again or cut and paste the dictation into the window.

You must give authorization for NaturallySpeaking to post to your Facebook or Twitter account the first time you use this command (as shown in the following instructions). You are, of course, still subject to all the Twitter or Facebook restrictions on your account as you would normally be.

To use DragonPad to post to Twitter, use the following steps:

1. **Open the DragonPad by saying,** "Open DragonPad."

   The DragonPad opens.

2. **Dictate your message.**

3. **Once you have your message the way you want it, say,** "Post that to Twitter."

   A text window with the title "Post to Twitter" will open and your message will be in it, as shown in Figure 8-3.

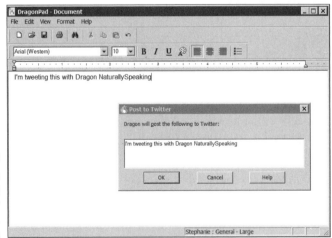

Figure 8-3:
The Post
to Twitter
window.

4. **Say,** "Click OK."

   An authorization window as shown in Figure 8-4 appears.

5. **Dictate or type in your e-mail and password.**

6. **Say,** "Click sign in" **and your message will be posted.**

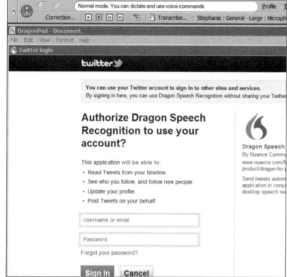

Figure 8-4:
Giving
Dragon
permission
to post to
your site.

Chapter 9

Dipping into Word Processing

In This Chapter

▶ Editing and moving text

▶ Listening to your text

▶ Understanding Natural Language Commands in Word

▶ Formatting and editing with Natural Language

▶ Inserting tables with Natural Language

▶ Working in OpenOffice.org Writer

*I*f you have used NaturallySpeaking for even a short amount of time, you know that there are many different ways of accomplishing the same thing. Some applications, such as Microsoft Word, PowerPoint, and Excel, and Corel WordPerfect, can be used with Natural Language Commands. (The Home edition does not support Excel or PowerPoint.)

In this chapter, I look at all the ways you can work in Word or WordPerfect for an easy, uncomplicated experience. I discuss how Natural Language Commands make it even more intuitive. At the time of this writing, Word 2003, Word 2007, Word 2010 (English), and WordPerfect X3, X4, and X5 are supported.

If you work with online applications, I look at using Open Office.org Writer as your word-processing program.

Saying the Right Thing

If you are new to using Dragon NaturallySpeaking with Word, you want to know the quickest ways to find the right thing to say. Here are some things to do when you're stumped:

- ✓ **Sidebar:** You can always say, **"What can I say?"** and the Dragon Sidebar will pop up with commands that pertain to the application you are working in. If the application is not supported with specific commands, you'll see global commands that work in most applications.

- ✓ **Open the Command Browser:** Go to Tools⇨Command Browser and use the Keyword Filter to find the right command. (See Chapter 18.)

- ✓ **Say,** "Give me help": The Dragon Help window opens and you can say or type a keyword. (When you are done, just say, **"Close Help."**)

- ✓ **Say what you see:** Natural Language Commands don't cover everything. You still need to use menus for some functions. You can either use your mouse or voice commands for menu choices. For example, say the menu item, like, **"View,"** and then choose from the pull-down menu that opens.

- ✓ **Mouse over with your cursor:** If you aren't sure what a particular item is called on the Word menu, mouse over it with the cursor and you'll see the name of the choice. Then use that name when calling that menu or button.

If you are using the Office Ribbon versions of Word, get to the File Menu items by saying, **"Office Button."** (It's the circle with the Windows icon to the far left of the upper menu in Word 2007.) The Office button then displays such items as New, Open, Save, and so forth. Say, **"File Tab,"** to open it in Word 2010.

Creating, opening, and closing documents

To get started with Word, you don't need any special Natural Language Commands. You're already familiar with them. Some of the commands you'll most likely use are

- ✓ **Open Microsoft Word**
- ✓ **Open new document** (You must have Word open already to use this.)
- ✓ **Save document**
- ✓ **Close document**

Playback and Read

A familiar set of features in Word are Playback and Read. Playback lets you play back a recording of your voice to help you proofread. (The Playback feature only comes with the Premium and higher editions.) Read is the

NaturallySpeaking text-to-speech feature. Chapter 7 provides the details of both Playback and Read, including the Playback toolbar that is in the Extras bar.

You can play back your text by menu command and voice command, as well as with the Extras bar. First, select the text you want to hear. The menu command for playback is Audio⇨Play That Back.

You can have NaturallySpeaking read your selected text out loud by using the **Read That** command.

Natural Language Commands for Word

The worst thing about dealing with computers is that you have to learn their language. Sure, NaturallySpeaking takes dictation. But when you want to tell it what to do with that dictation, you're back in the same old situation, right? If you don't like a 10-point font, you have to say something geeky like, **"Format that size 12."**

If there were an actual human setting type for you, you wouldn't say anything remotely like **"Format that size 12,"** would you? You'd say, **"Make it a little bigger,"** and the person would know what to do.

That's what a Natural Language Command is. It's a command that sounds like something you would naturally say, in your own language, rather than being something you would say only because you're talking to a computer.

Understanding Natural Language Commands

The engineers who built Natural Language Commands for Word believe in freedom of speech. They tried to anticipate any way in which you might want to command Word. I think this task is Herculean, given that people may say anything from, **"Bold that sucker"** to **"Slice this turkey into two columns."** (You're probably more restrained.)

Nonetheless, Nuance engineers do succeed in giving you a lot of flexibility with Natural Language Commands.

So, I would be crazy to try to document all the thousands of ways you can give commands, and you wouldn't be any better off. Instead, I mainly tell you what you can talk about, and tell you the best verbal commands to use.

How do you ultimately know what's best to say? NaturallySpeaking accepts commands in so many different forms that Nuance suggests you just try speaking a command and see whether it works.

Clever as NaturallySpeaking is, accidentally coming up with a "command" that doesn't work is still quite possible. And, to add injury to insult, if you have selected text in your document when you speak a "command" that NaturallySpeaking doesn't recognize, that text is replaced by the text of your "command"! If that happens, undo the error by saying, **"Undo That"** or pressing Ctrl+Z. (You may have to repeat that command to totally undo the error.)

If NaturallySpeaking doesn't perform your command, either NaturallySpeaking doesn't recognize it as a command or the command can't be accomplished because the context where you're trying to use it is incorrect. (See Chapter 21 to see what to do if this happens.) The following sections tell you how to perform many Word commands by using Natural Language Commands.

Dictating text

The simplest way to think about dictating with Natural Language Commands is that you can work with your favorite documents in their natural settings. Word and WordPerfect have similar commands, so for the purposes of my examples, I refer to Word.

Here are a few points to remember about dictating:

- ✔ Don't panic if **Undo That** doesn't seem to completely restore an error. Speak the command again. You may have to repeat the command several times to restore things as they were.

  Many NaturallySpeaking commands are actually multiple commands as far as your word processor is concerned. **Undo That** only undoes one Word or WordPerfect command at a time.

- ✔ NaturallySpeaking's idea of a paragraph isn't exactly the same as Word's or WordPerfect's idea. When you create a paragraph with the **New Paragraph** command, NaturallySpeaking (in effect) presses the Enter key twice. That action creates two paragraphs! (In Word, click the Paragraph [¶] button on the toolbar to see the paragraph marks.) To get a single Word or WordPerfect paragraph, you must use the command **New Line.**

- ✔ After a New Paragraph command, Dragon capitalizes the first letter of the next sentence. After a **New Line** command, Dragon does the same, but only if the last sentence ended in a period or question mark.

Editing and formatting text

Natural Language Commands bring to Word all the editing and formatting features of the NaturallySpeaking DragonPad (described in Chapters 5 and 6). See those chapters for the picky details. Here's an overview of those features and a couple of examples of the verbal commands each uses:

- Ordinary cursor control commands (**Go To Top** or **Move Back Three Words**)
- Ordinary selection (**Select Paragraph** or **Select Previous Three Words**)
- Through (**Select** *<beginning text>* **Through** *<end text>*)
- Correction (**Correct That** or **Correct** *<text>*)
- Insertion (**Insert Before** *<text>* or **Insert After** *<text>*)
- Cut and paste (**Copy That** or **Paste That**)
- Deletion (**Delete That** or **Delete Previous Character**)

Editing with familiar commands

Natural Language Commands for editing in Word are just what you would expect. Just say something and see if it works.

Here are some familiar ones:

- **Undo/Redo:** You have the same **Undo That** command in Word that you have anywhere with NaturallySpeaking. (You don't have a Redo command, but you can always say, **"Press Ctrl+Y,"** instead.)

- **Selection:** The basic form of the command is **Select** *<text>*, where *<text>* is text you can see. You can also use **Select All** to select the whole document.

- **Cut, Copy, and Paste:** You enjoy the same **Cut That, Copy That,** and **Paste That** commands you do elsewhere with NaturallySpeaking. Likewise, you have the **Copy All** command for copying the whole document.

- **Find and Replace:** To use **Find** or **Replace** when in your document, you just say, **"Find"** or **"Replace,"** and the Find/Replace box opens. You can also verbally press the hotkey: **Press Control F** (for Find) or **Press Control H** (for Replace). You can also say, **"Find in Replace"** as a single command.

- **Go To:** You can "go to" places (move the cursor) just as you can in any other application served by NaturallySpeaking. See Chapter 5 for the commands, which include such favorites as **Go To Top, Go To Bottom,** and **Go Back Three Paragraphs.**

A convenient way to go to a specific phrase is to use a Full Text Control command. First, say, **"Select *<phrase>*"** (substituting your word or phrase for *<phrase>*), then say **"Move Right One/ Move Left One."** Your cursor is now positioned just after that phrase.

One of the best editing features of Natural Language Commands has nothing to do with the Edit menu. It's the **Move That** command. With **Move That,** you can select text and then say, **"Move that down two paragraphs,"** for instance.

You can replace the word **That** with a reference to any number of words, lines, paragraphs, sections, or pages. For instance, you can say, **"Move next three paragraphs to bottom of document"** or **"Move previous three lines up one paragraph."**

Inserting

Natural Language Commands can be used for anything on the Insert menu. You can use the Natural Language **Insert *<something>*** command for page and section breaks, by just saying, **"Insert page break."** You can also use the command for other whitespace features like lines, tables, and columns. (*Whitespace* refers to stuff that doesn't actually put ink on paper.)

Say the word **"Insert,"** and then immediately say one of the terms in the following list of whitespace *<somethings>*:

- **Space**
- **Line** or **Blank Line** (both mean the same thing)
- **Paragraph**
- **Section Break** or **Section** (both mean the same thing)
- **Row** (referring to rows in a table)
- **Column** (meaning columnar formatting, or columns within a table)
- **Page Break** or **Page** (both mean the same thing)
- **Table** (see the section on creating tables, later in this chapter)

To insert just one of any in this list, use the singular form, as in **Insert Line.** To insert several, use the plural form and tell NaturallySpeaking how many you want. For instance, say, **"Insert ten lines."**

NaturallySpeaking makes a paragraph with two presses of the Enter key; a line is one press. In Word, that makes two paragraphs! If you want a single Word paragraph, use **Line** instead of **Paragraph.**

The verb **Insert** can also be used for formatting borders, numbers, and bullets. See the section "Formatting paragraphs," in this chapter.

Laying out pages

Natural Language Commands are available for various ways of laying out your document. If you want to verbally control those menus and see what's there, use the command and then choose from the drop-down menu. For example, you can say, **"Page layout columns"** and then choose the number of columns you want.

Printing

Natural Language Commands for Word offer commands for printing. You can print any number of pages, the current page, or selected text, and you can use Print Preview.

Say **"Print,"** then one of the following terms (substituting your chosen page numbers for *<page number>*):

- **Preview On/Preview Off**
- **Document**
- **Selection**
- **Page**
- **Page** *<page number>*
- **Pages** *<page number>* **Through** *<page number>*

So, for instance, say, **"Print Preview on"** or **"Print page."** You can say, **"Print this page"** or **"Print the current page,"** too, if you prefer.

Setting up page margins

Natural Language Commands have commands for margins, which are on the File (Office Button) menu. State your marginal commands by saying

"Set Left Right Top Bottom Margin To *<distance>* *<units>*"

For example, you can say, **"Set top margin to one point two inches."** The *<distance>* in this example is 1.2 and the *<units>* are inches. Allowable units are inches, centimeters, points, and picas.

What, which way, how much, and where

The objects that you can talk to Natural Language Commands about are the character, word, line, sentence, paragraph, section, page, column, row, cell, table, and document. (You can also talk about the whole or entire document, or "all.") You can move any number of these objects up, down, left, right, ahead, back, backward, or forward.

You can move some number of the next, last, forward, following, back, or previous objects. You can move them a distance, measured in some number of objects. "Huh?" you say. Okay, for instance, you can **Move the Next Three Words up Two Paragraphs.** Or you can move an object to a destination: the top or bottom, start or beginning, or end of another object.

You have to set something "to" a distance. For instance, you would say, **"Set top."**

Natural Language Commands for formatting

Formatting is where Natural Language Commands for Word really get interesting, mainly because there is so much more to talk about. You can make things larger or smaller or indent them more or less.

Formatting characters

In Word, you can format characters (choose basic fonts and styles, like bold) using the same commands you use in any other Full Text Control application. See Chapter 6 for instructions.

Natural Language Commands give you additional options for Word, however. I give only a few examples here, using my favorite **Format That** command, and point out where Natural Language Commands add flexibility.

- ✔ **Font faces:** Say, **"Format that Arial,"** for instance. Natural Language Commands recognize all the fonts in Word.

- ✔ **Font sizes:** Just as in the NaturallySpeaking window, or in WordPerfect with Natural Language Commands, you can say, **"Format that size 14,"** or you can add the font size to a font family by saying, **"Format that Arial 14."** You can't, however, say, **"Format that 14"** (without the font name or the word size). Sizes are limited to the ones Word lists in the toolbar and dialog box. (So, for example, you can't use odd-numbered sizes in the 20- to 30-point range. NaturallySpeaking types your command as text, if you try.)

✔ **Font styles, colors, and effects:** Say, **"Format that *<style>*,"** where *<style>* is anything in the following list. You can apply a style by itself with, for example, **"Format that Italics,"** or add the style at the end of a longer font command, as in, **"Format That Courier Italics."** Say, **"Make this,"** and then immediately follow with any of the following terms:

- **Black**
- **Navy**
- **Green**
- **Blue**
- **Gray**
- **Red**
- **Maroon**
- **Olive**
- **Teal**
- **Aqua**
- **Purple**
- **White**
- **Yellow**
- **No Highlight**
- **Bold, Bolded,** or **Bolding**
- **Italics** or **Italicized**
- **Double Strikethrough**
- **Embossed**
- **Engraved**
- **Hidden**
- **Shadowed**
- **Superscript**
- **Subscript**
- **Underline** or **Underlined**
- **Double Underlined**
- **Wavy Underlined**
- **Thick Underlined**
- **Strikethrough**
- **Bigger** or **Larger**

- **A Little Smaller**

- **Smaller**

- **Much Smaller** or **a Lot Smaller**

- **A Little Bigger** or **a Little Larger**

- **Much Bigger, Much Larger, a Lot Bigger,** or **A Lot Larger**

- **With Hyphens**

- **Lowercase** or **No Caps**

You can use an imperative verb form of command for certain styles. (Remember imperative verbs from English class? No, me neither, but that's what they are!) The imperatives for fonts are a short list, as follows:

- ✔ **Cap That**

- ✔ **Italicize That**

- ✔ **Bold That**

- ✔ **Underline That**

When you format something, **That** refers to text you have selected or previously uttered. You can say things other than **That** if you like. See the upcoming bullets that talk about equivalent terms.

As with most commands in Natural Language Commands, you can say them in different ways. Here are a few of the variations Natural Language Commands allow for font commands:

- ✔ **Make** and **Set** are equivalent to **Format.** For instance, you may say, **"Set that blue"** or **"Make that Arial 12 point."**

- ✔ You can use **Set It** instead of **Set that,** as in **Set it Normal.** You can also substitute **That** phrases with **Next Three Words** or **Previous Two Paragraphs** to avoid having to select the text first. You can direct your font commands to the previous or next 1 to 20 **Words, Lines, Paragraphs, Pages, Sections, Columns, Tables, Rows,** or **Cells,** or to the **Document.**

- ✔ You can use the command **Set Font** in place of **It** or **That.** You can use **Set Font Blue,** for instance.

Paragraphs

For formatting paragraphs in Word, I prefer (you guessed it) the **Format That** *<some formatting>* command. Because you can use **Format That** no matter whether you're formatting paragraphs, fonts, or anything else, it's easiest for my poor brain to remember.

When you format paragraphs, you can use two other types of commands. Table 9-1 gives the gory details. The top three rows give the conventional commands that work anywhere (left-, right-, and center-align). The remaining rows list commands that Natural Language Commands give you.

NaturallySpeaking gives you no Natural Language command for setting tabs. For most purposes, though, you can use indentation or table commands instead.

Table 9-1	Three Ways to Format Paragraphs in Word	
Say, "Format That" and Then	*Or Just Say*	*Notes*
Left Aligned	**Left Align That**	
Right Aligned	**Right Align That**	
Center Aligned or **Centered**	**Center That**	
Justified	**Justify That**	Means no ragged right edge.
Indented (Also **Outdented**)	**Indent That** (Also **Outdent That**)	Means increase indentation to the next default or user-added tab stop. (Outdenting decreases indentation.)
(nothing)	**Indent That** *<distance>*	For indenting a specific amount (for example, 1.5 inches). Substitute your indentation distance for *<distance>*.
Bulleted or **Bullet Style** or **A Bulleted List**	**Bullet That**	Repeat this command to turn off bullets.
Numbered or **A Numbered List**	**Number** (or **Unnumber**) **That**	Repeat this command to turn off numbering.
Double Spaced	**Double Space That**	
Also Single Spaced	Also Single-Space That	

For most work, I suggest my favorite command, **Format That** *<whatever>*.

That refers to paragraphs you have selected or what you previously uttered. See the bullets that follow for other words you can use instead of **That**.

As with font formatting, Natural Language Commands let you say paragraph formatting commands in different ways. Here are some of the variations Natural Language Commands allow you:

- You can substitute **Justified** for **Aligned.** (And, as you may suspect, you can also substitute **Justify** for **Align,** or **Justification** for **Alignment.**)

- You can use the term **Set** or **It** in place of the word **That.**

- You can use the term **Paragraph** in place of **That.** You can also substitute phrases like **Next Three Paragraphs** or **Previous Two Pages** to avoid having to select the text first. You can direct your paragraph commands to the previous or next 1 to 20 **Paragraphs, Pages, Sections, Columns, Tables, Rows,** or **Cells,** or to the **Document.**

- In Natural Language Commands, the verb **Make** works just as well as **Set** (described in Chapter 6) for changing the formatting of a font or paragraph.

Styles

Want a top-level heading? Say, **"Change style to heading 1."** Want to redefine what Heading 1 is? Format a paragraph (by voice or by hand), then say, **"Remember that as heading 1."**

If you aren't familiar with styles, here's the story in brief: Styles are combinations of font and paragraph formatting that go by a certain name, such as Heading 1. Word comes with certain predetermined styles. You, however, can change what font and paragraph formatting goes with any of the named styles.

You can't use verbal commands for style names that you create. For example, if you create a style called Indented Quote, you can't say, **"Format that indented quote."** Instead, try using the **Remember That As** command to redefine the standard Word styles, like Block Text. Then use those redefined styles. (Your new definition applies only to the current document. To apply it to other documents, you use the Word Style Organizer, but that's a whole other discussion!)

To apply a style, first click in a paragraph or select some text. Then say, **"Set that selection to,"** followed immediately by any of the following phrases:

- **Normal Text** (same as Normal)
- **Text** (same as Body Text)
- **Body Text**
- **Body Text 2**
- **Body Text 3**
- **Plain Text** (Courier)
- **A Quote** (same as Block Text)
- **Quoted Text** (same as Block Text)
- **A Caption**

- ✔ **A Heading** (same as Heading 2)
- ✔ **Heading 1**
- ✔ **Heading 2**
- ✔ **Heading 3**
- ✔ **A Heading 1**
- ✔ **A Heading 2**
- ✔ **A Heading 3**
- ✔ **A Major Heading** (same as Heading 1)
- ✔ **A Minor Heading** (same as Heading 3)
- ✔ **A List**
- ✔ **List 2**
- ✔ **List 3**
- ✔ **Bulleted List 2**
- ✔ **Bulleted List 3**
- ✔ **A Title**
- ✔ **A Subtitle**
- ✔ **Numbered List 2**
- ✔ **Numbered List 3**

Natural Language Commands don't perform all the Word styles, just the ones I list.

To see what these styles are like, choose Format⇨Style, and the Style dialog box appears (Home⇨Styles). In that dialog box, click in the box marked List, and then choose All Styles. The area marked Paragraph Preview shows you what the current paragraph formatting for that style looks like; the Character Preview area shows you the font currently in use. The Description section lists exactly what font and paragraph formatting the style contains. Many style descriptions begin with "Normal+," which means the style is based on (uses the same settings as) Normal style, then the settings are modified from there. If you change the Normal style, all the styles based on Normal will change.

Some of the style commands, like the ones for numbered and bulleted styles, sound very much like the paragraph formatting commands, but they really refer to named styles. The number **2** or **3** at the end of certain commands refers to how much the line is indented. A **3** is more indented than a **2**.

As with paragraph and font commands, Natural Language Commands let you say it your way. Here are three ways you can say things:

✔ If the term **Format** doesn't seem natural to you, you can use **Make** or **Set.** For instance you can say, **"Make that a quote."**

✔ You can use the term **Selection** or **It** instead of the word **That.**

✔ You can use the term **Paragraph** in place of **That.** You can also substitute phrases like **Next Three Paragraphs** or **Previous Two Pages** to avoid having to select the text first. You can apply your style commands to up to 20 of the previous or next **Paragraphs, Pages, Sections, Columns, Tables, Rows,** or **Cells,** or to the **Document.**

Spelling and grammar

How easy can this be? Following are the commands for the two Microsoft Word tools for spelling and grammar:

✔ **Check Spelling**

✔ **Check Grammar**

On the other hand, if you truly are dictating everything in your document using NaturallySpeaking, you should never need to run the spelling checker! NaturallySpeaking never makes a spelling error (unless you added a misspelled word to your NaturallySpeaking vocabulary).

Keep in mind that when you check spelling, the Word spell checker may not recognize words that are in your NaturallySpeaking vocabulary. The two programs maintain their own lists of acceptable words.

Tables

You can use Natural Language Commands to create Word tables with up to 20 rows or columns. Use the commands **Insert, Make, Add,** or **Create,** as you prefer. I prefer **Insert** because it's the same command I use for other whitespace insertions like spaces, paragraphs, and page breaks. Here are the different forms of commands you can use (using **Insert** as my example):

✔ **Insert Table** *<n>* **Rows By** *<m>* **Columns**

✔ **Insert** *<n>* **By** *<n>* **Table**

✔ **Insert** *<n>* **Rows by** *<n>* **Columns**

Substitute numbers between 1 and 20 for *<n>* and *<m>*. In any of these commands, you can say the columns first and then the rows, or vice versa.

You can leave out either the rows or the columns in any of these commands and then add them later. For instance, **Insert Three Column Table** leaves out any discussion of rows, and so creates a three-column table with one row.

After you have a table, you can verbally move your cursor around in the table, referring to rows, columns, or cells. Commands use either **Move** or **Go** and take forms like these examples:

- ✔ **Move Right One Column**
- ✔ **Move to Next Row**
- ✔ **Go Down Three Cells**

You can move Left, Right, Up, Down, Back, Backward, Ahead, or Forward.

You can add rows or columns using exactly the same sort of command you use to create a table: **Insert, Add, Make,** or **Create.** Place the insertion point where you want to add stuff, and speak the command.

As usual, I prefer **Insert.** You can insert a number of rows or columns or insert a new row or column. Here are a few examples, using my favorite command, **Insert:**

- ✔ **Insert a New Row**
- ✔ **Insert Five Rows**
- ✔ **Insert Two Columns**

You can select, delete, cut, or copy rows, columns, or cells just as you would words in regular text. For instance, you can use **Select Row** to select the row your cursor is in, or use **Select Next Five Rows.** You can also use **Delete Row** or **Copy Row.** Deleting rows only removes the data from the row, not the row itself. To paste a row, column, or cell you have copied, use **Paste That;** don't refer to a row, column, or cell in the command.

Inserting, deleting, and pasting by voice works just as it does when you insert, delete, or paste by hand. That is, rows are inserted above the current row; columns are inserted to the left of the current column.

Windows

Natural Language Commands don't give you any special commands for document windows in Word. If you want to do anything in the Word Window menu, you have to do it manually or with the **Click Window** command.

You can, however, make use of the key combination Ctrl+F6 to switch document windows (say, **"Press control F6"**). Ctrl+F4 closes a document window (say, **"Press control F4"**).

This isn't to say you can't switch between the Word window and other program windows. As in any application, you can say, **"Switch to <*program name*>"** (if that program is running) or **"Switch to previous/next window."**

You can always say, **"List all windows for <*program*>"** to get to the document window you are looking for.

Choosing OpenOffice.org Writer

Want an online suite of office products that you don't have to license? If so, check out OpenOffice.org. It is an open source program that includes a word processor called Writer and several other applications that resemble the MS Office suite.

People use it so they always have access to the most up-to-date version of the application. (Also, it's free.) In Version 11.5 of NaturallySpeaking, Nuance has added commands that can be used directly with OpenOffice.org Writer 3.1, 3.2, and 3.3.

The following are some tips you should know if you want to use Writer with NaturallySpeaking:

- ✔ With NaturallySpeaking version 11.5, Writer is a Full Text Control application. This means that you can create, edit, and format content.

  The only higher designation for dictation would be Natural Language Commands, as in Microsoft Word.

- ✔ You can use the general navigation commands to edit when you dictate. For example: **Go to, Select, Line up/ down, Page up/down.**

- ✔ You have a full range of familiar correction commands: **Scratch that, Correct that, Correct <word>, Correct <x> through <y>**

- ✔ Formatting commands are available. For example, **Bold/Italicize/ Underline/Cap <x>.**

- ✔ When several instances of a word are present, Dragon will number all of them and enable you to either Choose all, or choose the one you want.

Chapter 10

Working with Excel

In This Chapter

▶ Using NaturallySpeaking with spreadsheets

▶ Working in Quick Edition or Full Edition mode

▶ Using your cursor with spreadsheets

*E*arlier chapters explain what NaturallySpeaking offers to word-oriented people, but what about number-oriented people — people who have a lot of data to enter, to keep track of, and to process? Left-brainers, unite!

NaturallySpeaking enables you to work with spreadsheets (not available in the Home edition). In Dragon NaturallySpeaking Premium and higher, you can use Full Text Control, Menu Tracking, and Natural Language Commands for Excel 2003, 2007, and 2010.

Doing Excel-lent Works with Spreadsheets

Using spreadsheets with older versions of NaturallySpeaking was difficult because you couldn't directly address the names of the cells. You wanted to say something like, **"Cell A5"** or **"Select Column C."** But (sigh), no dice. Your assistant had no idea what you were talking about. Well, your assistant has "up-leveled" its skills!

You now can select a cell and go right to it. After you know how to move around in your spreadsheet, you will be surprised how easy it is. If you are stumped about what command to say, you can always call on your Dragon Sidebar with, **"What can I say?"** to see the appropriate commands. You can, of course, use the mouse for these sorts of operations, and dictate only the text that goes into the cells. That decision is up to you.

You also have another option to address the cells. Spreadsheets are designed by and for geeks who regard using a mouse as a sign of weakness, so for their sake, most popular spreadsheet applications contain (at last count) bazillions of hotkey combinations that do just about anything you would ever want to do. If you know the right hotkeys, you can use **Press <*keyname*>** voice commands to have a reasonably pleasant and efficient no-hands experience with your spreadsheets.

The examples in this section are demonstrated with Microsoft Excel. It's important to show you the kinds of activities that are possible with voice, keyboard, and mouse.

Getting in the mode

Excel has two voice modes in which you work: dictation mode and edit mode, called Quick edition and Full edition, respectively. Unlike the Recognition modes (see Chapter 3), you do not select the Quick or Full Edition mode manually. You invoke them based on the actions you take inside the spreadsheet.

It's important to know about them because they make life easier when you want to dictate or edit the cells. On the other hand, if you aren't aware of them, you can become frustrated when your NaturallySpeaking assistant does something you aren't expecting because of the mode it is in. Here is what you need to know about each mode:

✔ **Quick Edition mode:** This mode is the dictation mode. If you dictate into a cell, you see a yellow background. This tells you that everything you say will show up in the cell. So, for example, if you say, **"Select C5,"** and then started dictating, the program writes everything you say into that cell. Then you use commands to format what you say, just as you do in a text-editing application.

✔ **Full Edition mode:** This mode enables you to fully edit a cell by saying, **"Edit cell"** or **"Press F2."** After you do that, the background of the cell becomes blue. Then you can edit the cell in any way you want.

If you see a cell acting funny, check the background color.

✔ If the background is yellow, you're dictating into it.

✔ If the background is blue, you are commanding it.

Adjust your words accordingly.

Having a look around

Thankfully, moving around in an Excel spreadsheet is pretty intuitive. Start by saying, **"Open Excel."** Voilà, it does! The same thing goes for creating a new spreadsheet or closing it. Say, **"Open a new workbook"** or **"Close the workbook,"** and it does.

If you aren't sure what to do, either the Command Browser or the Dragon Sidebar will display all the commands you can use in Excel. Saying, **"What can I say?"** while you're in Excel opens the Sidebar. What could be easier?

The following commands are right at your fingertips (er, I mean right on your lips):

- ✔ **Moving around**
- ✔ **Selecting and inserting**
- ✔ **Cutting, copying, pasting, and deleting**
- ✔ **Formatting, saving, and printing**

Selecting cells

Selecting cells or blocks of cells in a spreadsheet is a snap. You can just say, **"Cell C2"** and it goes there. Or you can say, **"Select <x> through <y>,"** and it does. If you want to move to the next row, say **"Next Row."** Previous column? Say, **"Previous Column."** Wow, this isn't hard at all!

You can also just click in the cell you want to select, or drag a selection rectangle over a block of cells. If you want to do the mouse thing by hand, NaturallySpeaking won't stop you.

When you select cells by voice, consider using the International Communications Alphabet (ICA). In the ICA, the names of the letters all sound different, so you can spell aloud with confidence — if you know the ICA. For example, you can say, **"Alpha"** for A or **"Bravo"** for B. That means you say, **"Cell Bravo 12"** to move to cell B12.

You can find the ICA names of the letters listed in NaturallySpeaking Help. Choose Help↻Help Topics to display Help Topics, and then go to the Index tab and look up Spelling, Characters For. It's worth a peek.

Filling you in

If you like doing crossword puzzles you'll really enjoy filling in your cells in NaturallySpeaking. Here are some quick ways you can fill in your spreadsheet with the format you need.

To put in the days of the week, pick the cell you want to start in by saying, **"Cell <location>."** Then say, **"Sunday through Saturday down."** That column where the cell was now shows all the days Sunday through Saturday. You can then **"Bold that"** or format it in any other way you want.

To put in consecutive numbers, choose your cell as I explain in the preceding paragraph, and then say, **"One through ten across."** Those numbers will be put in the row you chose.

The same goes for months of the year or any other grouping of numbers or letters. If you have a consecutive sequence, you can use the **Through** command.

Using the cursor

The **Move Up/Down/Left/Right** commands can also be used when you work with spreadsheets. They do exactly what you need: move the cursor from one cell to another. If the currently selected cell is B2, saying, **"Move right two"** moves the cursor to D2. If you then say, **"Move down five,"** the cursor moves to D7. Unfortunately, the highest number of steps you can move with one command is 20.

For longer trips, **Press Page Up/Down** displays the next/preceding full screen of the spreadsheet. In Excel, **Press Alt Page Up** shows you the next full screen to the left. **Press Alt Page Down** displays the next full screen to the right.

Return to cell A1 by saying, **"Press Control Home."** Go to the extreme lower-right corner of the spreadsheet by saying, **"Press Control End."**

Go to any cell by selecting it using the Go To dialog box described in the next section.

Boxing up a block of cells

In Excel, the F8 function key anchors a selection box in the current cell. Moving the cursor to another cell automatically selects the block of cells "between" them (in other words, a block of cells in which these two cells are opposing corners). For example, you could select the C3:E7 cell block as follows:

1. **Move to cell C3.**

   Use any technique you want. See "Having a look around" earlier in this chapter.

2. **Say,** "Press F8."

3. **Say,** "Move down four."

   Now the C3:C7 block is selected.

4. **Say,** "Move right two."

   Now the C3:E7 block is selected.

If a block of cells is surrounded by empty cells, you can select the whole block in Excel by saying, **"Press control shift 8."**

Selecting rows and columns

To select an entire row or column in Excel, first move the cursor into the row or column. Then say, **"Press control spacebar"** to select the column, or **"Press shift spacebar"** to select the row.

How do you remember which does what? The words *control* and *column* both begin with the letter *C*.

Do you want column F with that?

After you select a block of cells, you can extend it by one cell in any direction by saying, **"Press shift <direction> arrow."** So, for example, if you have selected all of column E, you can add column F by saying, **"Press shift right arrow."**

This command works in many spreadsheets, including Excel, but not all.

Inputting and formatting data

Spreadsheets are all about manipulating numbers, so the obvious question is how to get the numbers into the spreadsheet in the first place. The basic idea of how to get a number or date or time (spreadsheets think of dates and times as numbers) into a cell is fairly simple. Here are the steps:

1. **Select the cell.**

   See "Selecting cells" earlier in this chapter.

2. **Dictate the number.**

   There are no special commands here, so think of NaturallySpeaking as if it were a keyboard. Whatever you want to see in the cell, say it. If, for example, you want the cell to contain the date 5/17/99, say, **"Five slash seventeen slash ninety-nine."** If you want to see 1.52E+01 in the cell, say, **"Spell One point five two Cap E plus zero one."** See Chapter 4, Table 4-5, for more ways to dictate numbers. A good spreadsheet should recognize any of the formats of Table 4-5 as numbers.

3. **Move to another cell.**

Spreadsheets like Excel are capable of displaying numbers, dates, and times in a nearly infinite number of ways. (You'd need a spreadsheet to figure out how many.) Your best bet is not to worry too much about how to format a number in NaturallySpeaking; just get the number into the spreadsheet in any old form, and then reformat it in the spreadsheet.

For example, suppose you were inputting a column of prices. You could dictate them as prices: **"Twenty-six dollars and seventy-two cents."** Or you could dictate them as numbers: **"Twenty-six point seven two."** After you dictate the column of numbers, then you could convert them to prices. Here are the steps:

1. **Select the column.**

   See "Selecting rows and columns" earlier in this chapter.

2. **Say,** "Click format, cells."

   The Format Cells dialog box appears, as shown in Figure 10-1.

3. **Display the Number tab in the Format Cells dialog box.**

   This tab may be on top when the box opens (or not!). Use the **Press Right/Left Arrow** commands to move from one tab to another.

4. **Say,** "Press Alt C."

   This hotkey moves the cursor into the Category List.

5. **Select Currency on the Category list.**

   The **Move Up/Down** commands are the easiest way to select items on the list.

6. **Say,** "Press Enter."

The Format Cells dialog box disappears, and the column is formatted as dollars and cents.

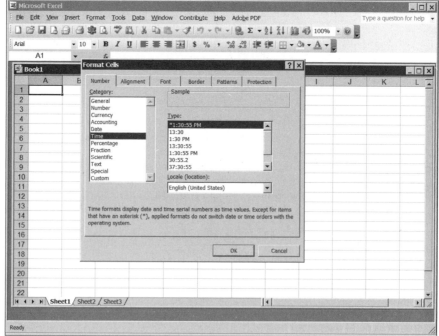

Figure 10-1:
A spread-sheet like Excel can format numbers, dates, and times in more ways than you can count.

Improving Your Vocal Functions

Spreadsheets have so many defined functions these days that nobody remembers exactly what their names are or what they do. (Remembering things is for people who *don't* have access to a computer.) All you have to do is pick the function out of a list (that the spreadsheet remembers for you) or add the function name to the NaturallySpeaking vocabulary.

All the popular spreadsheets have a menu command that brings up a dialog box listing all the available functions. In Excel, the menu choice is Formula and it produces the Function Library Ribbon.

To use this feature with NaturallySpeaking, do the following:

1. **On The Excel Menu Bar, choose formulas.**

   You see the icons of the functions available.

2. **Select the cell where the function belongs on your spreadsheet.**

3. **Say the category name of the function you want (for instance, math and trig).**

   A list is displayed. Pick the function by saying its letters. When the function arguments box opens, the cursor is in the number box.

4. **Say the number you want to insert.**

5. **Say, "Okay."**

If you use the same function over and over again, you can introduce it into the naturallyspeaking vocabulary. For example, you could introduce the "word" STDEV into the vocabulary and train NaturallySpeaking to recognize its spoken form, "Standard Deviation Function." Or you could give the function a pronunciation similar to its written form, like "Tansh" for the function TANH because it sounds like that. See Chapter 18 for details on how to implement vocabulary tricks like this.

in the formula section of Excel, TANH is the hyperbolic tangent of a number. If you aren't solving differential equations, you probably don't need to add this voice command.

Chapter 11

Using Recorded Speech

*T*hank Thomas Edison. He's the guy who figured out that you don't have to be standing there talking to your transcriptionist. Nope. Instead, you can record stuff in the privacy of your own office and hand it off to your transcriptionist later. Of course, in Edison's day, people had to yell into a big horn and their words were recorded on a wax cylinder. But the idea was a good one: Record now, transcribe later.

The idea was so good that now you can use any number of wonderful gadgets to dictate into while you're on the go. This chapter deals solely with a voice recorder. If you want to use NaturallySpeaking with mobile devices such as the Blackberry, iPhone, iPad, or iPod touch, see Chapter 15.

Why Record?

Perhaps the most attractive benefit of recording first and transcribing later is the same one that Thomas Edison probably had in mind. We suspect that he had no desire to master the manual skill of typing, preferring to let his assistant Watson do that job. Likewise, you can simply dictate your text and then let your assistant (if you're lucky enough to have one) handle the transcription. That way, you never have to master the intricacies of NaturallySpeaking itself. As did Thomas Edison, however, you still have to master the intricacies of using a recording device.

One of the nice things about recording on a portable recorder is that you can sit there talking into a little box in your hand (a recorder). It doesn't strain your eyes or cramp your fingers.

The second advantage of recording first and transcribing later is that, surprisingly, it's often more accurate! Because your recorder provides a digital audio file, NaturallySpeaking's transcription doesn't have to keep up with your rate of speech. It can take its time and read your speech from the file at its own rate. As a result, it will be more accurate.

The disadvantage of recording first and then transcribing is that you don't get to correct NaturallySpeaking on the fly. As a result, you may find that you have to make the same correction repeatedly throughout your document. Subsequent documents will, however, benefit from your corrections.

One fantasy to shoot down right now is the one in which you transcribe meetings using your recorder and NaturallySpeaking. One problem is that NaturallySpeaking has to be trained to each speaker's voice. What's more, the acoustic environment for meetings is invariably far too poor to get a decent recording from even one person. Besides, who really wants everything he said in a meeting to appear in a transcription?!

Setting Up to Use a Portable Recorder

Hopefully, if you already own a portable recorder, it will be good enough to work with NaturallySpeaking. Nuance lists on its website (`www.Nuance. com/compatibility`) recorders that they have tested with their products, as shown in Figure 11-1. In general, you need a good-quality recorder that outputs digital audio files. For serious remote dictation work, you want a recorder that enables you to store multiple separate recordings. Or do you feel lucky? You can try using your existing recorder and see how well it does.

You can improve the audio quality of some recorders by plugging a separate microphone into them. Look for a microphone jack on your recorder. Of course, a separate microphone often makes the recorder significantly less convenient and portable. "Stub" microphones (microphones on a short stalk) that do not make the recorder too unwieldy exist for this purpose. Check with a good audio equipment supplier.

You have to do a few things before you can make remotely recorded dictation work, including the following:

- ✔ You must be able to make a physical connection between your recorder and your PC. You can't just let the recorder play into the microphone.

- ✔ You must install any additional software required by your portable recorder.

- ✔ You must train NaturallySpeaking to recognize your voice the way it sounds after being altered by the processes of recording and transferring to your PC.

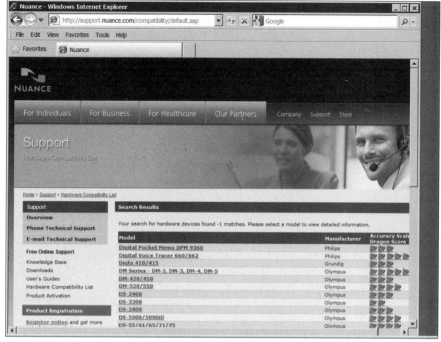

Figure 11-1:
Check the compat-
ibility list on
the Nuance
website.

Figuring out your connection

To get started, you need a physical connection between the recorder and your PC. If your recorder is not digital, you will have to use the Line-In connection discussed below.

Digital data transfer connection

Digital transfer most commonly takes place through a data cable, running from a connector on a digital recorder to a connector (usually a USB) on your PC. From this connection, you "copy the data" (your voice recording) to your PC's hard drive. Check your recorder's manual for details on how to make this connection.

Other possible ways to transfer digital data include a memory card that you remove from the recorder and place in a slot in your PC (or in a device connected to your PC). Check your PC's manual or your recorder's manual for instructions on copying the data from this memory card to your PC's hard drive.

If you have a digital recorder but it doesn't provide digital data transfer, use the Line-In connection (see the next section). Some other reasons for using the Line-In connection with a digital recorder are as follows: You may not have the digital cable you need; your PC may not have a connector available; or your PC may not be equipped to read the recorder's digital storage medium.

Line-In connection

If your recorder still uses tape (seriously?) or if the recorder is digital but you can't transfer the data for any of the reasons given in the preceding section, use the Line-In connection on your PC. This is also called an analog connection (as opposed to digital).

A Line-In connection requires a cable from the audio output jack (a round hole) of the recorder to the round Line-In jack on your PC. You can use this sort of connection with any recorder that has a Line-Out jack or a headphone jack (sometimes marked "ear" or "audio out"). If you use a stereo recorder for a Line-In connection, you need a special cable or adapter that creates a *monaural* (single-channel) output.

To be able to create a User Profile from another audio source (your recorder), you must have Administrator privileges. If you are the licensed owner of the software, you likely also are the administrator.

Adding a dictation source to your current profile

Most people think their voice sounds pretty terrible after it has been passed through a recorder. So does NaturallySpeaking. In fact, as far as NaturallySpeaking is concerned, your voice is so different that it needs to train with the recorder to recognize it.

Just like the first time you used NaturallySpeaking, you used the User Profile Wizard to train NaturallySpeaking. Training NaturallySpeaking to understand your recorded voice is just like training it for direct dictation, with one difference: You read the training material into your recorder, transfer the dictation to your PC, and then have NaturallySpeaking transcribe it.

The process is as follows:

1. **Choose Profile⇨Add Dictation Source to Current User Profile as shown in Figure 11-2.**

2. **Pick your source, as shown in Figure 11-3, from Microphone plugged into Line-in jack, USB Microphone, Bluetooth Microphone, Digital audio recorder, Dragon Remote Microphone Application, or Handheld or smartphone with recording application.**

3. **Choose "Digital audio recorder" from the list and click OK.**

    A screen pops up that says, "Recorder Training has not yet been successfully completed for this User Profile and dictation source." Here's your opportunity to do so.

4. **Click OK.**

As shown in Figure 11-4, you see a screen saying it will guide you through the five steps to get your recorder ready.

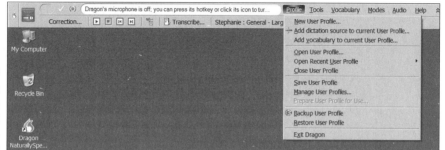

Figure 11-2:
Choose
from Profile
menu.

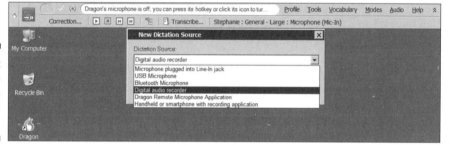

Figure 11-3:
Pick the
source from
which you
will dictate.

Figure 11-4:
The five
steps you
will take to
use your
recorder.

5. **Click Next.**

   You will now configure your recorder. If you haven't done so already, as noted above, click on the link shown in Figure 11-5 to check for Dragon supported recorders.

6. **Click Next.**

   The wizard displays, as shown in Figure 11-6, a selection of fine, edifying reading material to choose from in order to train your recorder. You are presented with several options to read.

7. **Make your selection and click the View the Selection button (or click the Print the Selection button if you prefer).**

   A window appears with your chosen text.

Figure 11-5:
Check
Nuance's
website for
supported
recorders.

Figure 11-6:
Choices for
reading text
into your
recorder.

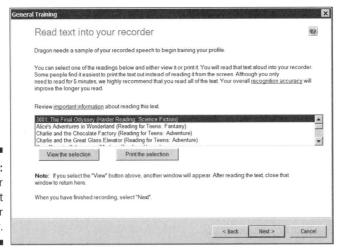

8. **Read the copy provided. When you are done, click the Back button to return to the previous screen (Figure 11-5), then click Next.**

   A screen, shown in Figure 11-7, tells you that you need to locate the file you just recorded.

9. **Click the Browse to Locate the File button to locate the file on your PC that you just recorded.**

   Find the file and choose it so that it appears in the window.

10. **Click Next.**

    You see a screen that shows the name of the file you have selected for training, as shown in Figure 11-8. If it is correct you can proceed to training.

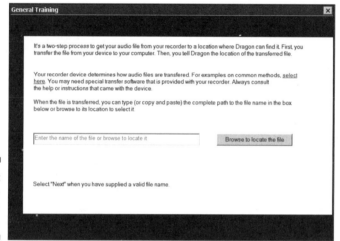

Figure 11-7:
Browse
to locate
the file.

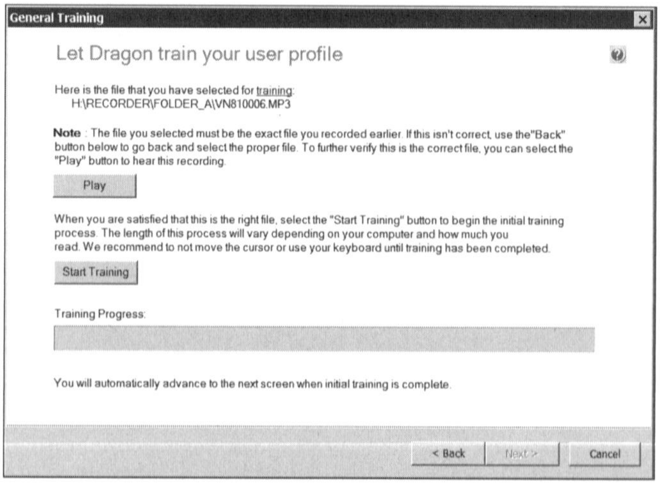

Figure 11-8:
The name
of the file is
shown.

11. **Click Start Training.**

The training process will take several minutes, so don't be impatient. It is recommended that you don't touch the computer keyboard or cursor until the training is complete. This gives you the opportunity to take some victory laps to refresh yourself.

When the training is complete, you see a congratulatory screen, as shown in Figure 11-9.

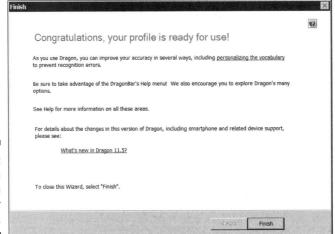

Congratulations, your profile is ready for use!

As you use Dragon, you can improve your accuracy in several ways, including <u>personalizing the vocabulary</u> to prevent recognition errors.

Be sure to take advantage of the DragonBar's Help menu! We also encourage you to explore Dragon's many options.

See Help for more information on all these areas.

For details about the changes in this version of Dragon, including smartphone and related device support, please see:

<u>What's new in Dragon 11.5?</u>

To close this Wizard, select "Finish".

Figure 11-9: You can now use your recorder.

The next time you open your list of User Profiles, you will see that a new profile has been added with your name and your audio source: Digital recorder.

When you dictate using a recorder, NaturallySpeaking remains in Normal mode. If you are going to do something that requires dictation of a specific type, switch to one of the other Recognition modes: Numbers, Spell, or Command mode. (See Chapter 10 for more information on Recognition modes.)

Getting better sound quality from portable recorders

For lots of reasons, you are more likely to have sound quality problems when you use a mobile recorder than when you dictate into your PC. Here are five tips to avoid problems:

✔ Avoid noisy environments: moving cars, traffic, machinery, wind, surf, weddings, car washes, rock concerts, or active airport runways.

- ✔ Don't move your fingers around on your recorder while recording, because this causes noise.

- ✔ Don't speak so directly into the microphone that it records puffs of breath when you speak. Keep the microphone of your recorder off to one side of your mouth. Keep the microphone a constant distance from your mouth.

    See if you can fit two fingers in between the microphone and your chin.

- ✔ If your recorder has different microphone sensitivity settings (or a microphone volume control), use the lowest sensitivity that still gives you a strong, clear recording. (Too high a sensitivity picks up background noise and sometimes distorts your voice.)

- ✔ Make sure your recorder is set for the highest quality of recording if it offers different quality levels. Check your recorder's instructions. Highest quality usually comes at the expense of maximum recording time, so choose the setting that gives the shortest recording time if quality level is not an option.

- ✔ Train in the environment in which you'll be dictating so that Dragon knows what to expect. If you train in a quiet room and dictate in a coffee shop, the accuracy will be dismal.

Recording Your Dictation

When you record text for NaturallySpeaking to transcribe, speak that text just as if you were dictating into NaturallySpeaking directly. Chapter 4 tells you how to do it.

Certain aspects of recording, however, make that process a little different than dictating directly to NaturallySpeaking. Using commands, for instance, is tricky because you can't see the transcription in progress. In addition, dictating into a portable recorder introduces some new issues that affect sound quality. The best thing to do is to limit your voice commands to dictation commands.

Because you can't see the result of NaturallySpeaking's transcription as you dictate, using certain commands in recorded speech is risky. NaturallySpeaking might, for instance, edit or delete the wrong text in response to a command. You wouldn't know that until you see your text on the screen.

Because of that risk, NaturallySpeaking ignores most editing commands it encounters while transcribing your recording. NaturallySpeaking does, however, accept dictation commands in your recorded text — the ones that control capitals and spaces. The safest procedure is to use commands that apply only to your next spoken word, such as **Cap** *<word>.* Even though NaturallySpeaking allows you to use the dictation commands that turn something "on," such as **Caps On,** NaturallySpeaking may occasionally miss the concluding **Caps Off** or other "off" command. You may end up making more work for yourself (or whoever does the final cleanup) by using those on/off commands.

Following are some of the commands that, in addition to punctuation, I think work most reliably in recorded speech:

- ✔ **All Caps** *<word>*
- ✔ **Cap** *<word>*
- ✔ **New Line**
- ✔ **New Paragraph**
- ✔ **No Caps** *<word>*
- ✔ **No Space** *<word>*
- ✔ **Spacebar**
- ✔ **Tab Key**

You can also use **Scratch That** (which deletes back to the last time you paused) if you make a mistake. Use it only if you're sure when you last paused, or you'll delete more or less than you intended! You can repeat the **Scratch That** command to back up through multiple pauses if your memory for pauses is very good.

To avoid having to remember your pauses, a better command for amending recorded dictation is **Resume With** *<word>*. This command enables you to back up to a specific word within the last 100 characters and then dictate new text beginning from that point. (Of course, it only works if NaturallySpeaking got your word right in the first place!)

See Chapter 4 for more about **Scratch That** and **Resume With.** Both commands are allowed when you transcribe from a recording. They are called the "restricted command set."

Transferring Files from a Digital Recorder

When you use your recorder, you need instructions from the manufacturer for transferring audio files to your PC. It may have its own program for handling file transfers that you need to install on your PC. Check your recorder manual for instructions.

Where on your PC's hard drive should you put the digital audio files from your recorder? You can put them anywhere, but the NaturallySpeaking transcription feature looks first in the Program folder in the NatSpeak folder on your hard (C:) drive, where NaturallySpeaking is normally installed. For convenience, put them in that Program folder.

If you have a digital recorder but it doesn't offer digital output or you do not have the necessary cable or software to make a digital transfer, you may be able to make an analog connection instead. See "Figuring out your connection," earlier in this chapter. Bring your recorder to an electronics store and ask for a cable to connect its audio output jack to a PC's audio line-in jack.

Transcribing Your Recording

Watching NaturallySpeaking transcribe a recording is kind of magical. You sit there and your words (or something like them) appear on the screen.

How does it work? NaturallySpeaking transcribes recorded speech from a sound file (a file with a .wav extension or a WMA, MP3, Vox, SRI, DSS, or DS2 format), created by a digital recorder, which you have stored on your PC's hard drive. (Oh, you haven't? See "Transferring Files from a Digital Recorder," earlier in this chapter.)

To transcribe a recording from a portable recorder, NaturallySpeaking must be set up with a special additional source User Profile specifically trained to handle recorded speech from that recorder. (See the earlier section, "Setting Up to Use a Portable Recorder.") You don't need to choose a special user to transcribe files from the NaturallySpeaking Sound Recorder (assuming the files were created on your PC); use the same user that you use for dictating directly to NaturallySpeaking.

Launch NaturallySpeaking if you haven't already, and take the following steps to transcribe:

1. **Open the User Profile you created especially for recorder input by choosing Profile⇨Open User Profile from the NaturallySpeaking menu, selecting the special "User Profile" that you set up for recorded speech, and then clicking the Open button.**

If your portable recorder uses the analog (Line-In) connection, NaturallySpeaking will expect a certain volume from your recorder. When you transcribe text, either make sure the volume is set to the same level you used for training or run the Audio Setup Wizard again at this point. To run the Audio Setup Wizard, choose Audio⇨Read text to improve accuracy and choose the Adjust Volume Only selection.

2. **In NaturallySpeaking, choose Tools⇨Transcribe Recording (or click the Transcribe button if your DragonBar has the Extras bar extended).**

The Transcribe From dialog box appears and asks you to select where Dragon NaturallySpeaking can find the audio file you want to transcribe, as shown in Figure 11-10.

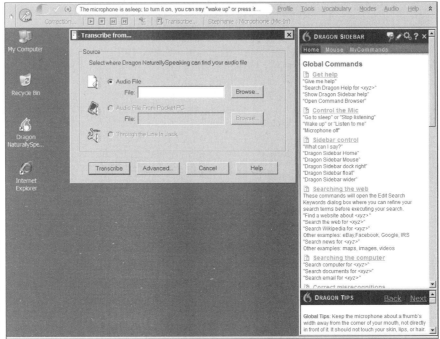

Figure 11-10:
Select the
source of
the file to
transcribe.

3. **Select the radio button of the type of file you have — Audio File, Audio File from Pocket PC, or Through the Line-In Jack.**

4. **Either type in or click the Browse button to select the file you want to transcribe from your hard drive.**

5. **Click OK.**

   The DragonPad opens and begins transcribing.

Transcribing with the AutoTranscribe Folder Agent

The AutoTranscribe Folder Agent saves you time if you have a recurring transcription. For example, if you record a weekly podcast, you can set up a specific folder for it. When you place a new audio file in that folder, it will automatically transcribe it.

If you want to set up the Folder Agent, do the following:

1. **Go to the DragonBar and choose Tools➪AutoTranscribe Folder Agent.**

   A new menu window opens.

2. **Choose Agent⇨Options.**

   A dialog box opens, asking you what you want to do with the file after it is transcribed. The choices are Delete It or Move It to the Output Directory.

3. **Select the radio button with your choice.**

   You will also see an option to "Generate DRA File." Choose this option to listen to the transcribed file and correct it.

4. **Click OK.**

5. **To set up the actual folder, choose Task⇨New.**

   A dialog box opens.

6. **Fill in the name of your input directory, its location, and what you want to do with the output file (if you didn't already choose Delete It).**

   Check that the correct User Profile is loaded with its associated vocabulary and that the dictation source Digital Audio Recorder shows.

7. **Click OK.**

   You see the input folder listed in the directory with the state listed as Idle. Obviously, it will show a working state when it is transcribing.

You can set up as many of these folders as you need for all your input sources. Your transcriptions will then be waiting for you when you return to the folder.

From the same Task menu, you can edit, disable, enable, or remove a task.

Correcting your transcription

It's kind of exciting to watch as your words are printed out magically on the screen. The hitch comes when you spot errors. Just like regular dictation, you need to proofread and correct your errors.

To proofread, I recommend that you transcribe into the DragonPad or your word processor and use your ability to play back your own voice if you are unsure about what you actually said. (This feature is not available in the Home edition.) Here's a method you can use:

1. **Begin reading your text. If you spot an error, you can say** "Select <*text*>" **and then,** "Correct that."

   The Correction menu pops up just as it does for your regular dictation. Choose the correct number of the correct version or say **"Spell that"** and correct it that way.

2. **Use Playback when you spot an error by selecting the incorrect passage and right-clicking. Choose Play That Back from the list of options, as shown in Figure 11-11.**

   You can alternate methods until you have corrected the entire transcription.

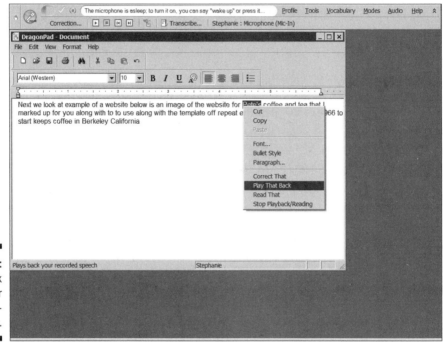

Figure 11-11:
Right-click to see your transcription options.

Correct Dragon's mistakes, not yours. If you hear yourself say something incorrect and NaturallySpeaking transcribes it, just go over it and correct it. Dragon didn't make a mistake, so it doesn't need to be corrected. (Yes, this is an operator error, not a software error! And for the record, it happens to the best of us!)

Are you lucky enough to have a staff member or other willing participant who will transcribe your recording for you? Make sure they transfer your User Profile to their PC before they begin. If they don't have your User Profile on their computer, the audio won't be recognized properly. (Of course, your faithful human transcriber also has to own Dragon NaturallySpeaking software in the Premium or higher edition to hear your voice when playing it back.)

Part III
Communicating Online

The 5th Wave   By Rich Tennant

Serch Injin
Optamazashun

Kee Werd
Stratageez

1. Top

"The good news is that he isn't programming
our dictation software."

In this part . . .

In Part III, it's time to see what your NaturallySpeaking assistant has learned about going online. When you run NaturallySpeaking with Internet Explorer, you find you can browse the Web by voice. With an e-mail or chat program, you can dictate your messages to people anywhere in the world.

In Chapters 12 and 14, your assistant is introduced to programs from the Lifestyle Speech Pack (a separate program). Many popular Web applications like Skype, iTunes, and Adobe Reader can now take dictation. In Chapter 15, you discover that your mobile devices even understand your dictation. Who knew? Now even smartphones are getting into the act!

Chapter 12

Sending and Receiving E-Mail

*U*sing NaturallySpeaking to command your e-mail application is an effective way to be more productive. Nuance has made e-mail-sending a priority. Several voice commands help you get things done faster. Programs like Outlook work with some Natural Language Commands. It is easy to learn and well supported.

This chapter delves into five e-mail programs: Outlook, Outlook Express, Thunderbird, Gmail, and Windows Live Mail. To use extended enhancements for Outlook Express and Thunderbird, I reference the LifeStyle Speech Pack. For instant messaging using the LifeStyle Pack, I cover Skype, Yahoo! Messenger, and Windows Live Messenger.

Chapter 14 details information about buying and using the Speech Pack. I assume you are familiar with the program. Also, if your preferred e-mail program is not on my list, it may work with some common commands. Try them. Now, just dive right in and start e-communicating, the NaturallySpeaking way!

Creating and Managing E-Mails

As you contemplate using NaturallySpeaking to send your e-mails, keep in mind these general recommendations that apply to most e-mail programs:

✔ **Check your previous e-mails:** Make sure you let NaturallySpeaking look at your previously sent e-mails before you send your next new e-mail. You want to give your NaturallySpeaking assistant a proper orientation, don't you? Your NaturallySpeaking assistant looks at your e-mail files to familiarize itself with e-mail addresses. To run this process, choose Vocabulary⇨Learn from Sent E-Mails on the DragonBar to enable NaturallySpeaking to look at them. See Chapter 18 for more information about this.

✔ **Use the Dictation Box:** If you have trouble dictating into your e-mail program, use the Dictation Box and then transfer the dictation back into the e-mail window. With your e-mail program open, access the Dictation Box by choosing Tools⇨Dictation Box on the DragonBar. See Chapter 8 for more information on the Dictation Box.

✔ **Know common e-mail commands:** Several commands work with most e-mail programs. Familiarize yourself with them before you start. Check the Command browser to see what other commands you can use. To do this go to Tools⇨Command Browser and use the Context pull-down menu to access specific program commands. Many commands are specific to Microsoft Outlook.

✔ **Use the Sidebar and Help files:** You can always get immediate help while you dictate your e-mails. Say, **"What can I say?"** to bring up the Sidebar. You can also say, **"Give me help."** There is no need to become frustrated trying to think of the right commands when help is almost literally on the tip of your tongue.

✔ **Format e-mail addresses:** You can make choices about how your e-mail and web addresses are formatted. Go to Tools⇨Auto-Formatting Options on the DragonBar and choose your preferences. Read more information about this in Chapter 18.

✔ **Add e-mail addresses:** If you frequently use a particular e-mail or web address, you can add it to your vocabulary like you do other "non-words." Otherwise, you can say an address, such as *person@company*. com, much like you would in conversation. Make sure everything is lowercase by saying, **"No Caps On,"** and then say the e-mail address. Then say, **"No Caps Off."** For the address itself (*person@company*.com, for instance), say, **"<*person's name*> at company dot com."**

✔ **Saying web addresses:** Speak a web address in the form, **"w w w dot company dot com."** For a full address (such as `http://www.company. com`) say, **"h t t p w w w dot company dot com."** Don't mention the colon or slashes. NaturallySpeaking adds the colon and slashes and recognizes the terms *com, gov, mil, net, org,* and *sys* just as you normally say them. If you prefer, you can verbally spell those terms letter by letter. Table 12-1 shows the NaturallySpeaking commands that are generally used for e-mail applications.

NaturallySpeaking works only with Internet Explorer and Mozilla Firefox when you use a browser with your e-mail application.

If NaturallySpeaking insists on capitalizing the *www* portion of a web address, correct the capitalization by using the Correction dialog box. (NaturallySpeaking has an obsession about capitalizing initials.) Or say, **"No Caps,"** then, without pausing, speak the address. To absolutely, completely suppress all capitals within the address, say, **"No Caps On No Caps w w w dot whatever dot com No Caps Off."**

Table 12-1	NaturallySpeaking Commands for E-Mail Applications
To Do This:	*Say This:*
Launch <*program name*>	"Start Microsoft Outlook"
Open your inbox	"Go to inbox"
Look at new mail	"Check for new mail"
Move to next e-mail	"View next unread message"
Send e-mail	"Send message"
Close e-mail	"Close all items"
Mark message to follow up	"Flag message for follow-up"
Open with e-mail address	"Send e-mail to <*person's name*>"
Add a file(s) to e-mail	"Attach a file"
Launch spell check	"Check spelling"
Print e-mail	"Print mail"
Reply to everyone in message list	"Reply to all"

You can substitute **message, memo,** or **e-mail** for the word **"mail."**

Interacting with Microsoft Outlook

Microsoft Outlook is the most widely used business e-mail client. When used in combination with NaturallySpeaking, it is a Full Text Control application that also provides some Natural Language Commands. Outlook keeps track of your personal information — at least appointments, addresses, and the like. Because of its extensive use in business organizations, I focus on several specifics that make using Outlook easier.

Outlook has a good collection of hotkeys that enable you to access features with the **Press <*hotkey*>** voice command. To see a list of Outlook's hotkeys, look in Outlook's Help Index under *keyboard shortcuts* for your version of Outlook.

Using the three-panel e-mail application window

Outlook uses the basic three-panel window arrangement (see Figure 12-3):

- ✔ **The folder list:** A vertical pane on the left displaying message folders or mailboxes

- ✔ **The message list:** A horizontal pane in the upper-right that lists the messages contained in the selected message folder

- ✔ **The reading pane:** A horizontal pane in the lower-left displaying the contents of the selected message

Move from one pane to another by pressing the Tab key or saying, **"Press Tab."** Move in the opposite direction with Shift+Tab.

Like Microsoft Windows 7, Outlook 2007 displays the Ribbon and the Office button. Use the cursor to mouse over the menu items to see what they are called. Then you can select them using that name. (See Chapter 16 for more about controlling and navigating in Windows 7.)

The folder list

The folder list in an e-mail application behaves like the folder list in Windows Explorer. (See Chapter 16.) When the cursor is in this pane, use the **Move Up/Down** commands to select a folder or mailbox. For example, **Move Down Five** selects the folder or mailbox five places below the currently selected folder or mailbox. Folders that contain subfolders or mailboxes have a +/– check box next to their folder icons. To display the subfolders or mailboxes, select the containing folder and say, **"Press Right Arrow."** To hide the subfolders or mailboxes, say, **"Press Left Arrow."**

The message list

The message list is, first and foremost, a list. When the cursor is in the message list pane of the e-mail application window, select messages in the list by using the **Move Up/Down** commands. To select the message three places above the currently selected message, say, **"Move Up Three."**

Reading messages

You can read a message in the reading pane of the application window, or you can get a little more reading room by opening a message window. Open a message window in Messenger by selecting a message in the message list and choosing File⇨Open from the menu. (Alternatively, you can say, **"Open mail message"** or **"Open message."**)

Whether the cursor is in the reading window or in a message window, the **Move** and **Go** commands move the cursor through the message. However, the most useful command when you're reading a message is **Press Page Down.** It displays the next window of text.

Switching between open mailboxes and messages

Say, **"Press Alt Tab"** to cycle through the items on the taskbar. Switch to a new mailbox by selecting it in the folder list. You can also say, **"List all open Windows"** to see what's open and select it from there.

Dictating messages

You can use some Natural Language Commands with Outlook just like when you dictate text into a word processor (see Chapter 9). In Outlook, a message composition window consists of a number of textboxes: several one-line boxes corresponding to the various parts of a message header, and one large textbox for the body of the message.

Move the cursor from one textbox to another by using the Tab key or saying, **"Press Tab."** Move in the opposite direction with Shift+Tab. You can also use the name of the field you want to access. To send your first e-mail, launch NaturallySpeaking and do the following:

1. **Say,** "Send e-mail to George Foster."

   Outlook (if it's your default e-mail program) opens a new e-mail form and inserts the e-mail address for George Foster (provided you already created e-mail addresses).

2. **Say,** "Subject."

   The cursor moves to the Subject field.

3. **Dictate your e-mail subject.**

4. **Say,** "Body Field."

   The cursor is now in the body of the e-mail and ready for you to dictate your complete message.

5. **Dictate your e-mail.**

6. **Proofread your e-mail.**

   If you find mistakes, select and correct them as you would in any other dictation process. (See Chapter 5 for more on quick correction of dictation.)

7. **After you correct all mistakes, say,** "Send Message."

   Your message is sent. You can now move on to reading or sending other e-mails.

Getting your mail read to you

Your NaturallySpeaking assistant can read your e-mail to you. Isn't that what you'd expect from a first-rate assistant? Use the text-to-speech feature to do this. Open the Extras toolbar from the DragonBar and click the Read That button. The text will be read back to you in the voice you have chosen from the options available to you. If you want to modify the voice of your assistant, go to Tools⇨Options⇨Playback/Text-to-Speech and look at the Text-to-Speech attributes. Where you see Voice, use the pull-down list to see your options.

If for any reason your application doesn't work that way, just copy the text of the message from the reading pane of your e-mail application into the NaturallySpeaking Dictation Box and say, **"Read Document."** The NaturallySpeaking voice and diction won't compete with James Earl Jones's voice, but you will understand what it is saying.

Keeping track of appointments

After you send an e-mail, you don't need to stop using voice commands in Outlook. You can schedule appointments through Outlook's Calendar window. Bring up the Calendar window (shown in Figure 12-1) by saying, **"Create a new appointment."** Opening the Calendar window adds the Calendar menu to the menu bar. Use this menu for all of your calendar-related activities. To create a new appointment in Outlook, do the following:

1. **Make sure NaturallySpeaking is running and say,** "Create a new appointment."

   The Outlook Appointment Form opens and the cursor is positioned in the Subject field.

2. **Dictate your subject.**

3. **Say,** "Move to location" **to go to the location field and dictate your location.**

4. **Say,** "Start time" **and dictate the date.**

5. **Move to time fields by saying,** "Press tab" **and add the times.**

6. **Say,** "Move to body field" **and dictate details.**

   Complete your message.

7. **Say,** "Save and close."

8. **To check if the appointment is there, say,** "Switch to the calendar folder" **to view it.**

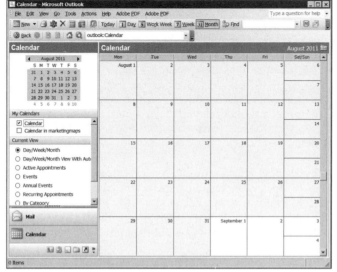

Figure 12-1:
Outlook's
Calendar
utility helps
you keep
track of your
appoint-
ments.

Six additional common commands you can use with Outlook appointments
are as follows:

- Show date
- View month
- Invite attendees
- Cancel invitation
- Create a meeting about
- Create an appointment at

Outlook Tasks are visible in the Calendar window, but they are most easily
added and deleted using the Task window. To open the Task window, say,
"Open, Tasks." Opening the Task window adds the Task menu to the menu
bar. To add a new task, say, **"New Task."**

Whether you add an appointment or a task, a dialog box with a number of
fields to be filled in confronts you. When the cursor is in a textbox, you can
dictate just as you would dictate into a word processor. Don't be afraid to
use those Full Text Control capabilities (see Chapter 8) to edit or correct
your entries.

Move from one field of a dialog box to the next by saying, **"Press tab,"** or jump
to any field you want by using the field's name. For example, in order to select
the All Day Event check box in the New Appointment dialog box, say, **"Press
All Day Event."**

Listing new contacts

Outlook keeps track of much more than e-mail addresses. As marketers like to say, "The money is in the list." They usually mean your customer mailing list — but for many people, their contacts list *is* their customer mailing list.

In this context, a *contact* is not one of those clear round things that falls out of your eye during a basketball game. It's a person you have contacted at some point in your life and created and stored his e-mail address (plus any other optional info you add).

Outlook handles contacts via the Contacts window. Open it by saying, **"View Address Book."** As an added bonus, the Contacts menu is appended to the menu bar. Anything you want to do with your contacts list is handled by this menu. For example, to add a new contact, say, **"Create new contact."** Outlook responds by displaying the New Contact dialog box, shown in Figure 12-2.

The New Contact window looks intimidating because it contains spaces for everything you may know about a person other than hat size. Nevertheless, the only field you have to fill out is Name. Other than that, you can skip around, using the hotkeys to pick other fields to fill. For example, to skip to the Web Page textbox, say, **"Press Alt W."** The New Contact window begins with the General tab on top. To switch to another tab, say, **"Press control tab."**

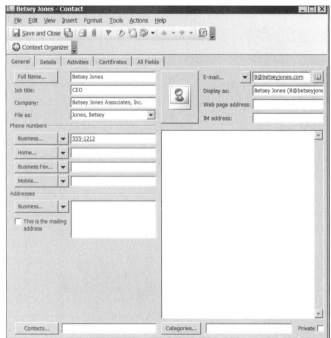

Figure 12-2:
The New
Contact
dialog box.

Making notes

Outlook Notes is a great place to jot down important things you don't want to forget. It works well with NaturallySpeaking because its main purpose is dictation, just like any word processor. If you want to dictate notes in Outlook, make sure that NaturallySpeaking is running and then do the following:

1. **Say,** "Start Microsoft Outlook."

   The Outlook application opens.

2. **Say,** "Open notes."

3. **Say,** "New note."

   A note opens for you to dictate into.

4. **Dictate your note.**

   After you dictate the note, proofread it for mistakes and make corrections as you would with any other type of dictation.

5. **Say,** "Save the note."

6. **Say,** "Close the note."

   If you want to view your note, say, **"Click Notes List"** to select the radio button and view your missive.

Easy, huh? If you like to create sticky-note reminders, this is much quicker (and neater and environmentally friendly and cheaper, but I digress!). Instead of sticking notes on your screen, use this.

Enhancing E-Mail with the LifeStyle Pack

NaturallySpeaking plays nicely with Outlook. When you add the LifeStyle Pack, you get some additional commands for Outlook Express and Thunderbird. If you use these e-mail applications, you'll be happy to know that voice commands are an option for them, too.

Outlook Express

Outlook Express supports Windows operating systems up through Windows XP. (Vista uses Windows Mail. Windows 7 users must use another e-mail client.) Outlook Express's most well-known feature is that you can use custom graphics. It also provides specially designed stationery templates for sending celebratory e-mails. It's likely that if you started using Outlook Express long ago and are comfortable with it, you'll be happy to add voice commands to your options.

As with the other e-mail applications listed above, Outlook Express also uses the three-panel window, as shown in Figure 12-3. By following the menu commands, you can navigate entirely with voice.

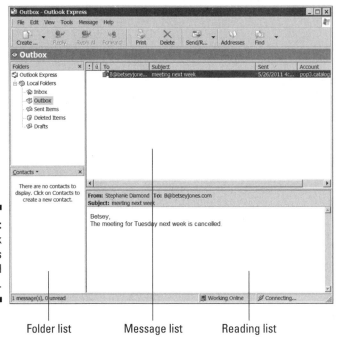

Figure 12-3:
Outlook
Express
three-panel
window.

Folder list   Message list   Reading list

In version 11.5 of NaturallySpeaking, Nuance added some voice commands for Outlook Express that were not in previous versions. To check out the additional voice commands you can use, see the later section, "Windows Live Messenger." The commands are the same; just use the name Outlook Express instead of Windows Live Mail when launching.

Thunderbird

If you use Thunderbird, Mozilla Foundation's free e-mail client, you know that it's an open source application and works cross-platform. This means that it is created by developers who donate their time and share code. It can be used with Windows, Mac, or Linux.

If you haven't used Thunderbird, consider it if you want to aggregate e-mails across several e-mail accounts. Thunderbird does not send e-mail on its own. It lets you combine your accounts and work from one main source. It has several add-ons and lets you configure your e-mail account in a way that makes sense for you.

After you set up and open Thunderbird, you notice that it looks like most other e-mail clients. It uses the three-panel window configuration: the folder list, a message list, and a reading pane.

Using the LifeStyle Pack, Thunderbird acts like a Full Text Control application. You can navigate by saying the menu and submenu names. Table 12-2 shows voice commands for Thunderbird in the LifeStyle Speech Pack.

Table 12-2	Voice Commands for Thunderbird Using the LifeStyle Speech Pack
From This Thunderbird Menu Choice:	*Use These Voice Commands:*
File	"New message," "New folder," "New account"
Edit	"Undo," "Delete folder," "Select all"
View	"Show all folders," "Sort by," "Search addresses"
Go	"Next unread message," "Go forward," "Mail start page"
Message	"Reply to all," "Copy message," "Tag message"
Tools	"Address book," "Delete junk in folder," "Open import"
Help	"Open release notes," "Help me," "Check for updates"
Options	"Spell check," "Send a copy to drafts," "Encrypt this message"

Dealing with Other E-Mail Applications

For most businesspeople, reading and answering e-mail takes up way too much time. Several books have been written about how to cope: when to check e-mail and how to manage your inbox. But, there's no good way to eliminate its presence. Dare I say e-mail is here to stay? NaturallySpeaking can be your ally in dispatching the job quickly.

Choosing Gmail

In NaturallySpeaking, Gmail is a Full Text Control application that doesn't work with Natural Language Commands. That means it has limitations in what you can do. If you were using Outlook and move to Gmail, you may be frustrated that it isn't as easy to use with NaturallySpeaking. For example, adding contacts is not supported. But it gets the job done, and if Gmail is your application of choice, fear not. It can work for you.

One secret to using Gmail with NaturallySpeaking is to use the **Click** command. Doing so enables you to manage e-mail tasks quickly. For example, you can say, **"Click reply," "Click delete,"** or **"Click report spam."**

The Gmail program doesn't have a reading pane, but closely follows the other structures of other e-mail programs. To send mail in Gmail after launching NaturallySpeaking and your Gmail window, follow these steps:

1. **Say,** "Click compose mail."

   The e-mail window opens with the cursor in the address box.

2. **Dictate the address and then say,** "Move to next field."

   Move through the subject field the same way.

3. **Dictate your e-mail.**

4. **Say,** "Click send."

Interacting with Windows Live Mail

If you move to the Windows 7 operating system, you must upgrade from Outlook Express to Windows Live Mail (WLM). WLM was created to work with the Windows 7 operating systems. To send an e-mail with WLM, make sure that NaturallySpeaking 11.5 is running and do the following:

1. **Say,** "Open Windows Live Mail."

   The application opens.

2. **Open the e-mail form by saying,** "Create a message."

   The mail form opens.

3. **Move through each field by saying,** "Go to *<field name>*."

   For example, say, **"Go to Subject field."**

4. **When you move into the body field, dictate your message.**

5. **Say,** "Send message."

   The e-mail is sent.

Four other commands you can use with WLM are

- **Go to address book**
- **Reply to author**
- **Forward the message**
- **Go to the outbox folder**

When NaturallySpeaking is unclear about the instructions for Live Mail, it shows numbered options as it does in most other applications. Just as you would anywhere else, select the option by saying, **"Choose *<number>*."** Once you get used to doing this, it's easy to get around.

Adding Instant Messaging Using the LifeStyle Pack

One of the great joys of the web is that it lets you chat in real-time with friends and colleagues for free. Programs like Skype, Yahoo! Messenger, and Windows Live Messenger enjoy great popularity. The world is now a connected place, or as Thomas Friedman wrote, it's "flat." For this reason, VoxEnable added instant messenger applications to its LifeStyle Pack. Use voice commands to navigate these chat programs hands-free from start to finish.

Basically, we all want two things out of a chat application: We want to get our messages out quickly, so that the conversation doesn't sound stiff and unnatural, and we want to get the messages out right, so that we avoid creating confusion.

NaturallySpeaking is a great help in getting a message out quickly, especially if you don't type fast. But always proofread first to avoid sending out the wrong message. NaturallySpeaking mistakes are correct English words that aren't obvious typos. If you're trying to tell somebody to "send an e-mail," you don't want it to come out "sand an e-mail" instead.

Skype

When I worked at AOL from 1994 to 2002, we used AOL Instant Messenger (AIM) to talk to internal colleagues on a moment-by-moment basis. Everyone was online and people in other companies were maybe a bit envious of AOL's closed little system. (That made it even more fun.)

When I started my own company, Digital Media Works, I was delighted to try a new application called Skype. Skype enabled me to instant message colleagues as I once did with AIM. (Well, that was before Skype signed on millions of users and was bought by Microsoft.) But, it's still as fresh as it was back then — and is still a free download. Of course, it has lots of new features, like video messaging.

To download Skype, go to `https://login.skype.com/account/signup-form` and create an account.

You can use Skype as a Full Text Control application. To figure out the right voice commands, look at the menu options. Table 12-3 shows more voice commands available from the LifeStyle Speech Pack.

Table 12-3	Voice Commands for Skype Using the LifeStyle Speech Pack
From This Skype Menu Choice:	*Use These Voice Commands:*
Skype	"Status away," "Edit profile," "Add video"
Contacts	"New contact," "Create contact group," Show Outlook contacts"
Conversation	"Send SMS," "Send voice mail," "Recent conversations"
Call	"Video call," "Ignore call," "Hold call"
View	"View conversations," "Change options," "Skype options"
Help	"Help me," "Welcome screen," "Check updates"
Other	"Down three contacts," "Start call," "Call contact Skype"

Imagine the fun of dictating your instant messages and calling your contacts — all hands free! Now, that's easy. If you want to try it, make sure Skype and Dragon NaturallySpeaking are running (along with your connection to VoxEnable). Then do the following:

1. **Say, "Start Skype."**

   The Skype application opens.

2. **Say the name of the contact's name exactly as it's listed.**

   The program chooses that name.

3. **Say, "Conversation."**

   The Conversation menu item opens the submenu.

4. **Say "Send," then say, "Instant message."**

   The cursor is in the box, ready to take dictation.

5. **Dictate your message and say, "Send message."**

   Your message is sent. You can now chat back and forth.

6. **When you are finished with your virtual live visit, say, "Close Skype."**

Yahoo! Messenger

Yahoo! Messenger works hard to compete with other popular messenger programs. Its latest version, 11.0, has video chat, an "always on" feature that lets you move your chat from your PC to your mobile device, and provides multiple-player game access. To download Yahoo! Messenger, go to http://messenger.yahoo.com/download/.

The key to using voice commands with Yahoo! Messenger is to remember that you can dictate into any open text window. If you remember that, you can move around and dictate easily. Table 12-4 lists some commands to try.

Table 12-4	Voice Commands for Yahoo! Messenger Using the LifeStyle Speech Pack
From This Yahoo! Messenger Menu Choice:	**Use These Voice Commands:**
Messenger	"Status available," "Preferences," Privacy options"
Contacts	"Add contact," "Address book contact," "Contact details"
Actions	"Instant message," "Send," "Video call," "Share photos"
Help	"Messenger help," "Set up," "Toggle diagnostics"

Windows Live Messenger

Do you already have a Windows Live ID from signing up for a variety of Microsoft online programs such as Hotmail, Office, Photos, or MSN? If so, you have a quick path to set up Windows Live Messenger. You just need to download and log in. Then you add contacts as you would with any other instant messenger client. Download Windows Live Messenger from the Microsoft website at http://explore.live.com/windows-live-messenger?os=other.

The Messenger chat screen is simple and takes the same format as Skype. Your contacts are on the left side, and the chat window is to the right.

When the cursor is in the input window, dictate what you want to say. Because Microsoft Windows Live Messenger is a Full Text Control application, you can use any of the selection and correction features described in Chapter 5. In particular, you can correct text by saying it. For example, if NaturallySpeaking misinterpreted **"Go back"** as "Go bad," you can say, **"Correct bad."** Table 12-5 lists some voice commands VoxEnable makes possible.

Table 12-5 Voice Commands for Windows Live Messenger Using the LifeStyle Speech Pack

In the Conversation Window from This Menu Choice:	Use These Voice Commands:
File	"Open received files," "Save conversation," "View message history"
Edits	"Undo," "Cut," "Copy," "Select all"
Actions	"Send e-mail," "Start video call," "Invite another contact"
Tools	"Toggle emoticons," "Audio setup," "Change display picture"
Help	"Help me," "Billing support," "About messenger"

Chapter 13

Working the Web

*W*ord processing may be the most obvious application of speech recognition, but it isn't the only one. Gadgets like BlackBerrys and iPads factor heavily into the equation, too. If you're like me, you spend more time than you care to admit on the web — browsing, tweeting, exchanging e-mail, and trying out new apps.

NaturallySpeaking command shortcuts for searching and dictating online are easy. The menu commands of the e-mail and browser applications provide all the specialized commands you need, and the rest is basically just word processing and window management. Nonetheless, in this chapter, I assemble a few tricks worth knowing.

Browsing the Web

Using NaturallySpeaking with Internet Explorer (IE) or Mozilla Firefox (Firefox) lets you do your entire web browsing by voice, efficiently, without having to touch a mouse or keyboard. Of course, you can use them if you want — do whatever is most comfortable for you. Be aware that you must choose either IE or Firefox when you use NaturallySpeaking, even if you regularly use some other browser. (Note that I use Internet Explorer in the following examples.)

Getting started

To start browsing the web, follow these steps:

1. **Start NaturallySpeaking.**

2. **Start Internet Explorer (or Firefox, alternatively).**

   It doesn't matter how you start Internet Explorer. You can start it with the **Start** command by saying, **"Start Internet Explorer,"** by selecting a Favorite from the Start menu, or by clicking its desktop icon with the mouse.

That's all there is to it. Your browser opens and is immediately ready to take your commands.

Choosing Firefox as your browser

If you enjoy using Firefox over Internet Explorer, the Nuance folks serve you well. NaturallySpeaking works equally well with Firefox, so you can just select links by saying them in that browser instead of IE. If you want to use Firefox with NaturallySpeaking, you can do it without much of a learning curve. Just remember the following when using Firefox:

✔ **Make sure Firefox is in the Start menu, so that you choose Firefox from there if that's the way you prefer to launch it.**

   As an alternative launch method, say, **"Open Firefox," "Launch Firefox," or "Show Firefox"** to launch it.

✔ Say, "Go to the Address Field" **when you want to get to the address box.**

One reason people started using Firefox was because they enjoyed using multiple tabs. You can use the following voice commands with Firefox tabs:

✔ **Add a new tab**

✔ **Open a new tab**

✔ **Click the next tab**

✔ **Click the previous tab**

✔ **Go to the next tab**

✔ **Go to the previous tab**

✔ **Close tab**

If you want to search something directly, use the shortcut examples in the "Using shortcuts created for the web" section in this chapter.

Giving orders to Internet Explorer

You can give Internet Explorer its marching orders in several ways:

- ✔ **Natural Language commands:** See Chapter 9 for a discussion of Natural Language.
- ✔ **Keyboard commands:** See Chapter 8 for a discussion of levels of control.
- ✔ **Menu commands:** See Chapter 16.

In addition, you can use the same **Move** and **Go** commands that work in the NaturallySpeaking DragonPad, like **Go To Top/Bottom** or **Move Down Three Paragraphs.** You can also use the mouse voice commands (see Chapter 16) to click toolbar buttons or links on web pages, but usually one of the other techniques achieves the same result more easily. Table 13-1 shows how to replace the Internet Explorer toolbar buttons with Natural Language, keyboard, or menu voice commands.

Table 13-1 Voice Commands that Substitute for the Toolbar Buttons

Toolbar Button	Voice Command	Menu	Key Combination
Back	Go Back	Click View, Go To, Back	Press Alt Left arrow
Forward	Go Forward	Click View, Go To, Forward	Press Alt Right arrow
Stop	Stop Loading	Click View, Stop	Press Escape
Refresh	Refresh	Click View, Refresh	Press F5
Home	Go Home	Click View, Go To, Home Page	Press Alt Home
Search	<none>	Click View, Explorer Bar, Search	Press Ctrl + E
Favorites	<none>	Click View, Explorer Bar, Favorites	Press Ctrl + I
History	<none>	Click View, Explorer Bar, History	Press Ctrl + H
Mail	<none>	Click Tools, Mail and News	<none>
Print	<none>	Click File⇨Print	Press Control P
Edit	<none>	Click File⇨Edit	<none>

Going Places on the Web

Web browsers provide multiple ways to open a web page or to get from one web page to another. Your first page opens when you start Internet Explorer (unless you start it by selecting an entry from the Start⇨Internet Explorer⇨Favorites menu). From there, you can move around on the web by choosing links; clicking toolbar buttons (refer to Table 13-1 for menu and keyboard equivalents); entering a web address into the Address box; or jumping to a page for which you have stored its location on the Favorites menu.

Linking from one web page to another

One useful feature you can use while browsing is the capability to click a link on a web page by saying all or part of its text label. For example, suppose that you are viewing the web page shown in Figure 13-1, the Newsroom page of the Nuance website, and you want to click the link labeled Always On: Must-Have Apps for New Smartphone Owners. All you have to do is say, **"Always on."** IE searches the links visible in the Internet Explorer window to see if any of them contain that text. Because one and only one such link appears on the page in Figure 13-1, the linked page is chosen.

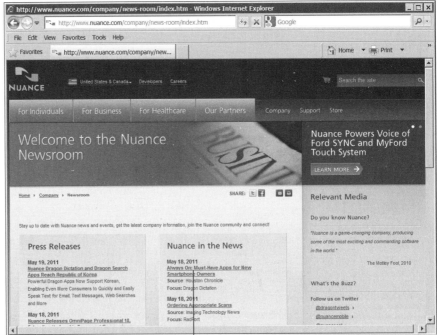

Figure 13-1: Naturally-Speaking checks for the occurrence of "Always on" on the page.

"Always On" line

Pick whatever part of the link's text label is easiest to say. For example, if you want to link to a news story "1331 injured in Ulan Bator earthquake," say, **"Injured"** or **"Earthquake."** Either should be sufficient to tell NaturallySpeaking which link you want.

If the link is an image, say, **"Image."** NaturallySpeaking selects all the images visible in your viewing window and numbers them. Then simply choose the number of the image you want by saying, **"Choose <image number>."** If you know the text label of the image (it is displayed while the image loads), select it by name, just as you would any text link.

Dictating to the Address box

The Address box is the textbox at the bottom of the browser's toolbar, the one that shows the web address of the current page. Say, **"Go To Address"** to move the cursor into the Address box. Then dictate the address you want and say, **"Go There."**

You can start a web search by dictating, **"Question mark <*search terms*>"** into the Address box and then saying, **"Go There."** For example, if you are looking for articles about McDonald's franchises in Antarctica, say, **"Question mark, McDonalds, comma, Antarctica."** When "?McDonald's, Antarctica" appears in the Address box, say, **"Go There."**

My tongue ties in knots whenever I try to say, "Double-you, double-you, double-you," so I came up with the following trick: I used the Vocabulary Editor to introduce the word "http://www" into the NaturallySpeaking vocabulary, and defined its spoken form to be **"Dubdubdub."** (I also created a second alias, **Triple-Dub.** See Chapter 18 for a detailed description of Vocabulary Editor tricks like this one.) So when I want NaturallySpeaking to type "http://www.yahoo.com," I just say, **"Dubdubdub dot yahoo dot com."**

The most recent 25 web addresses that were typed or dictated into your Address box are kept on a list that drops down from the Address box. To make it drop down, get the cursor into the Address box, and then say, **"Press Alt Down Arrow."** Naturally, **"Press Alt Up Arrow"** makes the list retract again. Move up or down the list with the **Move Up/Down** commands, like **Move Down Three.** After you select an address from the list, say, **"Press Enter"** to tell your browser to go there.

Using the Favorites menu

By far, the easiest way to connect to a web page is to store its location on the Favorites menu. Using this menu is also the simplest, quickest way to keep track of websites and return to them by voice commands. Use voice commands to go to a website on the Favorites menu as follows.

✔ If Internet Explorer is running in the active window, say, **"Favorites,"** then say the name of the favorite item you want from the menu. It doesn't matter where on the menu the favorite is. If, for example, you have a favorite called CNN in a folder called News Sites on the Favorites menu, you just have to say, **"Favorites,"** then say, **"CNN."** You don't have to say the name of the News Sites folder.

✔ Use the Favorites menu on the Internet Explorer menu bar, just as you use Start⇨Internet Explorer from the menu. If Internet Explorer is the active window, say, **"Click Favorites, News Sites, CNN."**

When you are at a site or page that you want to bookmark in your Favorites menu, say **"Add to favorites,"** and it will be placed on that menu list.

When you create favorites, give them short names that are easy for you to pronounce and easy for NaturallySpeaking to recognize. If the names of the favorites you already have are too long or too difficult, you can change them. Follow these steps:

1. **From the Start menu, go to Internet Explorer.**

   Don't select the favorite itself, because you don't want to open it right now. In the CNN example earlier in this section, you would say, **"Click Start, Favorites, News Sites."** The menu expands so that you can see the CNN favorite, but it is not selected.

2. **Use the Move Up/Down commands to highlight the favorite.**

   If CNN is the fifth entry in the News Sites folder, say, **"Move Down Five."**

3. **Say,** "Right Click, Rename."

   A Rename dialog box appears.

4. **Dictate the new name.**

5. **Say,** "Click OK."

Pinning websites or pages to the Start menu

If you are using Internet Explorer 9 or higher and running NaturallySpeaking 11.5, you can use voice commands to pin shortcuts to the Start menu. This is an added benefit when you are working quickly and want to grab something to look at later. A simple voice command will capture it. To pin it, do the following:

1. **Say,** "Pin this *<web page or website>* to the Start menu."

   You will see a dialog box with the web address (also known as One Box).

2. **If you want to edit the box, say,** "Go to the One box," **and edit accordingly.**

3. **To finish say,** "Click."

Moving around a Web Page

NaturallySpeaking has an automatic scrolling feature that I find very convenient for reading long articles. Just say, **"Start Scrolling Down,"** and the text
of the current web page starts moving up your screen like the credits at the
end of a movie. Adjust the scrolling speed by saying, **"Speed Up"** or **"Slow
Down."** (I love it — no computerese nonsense like, "Set Scrolling Speed Up
Five," or something equally obscure.) The **Stop Scrolling** command (and I bet
you already figured this out) stops the scrolling. To go backward, say, **"Start
Scrolling Up."**

If automatic scrolling makes you feel like you're in a speed-reading test, you
have other options for moving through a web page. Perhaps you are accustomed to using the scroll bar on the right edge of your browser's window to
move through a web page. As always, mouse-oriented techniques don't translate to speech as well as keyboard-oriented techniques do. The simplest way
to scroll through a web page by voice is to say, **"Press Page Down"** when
you want to display the next screen's text.

The **Move** and **Go** commands (see Chapter 5) also work with a browser,
but predicting what they're going to do is sometimes hard. The "lines" that
NaturallySpeaking moves when you say, **"Move down four lines"** don't precisely correspond to the lines of text that you see on your screen. (They're
usually a little bit larger than the lines of text. Don't ask me why.) And on
web pages that have several frames, images, animations, or other advanced
features, what a "paragraph" means is anybody's guess. "Top" and "bottom"
are still meaningful terms, though, and you will find that **Go To Top** and **Go
To Bottom** are good commands to remember when you're reading long documents on the web.

Entering information on a web page

Many web pages contain forms for you to fill out or textboxes into which you
can dictate longer messages. NaturallySpeaking has special commands for
entering such information or messages.

Before you can dictate text into a textbox, you must first move the cursor
there. You can, of course, move the cursor by clicking the mouse in the box,
just as you would if you weren't using NaturallySpeaking. But alternatively,
you can say, **"Click *<the name of the text box>*"** to move the cursor to the
textbox on the page.

For example, say, **"Click Name."** When the cursor is in the box (indicated by
a red arrow pointing at it from below), you can dictate, edit, and correct, just
as you would in any Full Text Control application. (See Chapter 8.) When you
finish with that textbox, repeat the process to move to a different box. Say,

"**Click <*the name of the textbox*>**" to move on to the next textbox, and so on. Go back to an earlier textbox by saying its name. You can also move to the next textbox by saying "**Next control.**" You can also say, "**Edit box,**" and Dragon will number every available edit box on the page so you can choose it.

To move the cursor to radio buttons or check boxes on a web page, just say, "**Radio Button**" or "**Check Box.**" The cursor moves to the first such object on the page. Say, "**Next**" to go to the next one or "**Previous**" to return to the one before. (NaturallySpeaking figures out from context what kind of object "**Next**" refers to.) To change the state of a radio button or check box, say "**Click That.**" You can also say, "**Edit box**" or "**Edit radio button,**" and Dragon will number every available edit box on the page so you can choose it.

To cycle through the objects on a web page, say, "**Press Tab.**" Say, "**Press Shift Tab**" to cycle in the opposite direction. This technique is useful when you want to go from one kind of object (like a textbox) to a different kind of object (like a radio button).

Here are some additional commands you can use to move around with tabs:

- ✔ Open new tab
- ✔ Switch to last tab
- ✔ View the next tab
- ✔ View the previous tab
- ✔ Close tab

Using shortcuts created for the web

Many of the activities you normally perform on the Internet are supported by new special shortcuts created by Nuance. Take advantage of these shortcuts because you can use them no matter where you are. Check the Command browser to see a complete listing, which includes the following commands:

- ✔ **Searching the web:** Use Google, Bing, or another search tool to find anything (well, not your misplaced car keys!). For example, say, "**Search Google for patio furniture,**" and your browser opens the search in Google and displays the results.

- ✔ **Searching using specific search categories:** These include images, video, news, maps, or products. For example, say, "**Search video for fossils.**"

✔ **Searching a specific well-known site:** Find exactly what you want at a specific website. Speak the website name, such as Google, Yahoo!, Bing, Amazon, and eBay, in your command. For example, say, **"Search Amazon for Dragon NaturallySpeaking For Dummies."**

✔ **Searching using a web address:** If you want to go to a specific website, say, **"Go to address bar"** and then say the URL you want to go to, as in **"Red Cross dot org."**

View the shortcut options for the web and other commands by choosing Tools⇨Options⇨Commands.

Chapter 14

Playing Media with the LifeStyle Speech Pack

*T*here are online applications that mean business. The applications I talk about in this chapter can be used for business or for laughing, dancing, and singing. You decide. You can skip this chapter if you have no interest in finding out about or using an add-on product called LifeStyle Speech Pack. I provide information about the bonus pack in this book because it enhances common web applications you may use and want to know about. (Nuance also has Gamer and Designer bundles. Check for them in the online store.)

Many of our entertainment centers no longer sit in our living rooms, thanks to computers and the web. We can access entertainment from any room in the house. When you add voice-enabled features, you really take these applications to the next level. This chapter shows you how.

Introducing the LifeStyle Speech Pack

Nuance has created a bundle called the LifeStyle Speech Pack (also called LifeStyle Bonus Pack) that you can buy in its online store. It is bundled with either the Home or Premium Edition of Dragon NaturallySpeaking. The add-on is published by VoxEnable.com, based in the U.K. You download it with a serial number given to you at the time of purchase in the Nuance online store. The pricing varies. At the time of this writing, the bundle for the Premium Edition with the LifeStyle Speech Pack is featured on promotion for $99.

The applications in the add-on bundle are discussed in two chapters of this book, this one and Chapter 12. Media applications that this chapter covers are speech-enabled commands for the following:

- Music:
    - iTunes
- Audacity
    - Spotify
- Digital media:
    - QuickTime
    - Windows Media Player
- Reading:
    - Adobe Reader

Chapter 12 covers voice-enabled commands for the following applications:

- E-mail:
    - Outlook Express
    - Thunderbird
- Instant messages and live video chatting:
    - Skype
    - Live Messenger
    - Yahoo! Messenger

Installing the LifeStyle Speech Pack

You may find the installation of the LifeStyle Speech Pack a bit complex. The trick is to know where to put the activation code at the right time. To install the Speech Pack, open the file with your activation code and then do the following:

1. **Download the files at** `www.nuance.com/speechpack` **to your desktop or wherever you like to put installation files.**

   Make sure that Dragon NaturallySpeaking is *already* installed on your computer before you install the LifeStyle Speech Pack.

2. **Double-click the icon you just downloaded.**

   The application starts and you see the screen shown in Figure 14-1.

3. **Click Next.**

   You'll be asked whether you want to create shortcuts.

4. **Click the boxes of the shortcuts you want and click Next.**

   You'll be asked to accept the terms of the Licensing Agreement.

5. **Click the Accept box and click Next.**

   You'll see the Install screen, as shown in Figure 14-2.

6. **Click Install.**

   The program installs.

Figure 14-1:
The
LifeStyle
Speech
Pack Setup
Wizard.

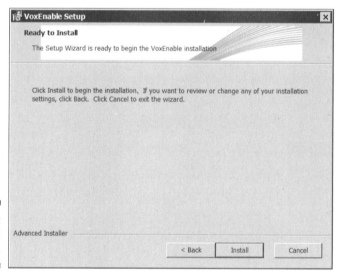

Figure 14-2:
The Install
screen.

7. **When you see the Install Complete screen, click Finish.**

A screen, as shown in Figure 14-3, pops up and says that Dragon NaturallySpeaking is being initialized.

Here comes the tricky part.

8. **Right-click on the VoxEnable icon that is now in your system tray.**

You see the choices shown in Figure 14-4.

9. **Click Supported Applications and you see the screen shown in Figure 14-5. Choose General in that list.**

Figure 14-3:
Files are being initialized.

Figure 14-4:
Right-click on the system tray icon for VoxEnable to see these choices.

Check Dragon Connection...
Supported Applications...
My Commands...
Social Networks...
Check for updates...
About VoxEnable...

Exit VoxEnable...

Figure 14-5:
Choose General in the list.

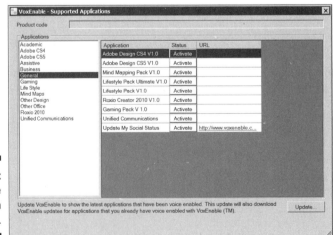

10. Click the Activate button next to Lifestyle Pack V.1.0.

When you click the button, a prompt box opens, as shown in Figure 14-6.

11. Type in your activation code and click OK.

You see a screen that says you have successfully activated the program.

12. Click OK.

You did it. Now let's get on to the serious business of playing songs!

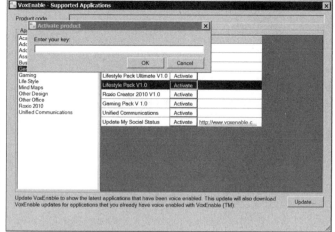

Rocking the Music

The lure of music has arguably made the web grow even faster than it might otherwise have. Downloading music got off to a rocky start with intellectual property at the heart of the controversy. Now, almost everyone who uses the web has some kind of music on their hard drives and gadgets. The app with the largest market share is iTunes from Apple.

Many applications help you edit your music files. The LifeStyle Speech Pack includes the music editor Audacity, which I cover here.

iTunes

If you have even a passing interest in online music, you likely know about iTunes. Apple owns iTunes and provides access to most of the popular digi-tized music available in the world. Its media players, the iPhone, iPod, and iPad (see Chapter 15 for information about using these with voice-enabled commands), have captured the lion's share of the market for mobile devices.

The good news is that with VoxEnable running, you can use iTunes as a Full Text Control application. This means that you can say the names of the menu commands and select the submenus you want to open. To see how using iTunes with voice-enabled commands can be done, let's look at a session you may want to customize for yourself. (The steps that follow are for iTunes version 9.2.1 and higher.) The scenario below assumes that you've already installed the LifeStyle Speech Pack and that NaturallySpeaking is running.

To voice-enable some music, flip up your laptop and do the following:

1. **Say,** "Sign into iTunes account."

   Your iTunes application opens.

2. **Say,** "Recently played."

   The list of recently played songs opens.

3. **Say,** "Play" **to play the first song in the list.**

4. **Say,** "Shuffle songs" **to randomize the list and play.**

5. **When you're done playing songs, say,** "Sign out of account."

You can also do music management in iTunes with voice commands, as shown in Table 14-1.

Table 14-1	NaturallySpeaking Commands for iTunes
To Do This:	*Say This:*
See your iTunes account	"View my account"
See if there are new downloads	"Check for downloads"
Run diagnostics	"Run diagnostics"
Start a new playlist	"New playlist"
Synch with your iPod	"Synch iPod"
View your songs in a list format	"View as list"
Rate a song five stars	"Rate five stars"

Audacity

Audacity is a free open-source sound editor and recorder that you can download from http://audacity.sourceforge.net/download/. Using Audacity, you can record podcasts, interview your favorite guru to post on your blog, or edit a recording you've already made.

If you've never used a sound-editing program before, the interface may seem intimidating at first. But it really is quite simple once you understand how things work. When you open a sound file with Audacity, you see the screen shown in Figure 14-7.

Like iTunes, you can use Audacity as a Full Text Control application. This means that you can say the names of the menu commands and select the submenus you want to open. As shown in Figure 14-8, you see the command you can use by looking at the open menus.

You'll find lots of tutorials available online from the Audacity website (see URL above). To get started, Table 14-2 shows some commands you can use.

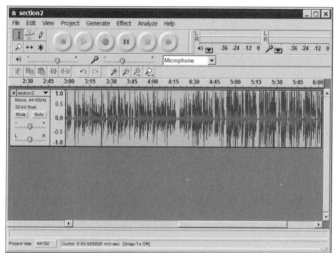

Figure 14-7:
An open
MP3 file.

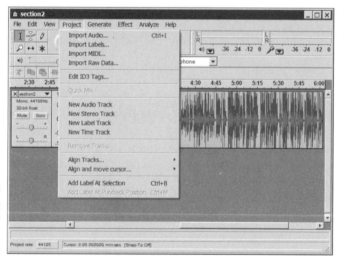

Figure 14-8:
Choice of
menu items.

Table 14-2   NaturallySpeaking Commands for Audacity

To Do This:	Say This:
Open a new file	"New file"
Open one of your recent files	"Recent files"
Zoom in on area to edit	"Zoom in"
Repeat the last effect	"Repeat effect"
Start or stop selected sound	"Play music"
Pause the audio playing	"Pause audio"
Close the program	"Exit"

Spotify

Spotify is an online music platform that has recently been introduced in the United States. It can be found at this URL: http://www.spotify.com/us/about/what/. It is different from other online programs in that it allows you to create your own playlists using Spotify's entire catalog of music — you don't need to buy individual songs. This gives you access to millions of songs the instant you join.

To sign up you need to choose one of the following three subscription levels:

- ✔ **Free:** You have to view advertisements.
- ✔ **Unlimited:** $4.99 per month and no advertisements.
- ✔ **Premium:** $9.99 per month. No advertisements and you can download your playlists on your mobile devices.

Spotify is easy to use with NaturallySpeaking. You treat it as you would any Full Text Control application by using the names of the menu items as commands.

Talking Back to Your Videos

Playing videos is one of the most popular online activities. It makes sense that you would want to make it as easy as possible. With voice-enabled commands, your next video is just a word away.

QuickTime Movie 7 and Windows Media Player 12 (WMP)

Originally, QuickTime and WMP were media players designed to support different operating systems — QuickTime for the Mac and WMP for Windows. Today, both players support both operating systems, so which player you use largely depends on the format of the media you want to play.

For advanced users, there are converters and editing programs, but for our purposes, it's likely that if you find a video that is in WMP format, you play it in that format.

Commands for these two media applications are Full Text Control. This means that you can find the right commands by looking at the menu names and using those as a starting point. Like most of the applications in this section, familiarity with them will make it easy for you to get around.

Lip-reading with Adobe Reader

The ubiquitous Adobe Reader has been in existence in one form or another since 1993. As an inveterate e-book consumer, I pop open the Adobe Reader and get lost in a book more times than I can count.

Adobe Reader is easy to use and stays in the background. Actually, it's pretty hard to avoid using it if you are a businessperson. The next time you want to read your latest PDFs, make sure NaturallySpeaking and VoxEnable are running and do the following:

1. **Say,** "Open *<name of file>*."

    Your PDF document opens.

2. **If it isn't the size you want, say, for example,** "Fit to width." The document fits to the width of your open screen.

3. **To move to the next page say,** "Go to next page."

4. **To change the display to a two-page format, say,** "Display page two up continuous."

    The pages are displayed in a two-page-per-screen format.

5. **If you want the pages read to you aloud, say,** "Activate read out loud."

    The digital voice starts reading the pages.

6. **If you want to pause reading, say,** "Pause read out loud" **and then say,** "Activate read out loud" **again when you want to read aloud again.**

7. **To close the document, say,** "Close document."

If you can't save time and actually enjoy reading your PDFs using this method, I suspect you just aren't trying. Give it a try!

Chapter 15

Dictating the Mobile Way

. . . .

. . . .

*I*t was inevitable that once we started talking into mobile phones, we'd want to talk *to* them as well. Now, thanks to Dragon NaturallySpeaking, you can have your phone or other mobile device take over the pesky task of typing your e-mails. If speed is your goal (and whose isn't?), you can dictate an e-mail to your mobile device — iPhone, iPad, iPod touch, BlackBerry, or Android — and quickly dispatch it to your waiting minions. It's (at least) five times faster than typing on that little keyboard!

This chapter covers the use of NaturallySpeaking dictation apps for your mobile devices. Typing with your thumbs makes most people feel like, well, "all thumbs." Now, a way to forget all furious fumbling is close at hand (pun intended).

Dictating with Apple Mobile Devices

Nuance's NaturallySpeaking mobile apps for the Apple devices, including the iPhone, iPad, and iPod touch, are incredibly easy. Mostly, you tap, speak, and send. If you like having to figure out how complex applications work, you're out of luck. The integration with Apple products is nothing short of dead simple. You'll be up and running as fast as you can download them.

Dragon NaturallySpeaking version 11.5 enables you to use the following apps with your Apple devices:

- ✔ **Dragon Dictation 2.0:** Dictate directly into your Apple mobile devices and send e-mail or post to Facebook and Twitter.
- ✔ **Dragon Search:** Easily search the most popular web search engines.
- ✔ **Dragon Remote Microphone Application:** Use your device as a microphone to dictate wirelessly to your PC.

Discovering Dragon Dictation

What's great about Dragon Dictation is that it turns your mobile device into a mini-NaturallySpeaking hub, and it's free. You get the same quality dictation with the added benefit of bypassing the mini keyboard for e-mail functions.

To get the Dragon Application, go to `http://nuancemobilelife.com/applications.html` and click the Download Now link, shown in Figure 15-1.

Then choose a way to download it. Your choices are an iTunes account, an SMS address, or an e-mail address, as shown in Figure 15-2.

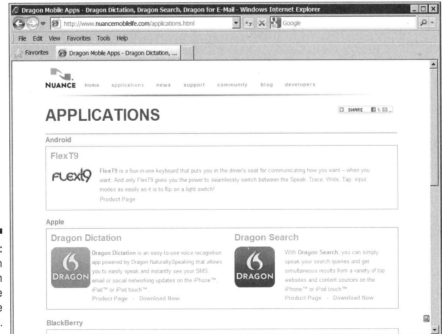

Figure 15-1:
Dragon
Dictation
App on the
Nuance
website.

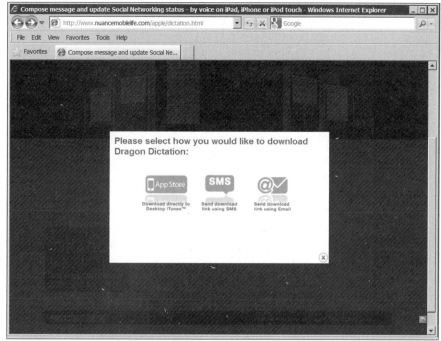

Figure 15-2:
Download
options for
the Dragon
Dictation
app.

Using your iPhone

This section explains how to dictate e-mails on the iPhone. Then I show you how to use Dragon Dictation with your iPad to post to Facebook and Twitter and create Notes.

To download the app from the iTunes store, do the following:

1. **Go online to the Apps Store on iTunes and find Dragon Dictation.**

2. **Open your account and download it as you would any app for your iPhone.**

   You will see the Dragon Dictation icon loaded in your Apple section.

3. **Go to your iPhone and look at the icons present on your home screen.**

   You will see a Dragon icon and the caption "Dictation."

4. **Tap the Dragon icon.**

   On the screen, you will see a red Recording button with the words "Tap and dictate" above it, as shown in Figure 15-3.

5. **To begin recording, tap the red button.**

   The screen indicates that you are recording, as shown in Figure 15-4.

Figure 15-3:
Recording
button on
your iPhone.

6. **When you are finished, tap the Done button.**

If you are dictating into your iPhone or iPod touch and are not using a wired headset, remember that the built-in microphone is located on the upper-left corner. Speak in that direction. On your iPad, you will see a message indicating where to speak when you dictate.

AT&T 📶 2:12 PM 🔋

Recording...

Cancel ⊗

DONE

Figure 15-4:
Dictation
is being
recorded on
your iPhone.

It is easy to end a recording, Tap the arrow icon (see Figure 15-5) on the bottom-right corner of the screen and choose Settings. Tap on the "Detect end of speech" setting to turn it on. Then, when you stop dictating, the recording stops without having to tap it. In that window, you also see other options for your dictation: SMS, Email, Copy, Facebook, Twitter, and Settings.

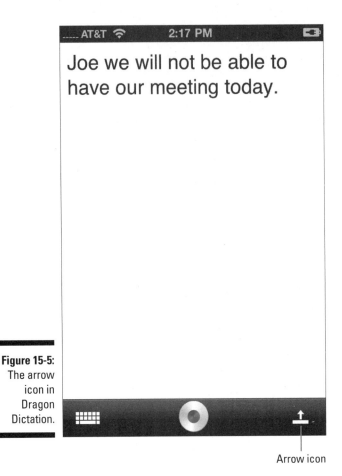

Figure 15-5:
The arrow icon in Dragon Dictation.

Arrow icon

7. **To send the message in an e-mail, tap the E-Mail icon, shown in Figure 15-6.**

   An e-mail form pops up, complete with your message. Send it as you would any other e-mail.

Extending dictation with the iPad

Like Dragon Dictation for your iPhone, you can use your iPad to send e-mail, and you can also

- ✔ **Post to social networks:** Without leaving the app, you can post directly to Facebook and Twitter.

- ✔ **Create notes:** Nuance has added a feature that allows you to dictate notes that you can store and use in a variety of ways.

Figure 15-6:
Use the
E-Mail icon
to send
e-mails on
your iPhone.

To post to Facebook and Twitter, do the following:

1. **Launch your Dragon Dictation icon from your iPad home screen by tapping it.**

   You will see the recording screen.

2. **Dictate the message that you want to post to Facebook or Twitter.**

3. **Tap the down-facing arrow icon on the upper-right side of the screen.**

   A window opens, showing you several choices (see Figure 15-7).

4. **Choose either the Facebook or Twitter icon.**

   A sign-in screen pops up, asking you to input your screen name and password.

5. **Enter your log-ins.**

   You will be asked if you want to send your message.

6. **Tap Send.**

Figure 15-7:
Choices for
sending to
Facebook or
Twitter on
the iPad.

After you set up your log-ins, you'll be able to seamlessly post your message.

To create notes with Dragon Dictation, follow these steps:

1. **With the Dragon Dictation app open on your iPad, tap the Notes button on the upper-left corner of the screen.**

   You see a split screen. On one side, you see your list of notes. On the other is the dictation of your last note, as shown in Figure 15-8.

2. **Tap the plus sign (+) to start recording, and then tap it again when you are done.**

   You see that your dictation is recorded and will be in your list of notes until you either delete it or do something else with it. With the Notes app, you can record and save passages of text, send them as an e-mail, or post to a social network.

Notes you dictate are automatically saved and put in your notes list. To manually delete a note, use the Trash icon. Your note will also be deleted if you send it as an e-mail or Cut it.

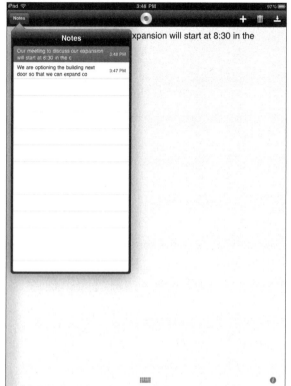

Figure 15-8:
The iPad
Notes
screen.

Correcting what you say

The correction process is a bit different when you dictate with your mobile device versus working on your PC. On your PC, you have the luxury of correcting on a good size screen where you can employ several ways to make corrections. You can select copy from a list of options, spell it, or type it. You can do that with the small screen (not the spelling function), but the experience is different because of the touch screen.

If you have NaturallySpeaking on your PC, you will quickly become familiar with all the different ways to command your assistant. Use this book and other Nuance training resources to build a backlog of knowledge and understand how the application works and what your options are. It becomes second nature, so that when you add a mobile device, you're more than halfway there. You'll instinctively know what to do.

On the flip side, if your first introduction to NaturallySpeaking is on a mobile device, you don't have the benefit of already knowing how things work in the PC version. You're starting from scratch. Given the high quality of the mobile apps, it's still easy to get things up and running. Form a frame of reference for how dictation corrections work. Following are four ways to make corrections that are specific to the Apple mobile devices:

- **Correcting/deleting a word:** To correct a specific word, tap on it. You are presented with possible options. If the correct spelling of the word is there, you can quickly select it by tapping on it. If the word has no options, a delete option appears. If you want, you can choose that.

- **Correcting/deleting a phrase:** If you want to correct a phrase, instead of tapping one word, drag your finger to select the phrase. It will be highlighted. Then you can select from the list or delete the phrase.

- **Voice correcting a word/phrase:** Do as indicated above to select the word or phrase, and then tap the red icon at the top of the screen to record a different word or phrase. That recording replaces the one you highlighted.

- **Typing over a word/phrase:** Do as indicated above to select the word or phrase, and then tap the keyboard icon at the bottom of the screen. Type in your correction.

Finding your way around with Dragon Search

Whether you're on the go or multi-tasking, your iPhone can be a real lifesaver. You can search the web to locate the nearest restaurant, find a new oven, or get sports equipment. The hitch is that it's hard to navigate on a tiny screen. Dragon Search simplifies the effort in two ways:

- **You can speak your search commands:** If your arms are loaded down with a briefcase or papers or you are in a room full of people, you can still do your search.

- **You can easily access several search locations without lots of extra navigation:** Dragon Search has a Search Carousel that is set up to go to Google (or Yahoo! or Bing, if one of them is your default search engine), YouTube, Twitter Search, iTunes, or Wikipedia.

This app is available only for the iPhone at the time of this writing.

To download the Dragon Search app, go to the Nuance website, `http://nuancemobilelife.com/applications.html#apple`. Click on the download. You will be asked how you want to receive it: by text message, e-mail download link, or into iTunes. Choose your preference and open it as you would any iPhone app.

To perform a search and customize the app for your own searches, follow these steps:

1. **Launch the Dragon Search icon on your home screen.**

   You are presented with a screen that says, Tap and Speak.

2. **Tap the red Record button in the center of the screen and say your search term.**

   It will be placed into the Google search box just as if you typed it.

   In this example, say, **"Best iPad apps."**

   Up pops the search results in Google. You can either tap a link or select one of the other icons above the search from the Search Carousel, as shown in Figure 15-9. The choices are YouTube, iTunes, Google, Wikipedia, and Twitter Search.

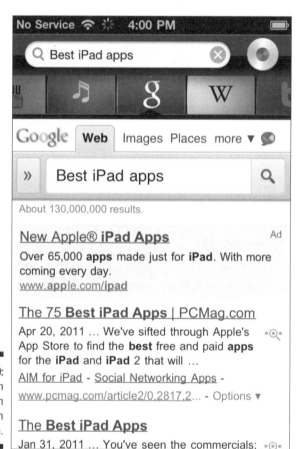

Figure 15-9: The Dragon Carousel in the Dragon Search app.

3. **To see what people are saying about the subject, tap the Twitter icon.**

   This shows you what Twitter users are saying about **"Best iPad apps."**

4. **Scroll through to see if there's anything interesting you want to tap on.**

   You can continue to do this or start a new search. Dragon Search makes it very easy to find what you're looking for — hands free.

At the time of this writing, Dragon Search is available only for use on the iPhone. This may change with future versions of NaturallySpeaking.

Having fun with Dragon Go!

If you like using Dragon Search, you'll love using Dragon Go! Nuance created this free downloadable app for use with the iPhone 3GS, iPhone 4, iPod touch (3rd generation), iPod touch (4th generation), and iPad. (You must have iOS 4.0 or later.)

Dragon Go! makes searching with your mobile device almost too easy. (I said *almost*.) If you haven't tried any of the other NaturallySpeaking mobile apps, this is the one to start with. You don't need any other Nuance software on your PC, and there is absolutely no software to train. You can use this app to find entertainment and shopping venues, or you can use it to find something serious and important. The choice is yours.

For this example, I use the iPad and do something fun. To get started, do the following:

1. **To learn more about Dragon Go!, go to the Nuance website at** `http://www.nuancemobilelife.com/apple/go.html` **or download it at iTunes:** `http://itunes.apple.com/us/app/dragon-go/id442975871?mt=8&ls=1`.

   Synch it as you would any other iPad app.

2. **Launch the Dragon Go! icon from your home screen.**

   You are asked if you would like to use your current location with this app.

   Nuance asks this question so that it has permission to use your personal location to search for things in your area and get driving directions.

3. **If you agree, click OK.**

   After you click OK, you are asked to select the region in which you live and are asked to accept the end user license agreement.

4. **Select the region and click Accept.**

   The main title screen appears and you see a forward arrow (>) next to the word *Tutorial,* as shown in Figure 15-10.

Figure 15-10:
The Dragon
Go! title
screen
with the
right facing
arrow for
the tutorial.

5. **Tap the Tutorial arrow.**

   It brings up the screen, as shown in Figure 15-11, that directs you to tap
   the red Record button and make a search request.

6. **Tap the forward arrow (>) in the upper-right corner again.**

   A new screen comes up and shows you examples of some of the things
   you can say to get a search started. For example, you can be general
   and say, **"Movie showtimes,"** or be specific and name a movie you want
   to see.

7. **Continue to tap the Tutorial arrow to see several more examples of
   things you can say.**

Figure 15-11:
The record
button to
tap to make
your search
request.

8. **To start a new search, tap the record button that is displayed on the screen.**

   In this example, I said, **"New movies, near me."** The addition of the phrase "near me" tells Dragon Go! to search theatres based on my location. A search is returned that shows my local movie theatres and the movies playing.

   To get a closer look at the movies, I pull my fingers apart to enlarge the screen, as shown in Figure 15-12, and then sweep my finger left to see the movie times. If they are available, I can buy tickets online.

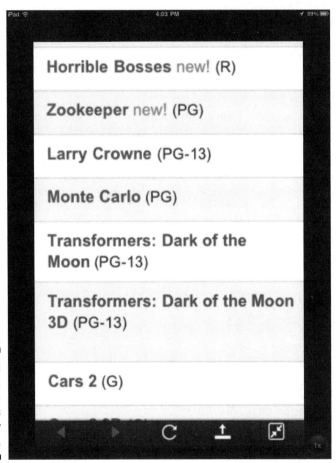

Figure 15-12: Zooming in to see the movies currently playing.

The searches are enhanced with the use of the Dragon Carousel that is shown in Figure 15-9. But in Dragon Go! you will also be directed to searches in the following search engines:

- **Fandango.com:** A popular search engine that searches movies by location and provides the capability to purchase tickets online for each show time.

- **Milo.com:** A search engine of major retailers that can be searched by location to find the exact product you are looking for in your neighborhood.

- **Yelp.com:** Here you can find reviews from your neighbors about local businesses and public services.

Of course, you can also use the other existing Carousel choices: YouTube, iTunes, Google, Wikipedia, and Twitter Search.

If you want to share what you've found with friends, all you have to do is tap the "up arrow icon" as shown earlier in Figure 15-5 and choose one of the URLs to send it to as shown in Figure 15-6.

Dictating wirelessly with the Dragon Remote Microphone Application

Mobile devices have really spoiled us. The idea that we might not be able to roam around wirelessly dictating our e-mails suddenly seems so "last century." After the thrill of dictating to your PC wears off, you go searching for the next big thrill. So, how about using your iPhone, iPad, or iPod touch 4 as a wireless microphone?

Using NaturallySpeaking version 11.5, you can download an app called the Dragon Remote Microphone Application. It turns your smartphone into a microphone. After you install it, you can dictate wirelessly from your smartphone to your computer using any Wi-Fi or home network connection. And guess what: It's free!

The application works really well right off the bat. To use it, you need to make sure you do the following things:

- Have iOS 4.2 or higher on your Apple iPhone, iPad, or iPod touch 4.

- Download the app from `http://Dragon.nuance.com/remote microphone`.

- Unzip the download and load it onto your mobile device with iTunes.

✔ Create a new User Profile specifically for the Remote Microphone Application.

✔ Use Bonjour (an Apple app that helps computers find each other if they both are running Bonjour) to connect your smartphone with your computer so it recognizes both halves of the wireless connection.

If you don't want to use iTunes to set up this app, you can use the iPhone Configuration Utility. Download it from `http://apple.com/support/iphone/enterprise`. If you have iTunes on your PC, I recommend that you load the application from there because it's so easy.

Once you install the app, launch it from the icon on your Apple device. You'll see a large Dragon icon button in the center of a speakerlike screen. Your User Profile name appears at the top of the screen. To operate remotely, with NaturallySpeaking running on your PC, try the following:

✔ **Tap the Dragon icon:** Notice that when you first tap it, the color around the icon changes from red to green. This means that your microphone is on — both on your PC and on your mobile device.

✔ **Tap the Dragon icon again when it's on:** The color returns to red. That means you've turned the microphone off.

What you don't see happening when you work remotely is that NaturallySpeaking is taking dictation into the app you specify on your PC.

For example, you can say, **"Open Word"** and your Microsoft Word application on your PC opens and is ready for dictation. If you want to dictate into the DragonPad, you can do that just as you would if you were dictating from headphones. Make sure to **Save** and **Close** your application. The material you dictate will be on your PC when you return to it.

When you work remotely, you can't see the dictation on your PC screen. For this reason, you should plan to proofread and correct your dictation when you are looking at it. Do all the same things you would normally do to make corrections on your PC.

Communicating Using Other Mobile Devices

Happily, NaturallySpeaking isn't limited to Apple mobile devices. You can dictate with both the BlackBerry and Android smartphones as well. (Check online at `http://www.nuance.com/for-business/by-solution/mobile-application/index.htm` to find out whether your specific model smartphone is currently supported.)

BlackBerry Dragon for E-Mail

As the name implies, BlackBerry Dragon for E-Mail is devoted exclusively to sending e-mail from your BlackBerry. It's free and it uses the built-in BlackBerry e-mail client, so everything works smoothly. Following are four key things to do when you install it:

- ✔ **Give permission:** You must give Dragon permission to use speech recognition on your phone.

- ✔ **Decide the location of your side key:** You need to pick a side key that lets you invoke speech recognition when you want it. This means that you choose whether the key will be enabled on the right or left side of the device by changing the designation to Nothing on the chosen side. When you are not in your e-mail application, the side key works in its default manner (for example, the left side key default is voice dialing).

- ✔ **Test your side key:** You will be asked to confirm that your side key is working as designated.

- ✔ **(Optional) Load in your e-mail contacts:** If you choose to, you can upload your e-mail contacts to the Dragon servers so they can instantly grab the requested e-mail address and put it in your e-mail.

After you install the app, you can e-mail as you normally do, with the added benefit of mixing voice with keyboard. To invoke dictation, press and hold the designated side key to enable voice recognition. You can then dictate into any field in your e-mail form.

You must have the cursor in the e-mail field in which you want to dictate. Unlike Full Text Control applications of NaturallySpeaking on your PC, you can't move the cursor by voice. So, for example, when you want to move from the Subject field to the Body field, you can't do it by saying, "Move to body field." You have to move your cursor into that field before you start dictating. It's still faster to dictate the body of your message rather than type it — five times faster.

Android Flex T9

Flex T9 is the Nuance application for the Android smartphone. I would be remiss if I didn't tell you that it isn't just limited to voice commands. It's like a booster shot for your Android keyboard. Using the same keyboard, it lets you communicate four ways:

- ✔ **Speak:** This is the dictation part of the app. You can dictate into open windows and your speech becomes text, just like in applications you use with NaturallySpeaking on your PC. This means that you can dictate e-mails, post to social media, send instant messages, and pretty much do anything that involves a text window, like web searching.

✔ **Trace:** With trace, you use the keyboard with continuous motion and you can actually see the tracing your hand is creating by tapping the letters. As you begin typing a word, you are given choices. If you see the right choice, tap it and save yourself the trouble of finishing the word. Over time, you can move pretty quickly working this way.

✔ **Write:** Use your finger to write as you do when you just can't find anything digital to write with. Then magically it becomes digital — whew, that was close! It recognizes what you type and turns it into text. What's interesting is that it takes handwriting recognition to the next level. The reason is that it takes advantage of the predictive nature of the NaturallySpeaking application. In order for Dragon to be able to pick the right word when you dictate, it has algorithms that predict which words most likely go together. By using those same statistics for handwriting recognition, it can be more accurate in the choices it presents to you.

✔ **Tap:** This is the normal tapping of the keyboard to write out your message. The secret sauce is that it corrects your spelling and sloppy texting input. Your English teacher would be proud.

To get started, you need to make the Flex T9 App the default keyboard choice. Then choose your language and input preferences. Presently, the app supports U.S. and U.K. English, French, German, Italian, and Spanish. Once you have everything set up, you work from the same keyboard for all input modalities.

To use this app, you must have the Android version 2.1 and ASTRO, a free app installer for Android, installed on your phone.

All this input flexibility gives you the opportunity to communicate in whatever method you need or prefer. That's quite an opportunity for creative output!

Part IV
Controlling Windows

The 5th Wave   By Rich Tennant

SPEECH RECOGNITION SOFTWARE
+
CHEAP LAPTOP

"Try speaking a little slower next time."

In this part . . .

Could it be a new-found assertiveness? Part IV really shows your NaturallySpeaking assistant who is boss! When you least expect it, you take voice control of menus, your mouse, and the Windows desktop in Chapter 16. You also begin to dialog with your boxes and tell your mouse where to go. Whew!

Then you move from application to application with only your voice, and you use the Start menu with voice commands, too.

Chapter 16

Controlling Your Desktop and Windows by Voice

*P*eople have been talking to their operating systems since the very early days of computing, but most of what they've been saying is not repeatable in public. Using voice recognition software, though, you can talk to your operating system and have it *do* something in response: run an application, switch to another window, move the mouse pointer, or choose a command from a menu.

You probably are used to controlling Windows's windows and applications through the keyboard and/or the mouse. You can easily imitate keyboard commands with the voice command **Press** — **Press Right-Arrow,** for example. You can also imitate mouse actions that click buttons or choose items from a menu with the voice command **Click** — for example, **Click OK,** or **Click File, Save.** (Unfortunately, this technique doesn't apply to toolbar and Ribbon buttons like Back. See Table 16-1 later in this chapter for keyboard and menu equivalents for the Computer and Windows Explorer toolbar and Ribbon buttons.)

By contrast, mouse actions that involve maneuvering the mouse pointer to click some tiny, nameless object (like the +/– boxes in Windows Explorer or the arrow that nets a drop-down list box) are less convenient to do by voice. You *can* maneuver the mouse pointer by voice (see "Do Mice Understand English?" later in this chapter), but doing so is seldom the most efficient way to accomplish your purpose. Fortunately, these mouse actions almost always have keyboard equivalents that you can use with the **Press** command.

And so, in addition to the obvious theme of this chapter — learning voice commands to control Windows — a secondary theme appears: learning keyboard commands to do tasks that you may be used to doing with the mouse.

Ya Wanna Start Something?

Plenty of people talk to their desktops, particularly when they are under great stress or have forgotten a loved one's birthday. Unfortunately, up until now, most of that talk has been unproductive. Desktops have seldom responded, and those that did respond came up with very few ideas that were worth putting into practice.

NaturallySpeaking, however, lets you talk to your desktop and actually see results. Now your desktop responds to your commands by starting applications, opening windows, and giving you access to menus, including the Start menu.

You can start applications or open files or folders by saying, **"Start <*name of application, file, or folder*>."** For example, say, **"Start WordPad,"** to open the WordPad application. You can also use voice commands to access anything on the Start menu — Pictures, Documents, the Control Panel, or anything else.

Starting applications by voice

Dictating text is nice, but the first feeling of real power you get from NaturallySpeaking is when you say, **"Open Microsoft Word."** The screen blinked, the hard drive ground, angels sang hosannas (okay, maybe I imagined that part), and the Word window appeared in all its glory.

The **Open** command opens any application whose name appears in one of the following places:

- ✔ **The desktop:** For example, if a Microsoft Excel shortcut is on your desktop, you can start it up by saying, **"Open Microsoft Excel."**

- ✔ **The top of the Start menu:** If you see the name of an application when you click the Start button, you can run it with the **Open** command.

- ✔ **In the Programs folder on the Start menu, or in any of the subfolders of the Programs folder:** For example, saying, **"Open WordPad"** opens it, even though it lies inside the Programs folder hierarchy (in Start/ Accessories — unless you moved it).

In general, use whatever name is on the menu or shortcut. NaturallySpeaking does recognize a few nicknames, though. If you say, **"Open Word,"** for example, it runs Microsoft Word. Saying **"Open Firefox"** opens Mozilla Firefox. Try opening your programs with the name you use to see if a shortcut exists.

You also aren't stuck with the names on the Programs menu. You probably didn't create most of those entries yourself. Some of them have been there since you unpacked your computer, while others have been created by the setup wizards that installed your applications. Delete them. If you have a long-winded, hard-to-remember entry on your Programs menu — something like "WinZip 15.0" — you can change it to something catchy, like "Zip." Then you can start it by saying, **"Start Zip."** Right-click any icon on your desktop, choose Rename, and give your program an easier moniker.

Using the Start menu

Anytime that NaturallySpeaking is running, you can say, **"Click Start"** to pull up the Start menu. You can then say the name of any object on the Start menu like: **"Shut down," "Log Off," "Restart," "Help and Support,"** or any individual applications, files, or folders that you have added to the menu. The resulting action is the same as if you had clicked the mouse on that entry in the Start menu:

✔ If the object is itself a menu, it expands when you click it. (For example, Documents expand to a listing of the names of about the 15 most recent objects.) Select one of those objects by saying its name. If the object is another menu, it expands, and so on.

✔ If the object is an application, it runs. (Run the application more easily by saying, **"Start <*application name*>."**

✔ If the object is a file or folder, it opens. The files could be documents or even web pages.

For example, if Skype appears on your Start menu, then you can access your Skype account online by saying, **"Click Start, Skype."** (The commas represent short pauses; don't say, "comma.") To open the Control Panel, say, **"Click Start, Control Panel."**

In addition to using the Start command, you can use the **Launch** or **Show** commands. For example, instead of saying **"Start Word,"** you can say, **"Launch Word"** or **"Show Word."**

Don't shut down the computer by voice, unless you have challenges that prevent you from doing it any other way. In general, shutting down Windows with a lot of applications running (especially robust applications like Naturally-Speaking) upsets the system. At the very least, it causes an application to do something illegal that makes Windows shut it down in an unnatural way. Some data could be lost in the process. Of course, some Windows operating systems run better than others, and you may get lucky. But why take the chance?

Does It Do Windows?

Yes, NaturallySpeaking does windows. Open them, close them, move them, resize them, switch from one window to another, use their menus, and interact with their dialog boxes — all without using your hands.

Listing all applications

If you want to know which applications are open on your computer, you can use the List command to say, **"List all windows."** A list pops up, showing what is running (see Figure 16-1). You see a numbered list of the applications. Choose it as the active window by saying, **"Choose <number>."** If you are not good about closing applications after you have used them, this is a very handy feature.

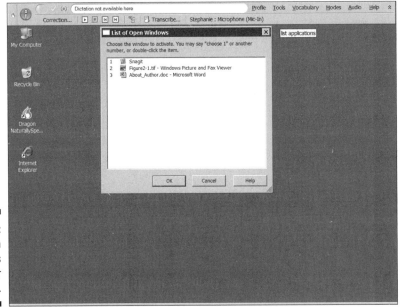

Figure 16-1:
List of open
windows
on your
desktop.

Opening Computer and other folder windows

You can open any folder on your desktop with the **Start** command. For example, say, **"Start Computer,"** or, more generally, **"Start <folder name>."** In this example, the Computer folder opens in a window, just as if you had double-clicked its icon on your desktop.

After a folder window is open, you can select any visible object inside the window by saying the object's name. You can then work on the object by using the menus. For example, open the Control Panel folder as follows:

1. **Say,** "Start Computer."

   The Computer window opens.

2. **Say,** "Control Panel."

   The Control Panel folder is selected.

3. **Say,** "<name of icon>."

After you have a folder window open, you can use the subcommands from its menu. You can also drag and drop within a folder window or from one window to another. (See "Dragging until you drop," later in this chapter.) Unfortunately, no direct way exists to use the toolbar buttons other than to maneuver the mouse pointer over one and say, **"Click."** The toolbar buttons in Computer or Windows Explorer have keyboard and menu equivalents that you can access by voice. You can duplicate the toolbar button functions with the keyboard and menu commands shown in Table 16-1.

Table 16-1	Voice Commands for Toolbar Button Functions	
Toolbar Button	*Voice Menu Command*	*Voice Key Combination*
Back	**Click Go, Back**	**Press Alt Left Arrow**
Forward	**Click Go, Forward**	**Press Alt Right Arrow**
Up	**Click Go, Up One Level**	**Press Backspace**
Cut*	**Click Edit, Cut**	**Press Control X**
Copy*	**Click Edit, Copy**	**Press Control C**
Paste*	**Click Edit, Paste**	**Press Control V**
Undo	**Click Edit, Undo**	**Press Control Z**
Delete*	**Click File, Delete**	**Press Delete**
Properties*	**Click File, Properties**	<none>*
Views*	**Click View**	**Press Alt V**

Commands marked with an asterisk (*) are also on the right-click menu.

Giving orders to Windows Explorer

Windows Explorer is an obedient application. If you say, **"Start Windows Explorer,"** it pops up, ready to take your orders. As with Computer, the Windows Explorer menus are available to your voice commands, but the toolbar and Ribbon buttons are not. (See Table 16-1.)

Windows Explorer has three main components, which are shown in Figure 16-2: the Explorer bar, the Contents window, and the Address box. How Windows Explorer responds to your commands depends on what component the cursor is in.

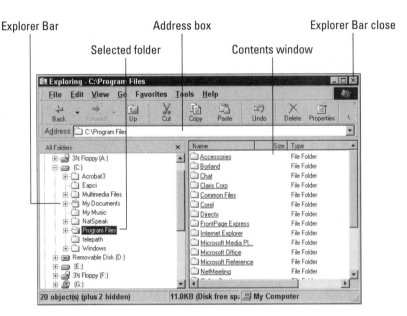

Explorer Bar   Address box   Explorer Bar close

Selected folder   Contents window

Figure 16-2:
Exploring
the parts of
Windows
Explorer.

Moving the cursor from component to component

Windows Explorer opens with the cursor in the Explorer bar. That's the left pane of the main window, the one that displays the overall structure of your file-and-folder system. Press the Tab key (or say, **"Press Tab"**) to cycle the cursor through the following three components of the Windows Explorer window (if you are using Windows XP):

- ✔ **Contents window,** the right pane of the main window, which displays the contents of the folder selected

- ✔ **Address box,** which displays the address of whatever file or folder is currently selected

- ✔ **Explorer bar,** the left pane of the main window that can contain a variety of things, depending on your choice in View⇨Explorer Bar

Depending on how Windows is set up on your system, a fourth component may exist — the Explorer bar's Close button, that little X in the upper-right corner of the Explorer bar. (It's kind of a silly thing to make a component out of, but what can I say — it's Windows.) When the Explorer bar's Close button is selected, you can make the Explorer bar go away by saying, **"Press Enter."** To get the Explorer bar back, say, **"Click View, Explorer Bar, All Folders."**

The Shift+Tab key combination moves the cursor through these components in the opposite order. Say, **"Press Shift Tab."**

Selecting and opening files and folders

The Explorer bar and the Contents window are each a list of folders and files. Select an item from the list by saying its name. That sounds great, but a few complications exist: You have to say the complete name, and if the file extension is displayed, you have to say it as well. Also, if the name of the item is not an English word that's in the NaturallySpeaking active vocabulary, the name won't be recognized unless you spell it.

Fortunately, you can also select items by using the **Move Up/Down/Left/Right** commands. The Explorer bar is treated as if it were one long vertical list. If you want to select the folder that's three lines below the currently selected folder, say, **"Move Down 3."**

The Contents window has both lines and columns. Use **Move Left/Right** to move from one column to another, and **Move Up/Down** to move within a column. So, for example, if the file you want is two columns to the right and three lines up from the currently selected item, say, **"Move Right 2, Move Up 3."**

After you select an item, open it by saying, **"Press Enter."**

Expanding and contracting lists of folders

Those plus (+) and minus (–) signs in little boxes next to the folders on the Explorer bar control whether a folder's subfolders appear on the list. You may be accustomed to clicking these little boxes with the mouse, but you *don't* want to try that technique with the vocal mouse commands. It's possible, but much too time-consuming.

Instead, select a folder on the Explorer bar, and then use the right- and left-arrow keys to expand and contract the list of subfolders. If the folder is contracted (that is, the + is showing), say, **"Press Right Arrow."** The folder expands. If it is already expanded (the – shows), say, **"Press Left Arrow."** The folder then contracts.

Switching from one application to another

If you have several application windows active on your desktop, you can switch from one to another just by saying so. You can do this in five ways:

✔ If the window represents an application or a folder, you can call it by the name of the application or the folder. For example, say, **"Switch To Word"** or **"Switch To Documents."** (Windows Explorer is an exception. Switch to an open Windows Explorer window by saying, **"Switch To Exploring."**)

✔ Return to the previously active window by saying, **"Switch To Previous Window."** This command is equivalent to pressing Alt+Tab. Repeating this command several times switches back and forth between two windows.

✔ Cycle through all the active windows (even the ones that are minimized) by repeating, **"Switch To Next Window."** This command is equivalent to pressing Shift+Alt+Tab on the keyboard.

✔ If the name of a document appears on the title bar, you can use the name of that document in a **Switch To** command. For example, if you're using Microsoft Word to edit a document called My Diary, the title bar of the window says "Microsoft Word — My Diary." (The block on the task-bar corresponding to this window says the same thing, though the block may not be large enough to accommodate the full title.) Switch to this window by saying, **"Switch To Word"** or **"Switch To My Diary."**

✔ As described earlier in "Listing all applications," you can use the **List Programs** or **List All Windows** command. For example, you can say, **"List Open Windows,"** and a list of the programs that are open on your desktop appears. Just select the program you want by choosing the number shown in the window.

Do Mice Understand English?

Once upon a time, you had to go to Disney World to find a mouse that understood English. Now, of course, you have one attached to your computer. The NaturallySpeaking voice commands let you move the mouse pointer anywhere on your screen and give you access to the full range of mouse clicks: right, left, and double. You can even drag and drop objects within a window, or from one window to another.

Telling your mouse where to go

NaturallySpeaking gives you two methods to move the mouse pointer. **MouseGrid** breaks up the screen (or the active window) into a series of squares, letting you zero in on the location you want to move the pointer to. The mouse pointer commands let you make small adjustments by saying things like, **"Mouse Up 5."**

How does it work? Surprisingly well, after you get used to it. Naturally, you have to adjust your expectations: Voice commands are not a high-performance way to move the mouse, so you won't break any speed records the next time you play a game. But your virtual, voice-commanded mouse, like the physical mouse attached to your computer, is remarkably intuitive. It makes a good backup system for those times when you can't remember the right hotkey or voice command.

Making your move with MouseGrid

In days of yore, before the invention of GameBoy, children amused themselves on long driving trips with number-guessing games. Here's a simple one: One kid picks a number and another makes guesses. The number-picker responds to each guess by saying "higher" or "lower." The guesser narrows down the range where the number can be until eventually he knows what the number is.

MouseGrid is like that, but in two dimensions. You pick a point on the screen where you want the mouse pointer to go, and NaturallySpeaking guesses where it is. Start the game by saying, **"MouseGrid."**

NaturallySpeaking's first guess is that you want the mouse pointer to be in the center of the screen. But just in case it's wrong, it turns your screen into a tic-tack-toe board, as in Figure 16-3. The nine squares are numbered like the keypad of a touch-tone phone: The square on the upper left is 1, and the square on the lower right is 9. The pointer is sitting on square 5. Look closely to see the numbers in the centers of the squares.

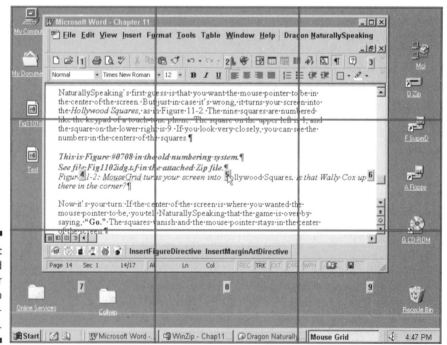

Figure 16-3:
MouseGrid turns your screen into a tic-tack-toe window.

Now it's your turn: If you want the mouse pointer in the center of the screen, tell NaturallySpeaking that the game is over by saying, **"Go."** The squares vanish and the mouse pointer stays in the center of the screen.

If the center was not the point you had in mind, say the number to tell NaturallySpeaking which square your chosen point is in. For example, you may say, **"Nine,"** indicating that the point is in the lower-right part of the screen. NaturallySpeaking responds by making all the squares go away other than the one you chose. Now NaturallySpeaking guesses that you want the mouse pointer to be in the center of that square. But just in case it's wrong, it breaks that square into nine smaller squares (see Figure 16-4). These squares are numbered 1 through 9, just like the larger squares were.

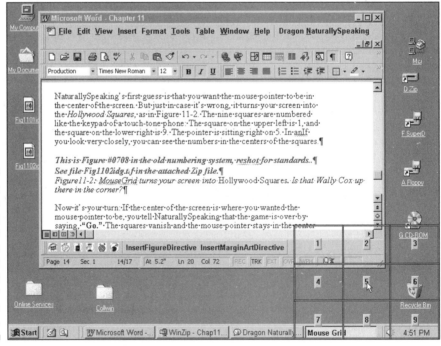

Figure 16-4:
Naturally-
Speaking
closes
in on the
destination
you have
chosen for
the mouse
pointer.

Again, you either say, **"Go"** to accept NaturallySpeaking's guess and end the game, or you say a number to tell it which of the smaller squares you want the mouse pointer to be in. It then breaks that square up into nine really tiny squares, and the game continues until the pointer is where you want it.

This description makes it sound as if you'll be old and gray before the mouse arrives at the point you had in mind, but, in fact, this process happens very quickly after you get comfortable with it. If you are aiming for something like a button on a toolbar, two or three numbers usually suffice. You say, **"MouseGrid 2, 6, 3, Go,"** and the mouse pointer is where you want it.

You can use **Cancel** as a synonym for **Go.** (This situation may be the only one in human history where "cancel" and "go" are synonyms.) I choose between them according to my mood: If I succeed in putting the mouse pointer where I want it, I say, **"Go."** If I just want out of the game, I say, **"Cancel."** It makes no practical difference.

If you want to move the mouse pointer to a place within the active window, you can restrict MouseGrid to that window by saying, **"MouseGrid Window"** instead of **"MouseGrid."** Now only the active window is broken up *Hollywood Squares* style. The process of zeroing in on the chosen location is the same (for example, **"MouseGrid Window 2, 7, Go").**

You can also get out of MouseGrid by giving a click command (which is probably why you were moving the mouse pointer to begin with). So rather than saying, **"MouseGrid 5, 9, Go"** and then **"Click,"** say, **"MouseGrid 5, 9, Click."** This trick works with any of the click commands, and also with **MouseGrid Window.** See "Clicking right and left," later in this chapter.

Nudging the mouse pointer just a little

If the mouse pointer is *almost* where you want it and just needs to be nudged a smidgen, use the mouse pointer commands **Mouse Up, Mouse Down, Mouse Left,** and **Mouse Right.** You need to attach a number between one and ten to the command in order to tell the mouse how far to move. So, for example, say, **"Mouse Up Four,"** and the mouse pointer dutifully goes up four.

"Four what?" you ask. Four smidgens, or four somethings, anyway. NaturallySpeaking Help calls them *units.* Ten minutes of experimentation has convinced me that a *unit* is about three pixels, if that helps. (Your computer screen is hundreds of pixels wide.)

All you really need to know about units is

- ✔ They're small, so **Mouse Right Six** isn't going to move the pointer very far. (For big motions, use MouseGrid.)
- ✔ They're all the same size, so **Mouse Down Three** is going to move the pointer three times as far as **Mouse Down One.**

As with MouseGrid, you can combine the mouse-pointer commands with the click commands. Instead of saying, **"Mouse Left Ten,"** and then **"Double Click,"** you can say, **"Mouse Left Ten Double Click."**

Clicking right and left

You don't usually move the mouse pointer just so that you can have a little arrow displayed on your screen in an aesthetically pleasing location. You move the mouse pointer so that you can *do* something, and doing something usually involves clicking one of the mouse buttons.

NaturallySpeaking gives you a full squadron of click commands:

- ✔ **Click** or **Left-Click,** which presses the left mouse button
- ✔ **Right-Click,** which presses the right mouse button
- ✔ **Double-Click,** which presses the left mouse button twice

If NaturallySpeaking has trouble understanding your **Click** commands, add the word **Mouse** to the command: **Mouse Click, Mouse Double-Click,** and so on. The longer command is easier to recognize.

Dragging until you drop

When you know how to maneuver the mouse pointer and click, you're ready to drag and drop. Drag-and-drop voice commands allow you to do almost everything that you can do with hand-and-mouse commands: Move objects from one window to another, rearrange objects within a window, select a number of objects within a window, resize windows, or move windows around on the desktop.

Perform all of these actions with the **Mark** and **Drag** commands (if you already put your cursor where you want it), following these steps:

1. **Move the mouse pointer until it's over the object that you want to drag.**

   This object could be an icon on your desktop or in a window, the title bar of a window that you want to move, or the lower-right corner of a window that you want to resize. It could even be an empty place in a window or on the desktop that you're using as one corner of a selection rectangle.

2. **Say,** "Mouse Mark."

3. **Move the mouse pointer until it's at the point where you want to drop the object.**

4. **Say,** "Mouse Drag."

You can combine **Mark** and **Drag** with the **MouseGrid** command. For example, instead of saying, **"MouseGrid 4, 5, Go"** and then **"Mark,"** you can just say, **"MouseGrid 4, 5, Mark."**

Suppose that your Computer icon is in the top-left corner of your desktop, and you want to move it to the bottom-right corner. Follow these steps:

1. **Say,** "MouseGrid 1, 1, Mark."

   From my screen, **MouseGrid 1, 1** was sufficient to get the mouse pointer over the Computer icon. Depending on your screen settings, you may need to say more than two numbers. For fine control, use mouse-pointer commands like **Mouse Up Two.**

2. **Say,** "MouseGrid 9, 9, Drag."

   The Computer icon disappears from its old location and reappears at the 9, 9 location, which is in the lower-right corner of the screen.

The **Mark . . . Drag** combination mimics certain familiar mouse actions, but it isn't precisely equivalent to any of them. For example, selecting an icon (with either a mouse click or by saying the icon name) doesn't mark it. Also, a marked object stays marked until something else is marked. You can, for example, mark an object on your desktop, go edit a document in your word processor, and then go back to your desktop to complete the drag-and-drop. The object is still marked, so all you have to do when you return to the desktop is move the mouse pointer to the appropriate location, and say, **"Drag."** Dragging and dropping by hand is not nearly so flexible.

Mark . . . Drag doesn't drag and drop text or illustrations within a word-processing document. Use **Cut That . . . Paste That** instead. (See Chapter 5.) Another deficiency of the **Mark** command is that it doesn't mark collections of objects. For example, if you have selected four objects inside a folder window (possibly by using **Mark . . . Drag** to drag a selection rectangle over them), you cannot now move them all by marking them as a group and dragging them elsewhere. Instead, choose Edit⇨Cut from the folder window, and then Paste from the Edit menu of the window where you want them (or Paste from the context menu of the desktop).

Dialoging with a Box

After you start talking to your desktop, it's only a matter of time before you find yourself conversing with a box. In fact, you may have been talking to NaturallySpeaking dialog boxes even before you started dictating to other applications. Don't fight it; dialog boxes are where Windows does its dirty work.

Dialog boxes are more difficult to deal with than menus, because dialog boxes can contain almost anything: radio buttons, drop-down lists, text-boxes, check boxes, tabs, browsing windows — sometimes all in the same dialog box. How the dialog box responds to a voice command depends on where the cursor is: If the cursor is in a textbox, the dialog box interprets spoken words as text that otherwise might select a file or change a radio button. Consequently, you must always pay attention to where the cursor is in a dialog box. The cursor location tells you what kind of input the dialog box is expecting, which determines how it will deal with any commands you give it.

These keys are hot!

People who don't have voice-recognition software (you may have been one of them until quite recently) use the mouse a lot when they are confronted with dialog boxes. Click here, click there, type something, double-click somewhere else, then click OK, and it's over.

NaturallySpeaking has mouse commands (see "Do Mice Understand English?" earlier in this chapter), but moving the mouse pointer around by voice is not as quick as moving it by hand. And hitting a tiny target like the down arrow on a drop-down list requires patience.

Fortunately, you don't have to do things that way. Most actions that are performed with a mouse can also be done through the keyboard, by using what are called "hotkeys." The Tab and Shift+Tab keys, for example, cycle the cursor through the various components of a dialog box.

The Alt key is used in most hotkey combinations. The Alt+↓ key combination makes a drop-down list, uh, drop down. Alt+↑ retracts a drop-down list. The **Press** command lets you use these key combinations by voice, as in **"Press Alt Down Arrow."**

Buttons and check boxes have hotkeys as well. You can find the hotkey by looking for the underlined letter in the accompanying text. In the Settings dialog box, as shown in Figure 16-4, for example, the text next to the Status Bar check box isn't really "Status Bar." It is "Status Bar" (note the underscored S). Check or uncheck the box by saying, **"Press Alt S."**

Moving the cursor around a dialog box

A dialog box may have any number of windows, textboxes, buttons, and so on. Before you can deal with any particular component, you usually have to get the cursor into its window. (Buttons are an exception. If the box has a Cancel button, for example, **Click Cancel** closes the box no matter where the cursor is.)

When you're working by hand, the simplest way to put the cursor where you want it is to move the mouse pointer there and click. You can do the same thing by voice if you want (see "Do Mice Understand English?" earlier in this chapter), but often you will find it simpler to cycle through the components of the dialog window with the Tab key. Say, **"Press Tab"** to move from one component of a dialog window to another. Repeat the command to cycle through all the components of the box. Say, **"Press Shift Tab"** to cycle in the opposite direction.

To see exactly how this works, go through some of the examples in "Looking at a few of the most useful dialog boxes," later in this chapter.

Dealing with dialog box features

Many menu commands lead directly to dialog boxes. For example, in the NaturallySpeaking window itself, the menu selection Tools⇨Options⇨View opens the dialog box (shown in Figure 16-5), which illustrates a number of the simpler standard features of dialog boxes: buttons, radio buttons, check boxes, and tabs.

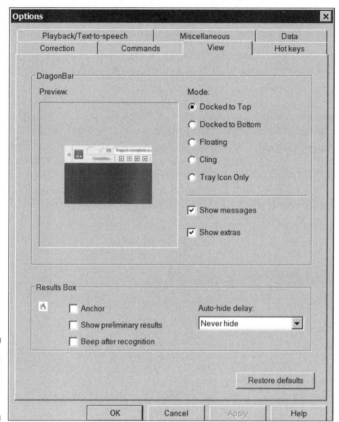

Figure 16-5:
The Options View dialog box.

✔ **Buttons:** Click a button by saying, **"Click *<button name>.*"** You can make the dialog box (refer to Figure 16-5) go away by saying, **"Click Cancel."** You can also say, **"Press Enter"** as an alternative way to click the OK button or whatever button is currently selected (the one that has the darkest outline).

✔ **Radio buttons:** Choose an option by saying its text label. Saying, **"Docked To Bottom"** changes the placement of the DragonBar to be at the bottom of the screen (refer to Figure 16-5), for example.

In general, this technique works when you have a single set of radio buttons (that is, a setup in which selecting one button deselects the others). More complicated multi-radio-button configurations require a **Click** command.

✔ **Check boxes:** Check boxes are on if they are checked and off if not. Change from On to Off or Off to On by saying the text label. In Figure 16-5, saying, **"Anchor"** anchors your Results box. Saying, **"Show Extras"** removes the check mark from the Show Extras check box.

✔ **Tabs:** Switch to another tab by saying its name. Using Figure 16-5 as an example, you could say, **"Click Corrections Tab,"** to switch to the Corrections tab.

The Open dialog box shown in Figure 16-6 has a more complex set of features: drop-down lists, a textbox, toolbar buttons, and a list of files and folders. Although I obtained this dialog box by choosing File⇨Open from the NaturallySpeaking window, it's typical of a type of Windows dialog box. It also illustrates a standard problem: The Open dialog box first appears with the cursor in the File Name textbox. Any text you say other than **"Click,"** **"Press,"** or **"MouseGrid"** will be interpreted as the name of a file.

Figure 16-6:
The Open dialog box illustrates a common problem: How do you get the cursor out of the File Name text box?

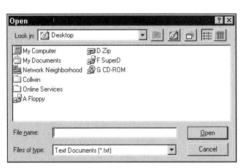

Deal as follows with the features exemplified in this box.

✔ **Drop-down lists:** The Open dialog box has two drop-down lists: Look In and Files of Type. You can recognize them as drop-down lists because of the little down arrow at the right edge of the text. To bring the cursor into the list say, **"Click <text label>."** For example, say, **"Click Look In."** In some cases, this command also causes the list to drop down, but if it doesn't, say, **"Press Alt Down Arrow"** to display the list. After the list drops, change the selected item on the list either by saying its name or by using the **Move Up/Down** command. Say, "**Move Down Five,**" for example. To retract the list and lock in the new selection say, "**Press Alt Up Arrow.**"

✔ **Textboxes:** The Open dialog box opens with the cursor in the File Name textbox. Enter text into this box by saying it. To get the cursor out of this box, use the **Click** command to click a button or a drop-down menu; use the **MouseGrid** command to click the mouse inside some other part of the dialog box; or say, "**Press Tab**" or "**Press Shift Tab**" to move the cursor into Files of Type or the file and folder list in the main window, respectively.

✔ **Toolbar buttons:** Unlike the big buttons (OK, Cancel, and so on), toolbar buttons in dialog boxes usually don't respond to their names. If you want to use them, you must click them with the mouse.

✔ **Lists of files and folders:** The tricky thing about using the list of files and folders is getting the cursor into its window. That's because there is no **Click** command that puts it there unless you maneuver the mouse pointer into the window. Instead, say, "**Press Shift Tab,**" if the cursor is just below the window in the File Name textbox, or "**Press Tab**" if the cursor is just above the window in the Look In drop-down list. After the cursor is in the main window, select files and folders either by name or by using the **Move Up/Down/Right/Left** commands. Open a selected file or folder by saying, "**Click Open**" or "**Press Enter.**"

When you open a folder from a list of files and folders in a dialog box, either **Click Open** or **Press Enter** does the job. However, **Click Open** returns the cursor to the File Name textbox, and **Press Enter** leaves the cursor in the main window, which now displays the contents of the opened folder. I prefer **Press Enter.**

Looking at a few of the most useful dialog boxes

Now we get down and dirty and slug it out with a few of the dialog boxes that you're going to run into again and again. These are "Look Ma, no hands" examples. Everything is done with voice commands. Naturally, sometimes you can accomplish the task faster by pecking a key or moving your mouse, but I assume you know how to do that already. Over time, you'll work out your own compromises between voice commands and mouse-and-keyboard commands. By giving these pure-vocal examples, I leave the compromising to you.

For the following searches, NaturallySpeaking supports these search engines: Google Desktop, Windows Vista Search, and Windows 7 Search.

Searching documents

Suppose that a couple of days ago you found a great article about Mind Maps somewhere on the web, and you know you saved it somewhere. Probably you used "mind map" somewhere in the filename, but in the heat of the moment, you aren't sure what you called it. It's bound to be somewhere on your hard drive. Find it by following these steps:

1. **Say,** "Click Start, Search Documents For Mind Map."

   The dialog box, opens. The search engine shows you all the indexed items that have "mind map" in the title.

2. **Say,** "Click Search."

   You see all the documents relating to mind maps on your hard drive.

3. **Choose the one you want by saying,** "*<Document Name>*."

   The document opens. (Say, **"Cancel Document"** to close it without saving.)

Searching your computer

If you think you misplaced an important invoice from the Widget Co. somewhere on your hard drive, find it by doing the following:

1. **Say,** "Search The Computer For Spreadsheets."

   A list of all the items that match that search are listed.

2. **To choose the one you want, say the name of the spreadsheet.**

Finding and replacing text

Suppose your daughter has used the NaturallySpeaking window to dictate a report for Show-and-Tell about your new dog Spot. The report is excellent, except for one small problem: She believes that Spot is a cat. How can she repair this error in her report?

1. **Say,** "Click Edit, Replace."

   The Replace dialog box opens. The cursor starts in the Find What textbox.

2. **Say,** "Cat."

3. **Say,** "Press Tab."

   The cursor moves to the Replace With textbox.

4. **Say,** "Dog."

   You're almost done. But unless you want the word "Category" replaced with "Dogegory," you need to do one more thing.

5. **Say,** "Click Match Whole Word Only."

   The corresponding check box is checked.

6. **Say,** "Click Replace All."

Part V
Working Smarter

The 5th Wave   By Rich Tennant

HELP DESK

TECHNICAL

ETHICAL

In this part . . .

*E*ven the best-behaved NaturallySpeaking assistant occasionally drops the coffee pot, crashes the mail cart, or eats the boss's lunch. If NaturallySpeaking is seriously cutting up (unwilling to go to work, not playing well with others, or breaking the Windows in the Microsoft grass hut) you need to chat with the folks at Dragon Systems about treating the beast for bugs.

If, however, your winged companion is simply not quite as accurate as you think it should be, it may have a good reason. (Or possibly not. Technology is treading awfully close to magic here, and occasionally NaturallySpeaking just seems to be going through a bad spell. Hey, maybe that's why it has so many wizard managers. Maybe it needs a "spell" checker, too.) In this part, I help you figure out what might be limiting your smart assistant's success.

Lots of different things can have an effect on NaturallySpeaking's accuracy. As with any office assistant, training and vocabulary building can make a big difference. It helps to speak to it nicely and make sure its microphone is in place. If you are giving it new customized commands to learn, you need to follow some rules. And finally, if you're moving NaturallySpeaking to another PC, upgrading, or otherwise making changes, you need to help your Dragon assistant cope with change. In this part, I show you different ways to achieve and maintain the precision you expect.

Chapter 17

Speaking More Clearly

Say, "I want a Fig Newton and a glass of milk." Go ahead. Say it the casual way you would in a diner. (Presuming, for the moment, that you like Fig Newtons and milk.)

If you're like me, you probably said something like, "Eyewanna FigNew'n 'na glassa milk." You probably skip the final "t" of "want" and slur "want a" ("wanna"), omit the "to" of "Newton," skip the "a" and "d" of "and" ("n"), and don't really pronounce either letter in the word "of."

We North Americans don't waste time or effort. Often, we ignore short words, initial vowels, and the final consonants of many words. And we unnerstan 'chother perfeckly, raht? Riot. So whah cain't t' dang computer unnerstan goodol 'merican English?

Most Americans would understand the Fig Newton line perfectly because of our love affair with cookies and milk. The computer, on the other hand, is rarely fed Fig Newtons and milk, except for what you drop into the keyboard or what your kids stuff into the DVD drive for the dog to lick out. The result? A computer relies on all those little things we normally skip but that distinguish one word from another. Without them, Dragon NaturallySpeaking may translate the line something like, "I have Fig Newton awesome milk." That translation may inspire a popular new dairy or fruit beverage, but it wouldn't be exactly what you had in mind for your computer activity.

So, should you learn to speak better, or should you train your NaturallySpeaking assistant to love you just the way you are? As with most things in life, the answer is "yes" — to both questions.

Do You Need to Speak Better?

You probably do need to speak a bit better. Improving your speech habits is one of the best and cheapest ways to cut down on errors in NaturallySpeaking.

On the other hand, don't go nuts. For instance, try to pronounce that example sentence about Fig Newtons *without* slurring any consonants or dropping any a's. (Say, "I want a Fig Newton and a glass of milk," being sure to speak all the underlined letters.)

Hard work, huh? You'd probably get tired of speaking like a BBC announcer after a very short while, or else develop an urge to go to cricket matches. Moreover, Dragon NaturallySpeaking still may not perform perfectly. For instance, you may get, "I want a Fig Newton in a glass of milk." If you try too hard to enunciate phrases like "Fig Newton," you get "Fig a Newton." Go fig ewer.

So, the first question is: Should you try to speak better than you do normally? If you suspect that your speech is naturally a bit sloppy, or if you've never thought about it much, you probably should try to do better.

If you find yourself working too hard to get better accuracy, stop. You will get tired quickly, start making even more errors, and your NaturallySpeaking assistant will never learn to recognize your natural speech.

If you have an accent (and who doesn't?), don't worry much about it. NaturallySpeaking adapts to your accent during training. What it has most trouble adapting to is missing words and sounds. If your accent is particularly strong, certain words may sound like other words to NaturallySpeaking. (You can correct it using word training. See Chapter 18.)

If you aren't sure you'd know good speech if you heard it, listen to some professional broadcast journalists on the radio or television. But listen to people hired specifically as news readers (as opposed to disk jockeys, "personalities," and retired sports heroes now working as sportscasters). News readers — particularly news readers at larger radio stations or broadcasting companies — are hired partly for their careful speech.

If your speech is pretty clear, but you continue to get recognition errors, consider some of the other remedies in this part of the book. Training (Chapter 18) and better audio input (Chapter 19) can make a big difference. For example, Figure 17-1 shows that the correct placement of the microphone is crucial for accuracy.

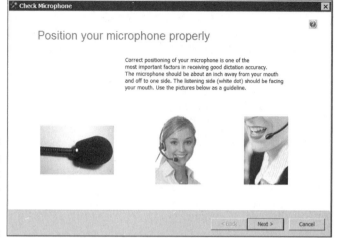

Figure 17-1:
Correct
place-
ment of the
microphone.

If NaturallySpeaking mis-recognizes special phrases, words, or acronyms in your vocabulary, for instance, the solution is more likely to be training or vocabulary work than improving your speech.

How Do You Do It?

Changing any habit is hard, and speech is one of the most habitual activities any of us do. (Well, besides drinking coffee.) Apart from taking our thumbs out of our mouths, we've been talking the way we have since childhood. How does a person improve his or her speech? Following are some fairly painless tips for speaking better:

- ✔ Speak every word, without fretting at first about the enunciation of the word itself. Avoid skipping words. NaturallySpeaking relies on the adjoining words to help figure out a word. If you skip or slur words, NaturallySpeaking will make more mistakes.

- ✔ Speak long phrases or full sentences. The more words in an utterance, the better NaturallySpeaking can figure out your words from context.

- ✔ Make sure you pronounce even small words like "a" and "the." If, like most people, you normally pronounce the word "a" as "uh," keep doing so. Don't switch to "ay," as in "hay."

- ✔ Avoid running words together. The tiny breaks between sounds help distinguish one word from another.

✔ Focus your effort on pronouncing words differently that *should* sound a little different, and which Dragon NaturallySpeaking may otherwise confuse. Trying to pronounce "hear" differently from "here," for instance, won't gain you much: They are supposed to sound alike. (They are homonyms.) Nor will you benefit from trying to pronounce the "t" in "exactly," because that word won't be confused easily with any other word, even if you pronounce it "zackly." But pronouncing the "th" in the word "the" — even if you do it very lightly — will help NaturallySpeaking distinguish that word from the word "a."

✔ If you're speaking every word and still have problems, work on your enunciation of words themselves. Pay attention to how a word is spelled. Try to speak all the consonant and vowel sounds in a word, especially ones that begin and end the word — unless they make the word noticeably awkward or the word sounds wrong as a result. ("Psychology" comes to mind. Don't pronounce the *P*, of course.)

✔ If you're getting small words in your text that you didn't say, like "a" or "and," the microphone may be picking up small puffs of breath. Try moving the microphone more to the side. Then run the Audio Setup Wizard, by clicking the Audio button on the DragonBar. Select the Check Microphone option. You are forced to run both the volume and quality checks. (See Chapter 18.)

✔ Sit with good posture, not bent over. Relax. Breathe freely. Think peaceful thoughts. Visualize twirling stars. You are getting very sleepy. . . .

✔ Don't speak too rapidly. You don't have to speak slowly, but in today's high-pressure environment, many people begin to sound like a chipmunk with a Starbucks habit.

✔ If your throat gets dry or scratchy, drink water or warm tea. (Creamy, cheesy, or overly sweet foods or drinks can goo up your throat. They can make you sound murky or cause you to clear your throat a lot.)

✔ If your voice changes volume over time, and errors increase, run the Audio Setup Wizard again, choosing to adjust volume. If you have a cold or allergies, or any other long-term change to your voice, consider doing some more general training, discussed in Chapter 18.

✔ Speak the way you trained. When you trained NaturallySpeaking, you read text aloud. Use your reading-aloud voice when you dictate text for highest accuracy.

✔ Talk to a voice trainer or singing instructor. A single session with a professional can give you a lot of tips about speaking more clearly. Who knows, you may find a whole new career.

Shouldn't NaturallySpeaking Meet You Halfway?

Despite all the tips in this chapter for speaking better, NaturallySpeaking is pretty adaptable to a wide variety of speech habits. The only speech flaws that can't be compensated for, in some way, are these two:

✔ Skipping or slurring words

✔ Pausing between each word (not using continuous speech)

Nearly every other speech peculiarity can be compensated for by training. On the other hand, it may take a lot of training, and maybe you can improve your speech, instead, with less effort. See Chapter 18 for more about word training, general training, and vocabulary work.

For instance, if NaturallySpeaking consistently gets the same word wrong, the problem may be that your pronunciation is a bit unusual. I, for instance, thought I heard a reference to a "9 o'clock chicken" when riding to the airport in New Zealand. I thought it was a colorful Kiwi phrase for a small commuter plane. The speaker was referring to a "check-in." Chickens aside, rather than retrain yourself, you can word-train NaturallySpeaking, or enter a phonetic spelling for the "spoken form" of the word using the Vocabulary Editor. (Of course, if you say "chicken" for "check-in," what will you say for "chicken?")

For the most part, NaturallySpeaking is not sensitive to how fast you talk. But very rapid or slow speech may require adjusting NaturallySpeaking settings for better accuracy. NaturallySpeaking looks for a pause as a cue that the next text may be a command. Normally it works best using a quarter-second (250-millisecond) pause, but you can adjust it. Choose Tools⇨Options, and then click the Commands tab. Drag the slider for Pause Required Before Commands to the right for longer pauses, left for shorter. If this setting is too short, words may get chopped up. If it is too long, NaturallySpeaking may translate commands as text.

Chapter 18

Additional Training for Accuracy

· ·

· ·

*I*f your NaturallySpeaking assistant doesn't appear to be quite as sharp as you'd like it to be, you can teach it to do better. Dragon gives you a central place from which to improve its skills. If you start there, you will find all the tools you need at your fingertips. You can also find training options in other DragonBar menus, but if you are new to the software, this is the best place to start.

Using the Accuracy Center

Training and improving NaturallySpeaking is the key to an almost flawless experience over time. Take the time to work with the software and train it to understand your special way of communicating.

Go to the Accuracy Center from DragonBar Go To Help⇨Improve My Accuracy, or say, **"Open Accuracy Center"** from the Help Menu. You'll see the following sections, as shown in Figure 18-1.

✔ **Personalize your vocabulary:** In this section, you use the Vocabulary Editor to build your personal library of words and let your assistant build your special vocabulary by "reading" your documents and e-mails.

✔ **Set options and formatting:** Here you see how to set the Options menu to personalize your settings.

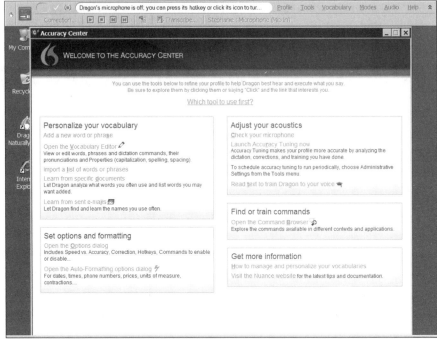

Figure 18-1:
The
Accuracy
Center.

✔ **Adjust your acoustics:** In this section, you launch your Accuracy Tuning and check your microphone.

✔ **Find or train commands:** This section shows you what commands are available to you in a variety of different contexts.

✔ **Get more information:** Here you find information directly from the NaturallySpeaking Help Menu pertaining to vocabularies.

Yikes, lots of choices! Nobody said that educating software was effortless, but this chapter familiarizes you with what to do, and when and how to do it.

Personalizing Your Vocabulary

Personalizing your vocabulary involves two functions. The first is vocabulary editing, which lets you add words to the NaturallySpeaking vocabulary and, optionally, train NaturallySpeaking in how you say those words. It also lets you add custom phrases that translate into text. For example, you can say, **"My Address"** and NaturallySpeaking types your address. The second function is vocabulary building, which uses documents and e-mails to build your existing vocabulary. I cover both of those in the following sections.

Vocabulary editing

You can directly add words to the NaturallySpeaking active vocabulary. The Vocabulary Editor is your tool to add or delete any word you have added but no longer use. It also has special features that allow you to do any of the following:

- ✔ Train NaturallySpeaking in your own, personal pronunciation of a word, for better recognition.

- ✔ Add special words or phrases to the vocabulary, like your company name, properly capitalized or hyphenated, or jargon that you use in your profession.

- ✔ Give awkward words or phrases a different "spoken form" to make dictation easier, like saying, **"My E-mail"** for `voiceguy@yourcompany.com`. These are called *shortcuts*.

- ✔ Come up with alternative ways to say words, punctuation, or whitespace characters, like saying **"Full Stop"** for a period.

Although I talk about mouse commands here, you can use voice commands to control the Vocabulary Editor, too.

Adding a new word or phrase

Adding a word tells NaturallySpeaking that you want to include something new to its vocabulary. The accompanying Word training also teaches NaturallySpeaking how *you* say a word.

No matter whether you say the word *bear* as "beer," "beyah," or "bayrrr," word training can tune NaturallySpeaking's ear to your pronunciation. If NaturallySpeaking is having trouble recognizing specific words, word training may be your solution. Word training is most helpful if the problem is that your pronunciation of a word is unique or not at all like its spelling. For example, in New York, Houston Street is pronounced "Houseton." In Texas, it's pronounced "Hueston."

To add a new word or phrase, from the Accuracy Center click, Add a New Word or Phrase. Up pops the Add Word or Phrase box, as shown in Figure 18-2.

You can train words without going to the Accuracy Center, too. Just select a word in your document, and choose Vocabulary➪Add New Word or Phrase and the same dialog box appears (refer to Figure 18-2).

Figure 18-2:
Use the Add
Word or
Phrase box
to add new
words or
phrases.

To add words, follow these steps:

1. **Spell or type the word you want to add in the left prompt box.**

2. **In the right prompt box, type or spell the spoken form of the word.**

   NaturallySpeaking uses a pronunciation guesser to figure out how most terms sound from the spelling. However, lots of jargon, acronyms, and other terms don't conform to standard rules of English pronunciation. Sometimes you can type a spoken form that gives NaturallySpeaking something better to guess from.

   But, whether you enter a written and spoken form or just a written form, if the pronunciation you're going to use isn't obvious from the spelling, you should train NaturallySpeaking in how you pronounce the word. That's why you see a check box that lets you choose to train the pronunciation of the word or phrase. You can use the word training feature to make sure NaturallySpeaking recognizes your word or phrase.

    For example, you may want NaturallySpeaking to write "Boston and Maine Railroad" when you speak the phrase "B&M." Enter the written form and the spoken form

3. **After you type in the word or phrase, click OK.**

The Train Words dialog box displays in large type the spoken form of the term (or the written form if you haven't entered a spoken form), as shown in Figure 18-3. I chose to train the word "prewash."

4. **Click Go.**

Speak the phrase into your microphone exactly as you always say it.

5. **Click the Done button after you've spoken the term.**

What if word training isn't enough? Perhaps you speak your newly trained word, and NaturallySpeaking still gets it wrong. If two terms sound alike, NaturallySpeaking chooses one by looking at how you have used the term in the past, in context.

If you have recently added this term (say, in the Vocabulary Editor), NaturallySpeaking has little or no context for the term. You haven't used it in a phrase, so NaturallySpeaking is more likely to choose the term with which it has more experience. The solution is to dictate your new term in context and then correct NaturallySpeaking with **Correct That** when it chooses the wrong term. If you dictate the new word and correct NaturallySpeaking with the Correction dialog box, it will catch on and use the new term.

Figure 18-3:
Training words in the Train Words dialog box.

Adding shortcuts in the Vocabulary Editor

To add custom terms to the NaturallySpeaking active vocabulary, click the Open the Vocabulary Editor link from the Accuracy Center (or you can launch the Vocabulary Editor by choosing Vocabulary⇨Vocabulary Editor from the DragonBar menu or speak the commands). Then follow these steps:

1. **Enter the term in the Written Form textbox at the top of the Vocabulary Editor.**

   In Figure 18-4, for example, I entered an e-mail address, `info@SavvyExecutiveInstitute.com`.

   To see what's in the vocabulary, you can either scroll the list in the Vocabulary Editor or type the term in the Written Form box. As you type, the list scrolls to match your typing.

   If you want to speak something other than what's typed, enter it in the textbox labeled Spoken Form (If Different). For example, I entered my e-mail there. I now can simply say, **"My E-Mail"** and have NaturallySpeaking type **dragon@gurus.com**. If you use a term in the Spoken Form box that NaturallySpeaking doesn't already have in its vocabulary, it pops up a dialog box letting you know that fact. It also asks whether you want it to "assign an approximate pronunciation." Click OK.

Figure 18-4:
E-mail
address
typed
into the
Vocabulary
Editor.

2. **After you enter a written (and, if different, spoken) form of the term, click the Add button.**

   If you think the pronunciation will be difficult, click the Train button and record the word as directed. The Vocabulary Editor adds the term to the vocabulary list and marks it with a plus sign (+). You can delete any custom term you add. Just click the term, then click the Delete button. You can also select multiple terms to delete by holding down the Ctrl button as you click.

3. **Click the Close button.**

Creating different ways to say the same thing

The period at the end of this sentence has more aliases (alternative names) than most criminals. The words *period, decimal point, dot, point, stop,* and *full stop* are all valid names for that same symbol in different contexts. NaturallySpeaking doesn't currently recognize all those alternative spoken names, but you can add them to the vocabulary.

If you have an alternative spoken name you would like to use for a word, phrase, or symbol, use the Vocabulary Editor to add that name. Unfortunately, you can't change any of the existing names, even if you don't like them. You can only add an alternative.

To add aliases, whether for symbols, numbers, or other terms, launch the Vocabulary Editor (choose Vocabulary⇨Open Vocabulary Editor) and then do the following:

1. **Type the term or symbol that needs an alias in the Written Form textbox.**

   The list scrolls to show the current written and spoken forms.

   To see all the currently defined symbols and dictation commands in the Vocabulary Editor, you must scroll up above the terms beginning with "a."

2. **Type a new term in the Spoken Form box, and then click the Add button.**

   A second copy of the word appears in the vocabulary list, with your new alias and a plus sign (+) to mark the alias as a custom term. (If the alias doesn't work out, you can delete it. Just click the line and then click the Delete button.)

To add a symbol that isn't on the keyboard, follow these steps:

1. **Insert the symbol into a document, and then copy and paste it into the Written Form textbox.**

   For example, in Word, choose Insert⇨Symbol to insert a symbol into a Word document. Select the symbol, and then press Ctrl+C to copy it to the Windows Clipboard.

2. **Click in the Written Form textbox of the Vocabulary Editor, and then press Ctrl+V to paste the symbol.**

3. **Enter whatever name you would like to speak for that symbol in the Spoken Form textbox, and click the Add button.**

Import a list of words or phrases

If you're likely to use terms from some specialized vocabulary in the documents you dictate, you can make a list of such terms and give them all to NaturallySpeaking in one fell swoop. For example, Queen's Gambit Declined is the name of a chess opening. Each of the three words is surely already in the NaturallySpeaking General English vocabulary, but NaturallySpeaking doesn't know that these three words have a special capitalization pattern when they appear together. If you were to dictate documents about chess, you would want to include Queen's Gambit Declined on one line of your list.

You can create a list and use the Add Words from Word Lists box, as shown in Figure 18-5.

Follow these steps:

1. **Create a text file in which each line is the written form of a vocabulary entry you want to add.**

2. **At the end of any line where you want a different spoken form, add a backslash (/) and then the shorthand alias you want to speak.**

3. **From the Accuracy Center, click the Import a List of Words or Phrases link or use the mouse or commands, and from the DragonBar go to Vocabulary⇨Import List of Words or Phrases.**

   A wizard pops up and says it will add the words.

4. **Click Next.**

   You are asked to add the file.

5. **Click the Add File button.**

   The file is analyzed.

6. **Click Finish.**

   A Summary box shows you how many words were added to your vocabulary.

Figure 18-5:
The Add
Words from
Word Lists
box.

A few wise ideas can save you time and trouble while adding words by using the Import method:

- ✔ Review the list of words to make sure they are real words that you really want.

- ✔ Don't add words that you use infrequently. This is especially true if they sound like some other word that you use often.

- ✔ Sometimes individual proper nouns that you want from a document are actually common words, except that their capitalization (or lack of capitalization) makes them special for you — a sports team named Bingo, for example, or an Internet domain that uses a person's name, `<personsname.com>`.

Learning from specific documents

At this step, you provide your NaturallySpeaking assistant with documents so that it can look at them and pick out any words or capitalized phrases it doesn't recognize. (In essence, it's automatically building a list like the one you may have provided, as the preceding section describes.) The more documents you give Vocabulary Builder, the better. In particular, give it documents that resemble the documents you want to dictate — your previous best-seller, for example, or a collection of your office memos.

Spell-check the documents before you analyze them. The vocabulary-building function looks for words it doesn't already know, and it thinks it has found one whenever it runs into a misspelled word. You save yourself some time if you spell-check your documents and correct any misspelled words before giving the documents to Vocabulary Builder.

To add words from specific documents in Word, WordPerfect, plain text, RTF (Rich Text Format), and HTML (web) documents, follow these steps:

1. **From the Accuracy Center, click the Learn from Specific Document link or choose Vocabulary⇨Learn from Specific Document from the DragonBar.**

   An Add Words from Documents screen pops up, as shown in Figure 18-6. On this screen, you have the option to Find Unknown Words (in various forms) or Adapt to Writing Style.

2. **Click the check box next to each option you want to add and then click Next.**

   A new screen appears with buttons to add either folders of documents or single documents to analyze.

3. **Click the buttons to add your files.**

   Your Windows Browse window opens, allowing you to choose the files as you normally do. Next the files show up in the window of the Add Words from Documents screen.

4. **Click Next.**

   Your documents are analyzed. A check mark appears next to the names of the documents analyzed. All the words that were new to your vocabulary are shown with check marks and the frequency with which they occurred.

5. **If you want to add all the words on the list, click Next.**

   You see a list of the words and the screen asks you to check the words you want to train.

6. **Check the ones you think should be trained for pronunciation.**

   The Train Words dialog box displays, in large type, the written form of the term.

7. **Click Go.**

   Speak the phrase into your microphone exactly as you would say it.

8. **Click Next.**

   A Summary box shows you how many words were added to your vocabulary.

9. **Click Finish.**

Figure 18-6:
Add Words
from
Documents
screen.

Adding words from somebody else's documents

Normally, you use your own documents to teach NaturallySpeaking about your vocabulary. What can you do, however, for a subject that you have not written much about?

Answer: Grab words from documents other people have written. The web, for example, is full of documents about nearly any subject you can name. The trick is to have NaturallySpeaking pick up on the words, but not the writing style, of this other author (unless you intend to write just like him or her).

To use someone else's documents, first you must get the documents! NaturallySpeaking can read Word or WordPerfect documents if you have Word or WordPerfect installed. It can also read plain text, RTF (Rich Text Format), and HTML (web) documents. To get documents from the web, browse to the page you want, and then save the page as an HTML file. In Internet Explorer, for example, choose File↷Save As, enter a filename in the dialog box that appears, and click Save.

Use these documents in the Add Words from Documents box as you would any other documents. When you get to the Adapt to Writing Style check box, unclick it so your NaturallySpeaking assistant won't assume that you write like that other writer.

Learning from sent e-mails

Analyzing e-mails is another way for your NaturallySpeaking assistant to build your vocabulary. This process helps in two ways. It learns from the style of your e-mails and it can automatically add e-mail addresses you currently use. It works with Microsoft Outlook, Outlook Express, Lotus Notes, and Windows Mail.

From the Accuracy Center, click Learn from Sent Emails or go to Vocabulary➪Learn from Sent E-mails from the DragonBar. A screen called Increase Accuracy from E-Mail pops up, as shown in Figure 18-7.

Follow these steps to complete the process:

1. **Click Next.**

   Choose from the options presented by clicking the check boxes.

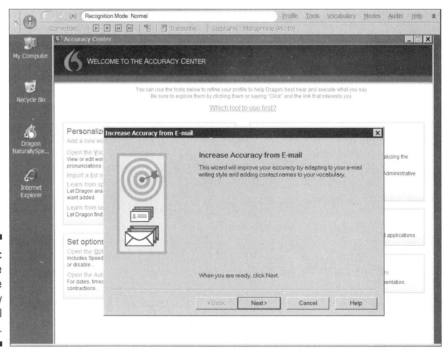

Figure 18-7:
The
Increase
Accuracy
from E-Mail
screen.

2. **Click Next again.**

   The e-mails are analyzed.

3. **Click Next again.**

   Any new words will be displayed for you to train (see "Learning from specific documents," earlier in this chapter).

4. **Click Finish.**

Setting Options and Formatting

This section of the Accuracy Center is key. It contains several ways for you to customize NaturallySpeaking to make your assistant do things your way. Remember to revisit your Options settings periodically when you are using NaturallySpeaking. You may want to alter the settings you chose when you first got started.

Opening the Options Tabs

It's important to set personal options from the Options tab on the Tools menu. From the Accuracy Center, access it by clicking the Open the Options dialog box. This is where you set up preferences for the NaturallySpeaking assistant to work your way. See Chapter 3 for a full discussion.

Opening the Auto-Formatting dialog box

Auto-Formatting is important so don't skip it. Access it from the Open the Auto-Formatting Options dialog box in the Accuracy Center or go to Tools⇨Auto-Formatting Options.

As shown in Figure 18-8, you can see the range of options you have for pre-setting the way you want such things as dates, times, street addresses, and phone numbers to display.

If you get overzealous and regret some of the changes you made, use the Restore Defaults button.

To save time, consider setting these default options:

✔ **Format Numbers, Telephone Numbers, Currency, and Times Automatically:** These check boxes allow typical formatting without your attention.

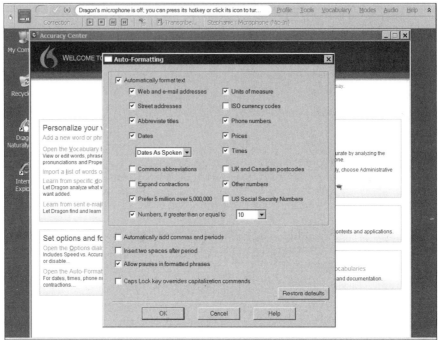

Figure 18-8:
The Auto-
Formatting
dialog box.

- ✔ **Dates:** You have the option to set a specific date format from a drop-down menu.

- ✔ **Format Web and E-mail Addresses Automatically:** To set this option, click the check box. If you have to do these a special way and can't use auto-formatting, you may want to train them individually.

- ✔ **Allow Pauses in Formatted Phrases:** A nice feature, because you often pause to check numbers when speaking phone numbers. If you clear this check mark, NaturallySpeaking may put spaces where you pause.

Adjusting Your Acoustics

The Accuracy Center provides three ways to help your NaturallySpeaking assistant improve your acoustics. They are as follows:

- ✔ **By checking your microphone**
- ✔ **Launching Accuracy Tuning**
- ✔ **Reading text to train Dragon to your voice**

I discuss these in the following sections.

Checking your microphone

Obviously, the microphone is an all-important part of your software. Make sure your NaturallySpeaking assistant doesn't have a "hearing" problem. Does NaturallySpeaking make errors on lots of words and phrases, not just a specific few? Your problem could be with speaking unclearly, with your microphone position or quality, with your sound card quality, or with the microphone volume set by the Audio Setup Wizard, as shown in Figure 18-9.

To rule out a hearing problem, rerun the Check Microphone Wizard from the Check Microphone link in the Accuracy Center. You can also access it from the Audio Check Microphone. If the Audio Wizard thinks your audio is fine, and you still get errors on lots of words after running the wizard, try the voice tips in Chapter 17. You can also run the audio setup test if you're dictating in a new environment and see if that helps.

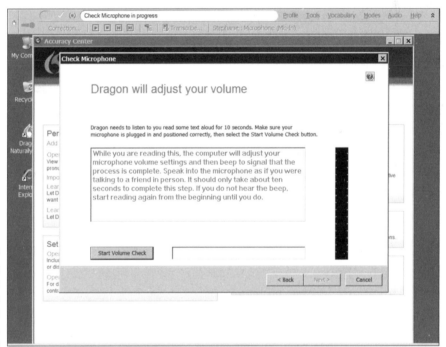

Figure 18-9: The Microphone Volume setting.

Launching Accuracy Tuning

Here's where the correction and fine-tuning of your dictation really pay off. From the Launch Accuracy Tuning Now link in the Accuracy Center (or from Audio⇨Launch Accuracy Tuning), you'll be presented with the

Acoustic and Language Model Optimizer screen. Don't be intimidated. Your NaturallySpeaking assistant does all the heavy lifting.

As shown in Figure 18-10, the check boxes for both Perform Acoustic Optimization and Perform Language Model Optimization are checked by default. Leave them checked. Then do the following:

1. **Click Go.**

   You are given an estimated time for completion of this process. Don't be shocked if the initial estimate says 450 hours! It quickly changes to a couple of minutes as it's working. Perhaps your NaturallySpeaking assistant has a weird sense of humor.

2. **After the process completes, click Done.**

   You'll be asked to save the newly optimized files.

3. **Click Yes and you're done.**

See? Your NaturallySpeaking assistant does all the work. (Isn't that why you pay it the big bucks?)

Reading text to train Dragon to your voice

If NaturallySpeaking seems to be making more mistakes than it used to, ask yourself if *you* have changed since you first trained Dragon. Has your voice, manner of speaking, or working environment changed?

For example, are you getting more experienced at dictation? Have you changed your office or changed something that makes or absorbs sound in your office? If so, try running General Training. (Because you ran General Training when you set up NaturallySpeaking, access it now by going to the DragonBar menu and choosing Audio⇨Read Text to Improve Accuracy.) General Training helps NaturallySpeaking get a more accurate picture of your voice and speech habits.

The Text dialog box, and all the ones that follow, are the same ones you saw when you first performed General Training to set up NaturallySpeaking. For details on using them, refer to the discussion of General Training in Chapter 2.

Running General Training after you've had some experience with NaturallySpeaking is a good idea. Often, you speak differently after a few days.

The plan in General Training is to read something to NaturallySpeaking so that it can figure out how you speak. This time around, you may find some additional reading material in the Select Text dialog box that is shorter to read than the selections that were available when you first set up NaturallySpeaking. You don't need to read more than a few screens of text.

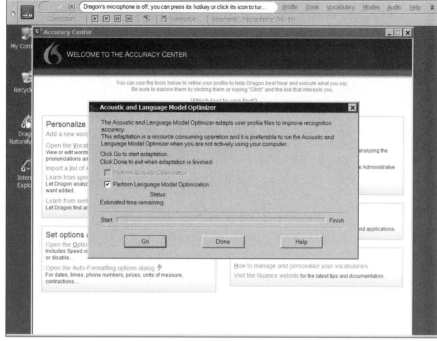

Figure 18-10:
The
Acoustic
and
Language
Model
Optimizer
screen.

A fundamental problem with General Training is that many people read differently than they dictate. Try to speak the way you would if you were the author and were thinking this stuff up for the first time.

Don't say, **"Cap"** or any other dictation commands during General Training. Don't say any punctuation, either. Click the Back Up button if you really mess something up, and try again. Click the Pause button if you need to take a break.

Finding or Training Commands

In version 11 of Dragon NaturallySpeaking, Nuance gives you several ways to identify commands. The addition of the Sidebar makes it really easy to find them on the fly. (See Chapter 22.) Because the Sidebar is context-sensitive, you will always see the commands that are helpful for the application you are in.

Opening the Command Browser

If NaturallySpeaking isn't obeying your commands, it may not be recognizing your pronunciation. You can improve its recognition for many commands exactly as you would for word or phrase training. See the steps in the preceding sections for instructions.

Make sure you capitalize the words of the command properly. Check the documentation that comes with NaturallySpeaking for proper capitalization. Most words in NaturallySpeaking command phrases are initial-capped except for articles, prepositions, and other short words.

You can't, however, train "dictation commands" this way. These commands are the ones that control capitalization and spacing, like **No Caps On.** To train those commands, use the Vocabulary Editor. Scroll to the top (above the "a") of the list of words in the Vocabulary Editor. Click a command and then click the Train button.

Before you try command training, make sure that you pause correctly before and after a command. If NaturallySpeaking gets the words right but types them instead of doing them, pausing is more likely to be your problem than pronunciation. Chapter 4 talks about solving this problem.

To access the Command Browser from the Accuracy Center, click on the Open the Command Browser link. Or you can choose Tools➪Command Browser.

You can also add a new command by choosing Tools➪Add New Command. Here you can easily type in and train a new command.

When using the Command Browser, as shown in Figure 18-11, you have several options:

- ✔ **Find specific applications:** Use the pull-down window to see if the particular application you are using has specific commands in NaturallySpeaking. Then you can peruse them to see what you need.

- ✔ **Train commands:** By clicking on a particular command, you can use the Train icon on the left side to train that command to understand your pronunciation.

- ✔ **Look at scripts:** By choosing the Script icon on the left side, you switch from Browse mode to Script mode. Here you can directly create, delete, edit, or copy commands.

    Unless you know what you're doing, stay in Browse mode.

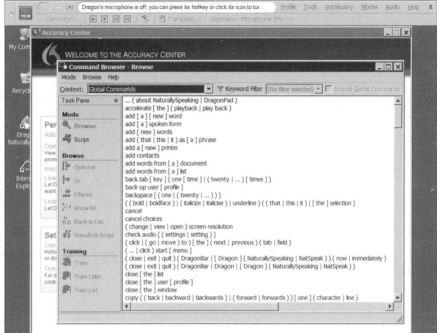

Figure 18-11:
The
Command
Browser
window.

Getting more information

This is section of the Accuracy Center where you find information about your vocabulary and a link to the Nuance website, shown in Figure 18-12. Take a look and see how the vocabularies are described.

When you click the link in the Accuracy Center under How to Manage and Personalize Your Vocabularies, you are taken to an explanation of the types of vocabularies available. Recall that when you installed your NaturallySpeaking software, you were asked several questions about your accent and what region of the world you live in. This Help section gives you more information about those vocabulary choices.

The Nuance website is chock-full of information, training, help, and tech support. Chapter 22 covers this extensively.

Figure 18-12:
The Nuance
website.

Chapter 19

Improving Audio Input

*T*he old expression "garbage in, garbage out" takes on a different twist when you talk about speech recognition. If garbage goes in, NaturallySpeaking reconstructs it into perfectly good words. It acts like a trash compactor: It makes garbage look better.

Of course, you aren't talking trash. Nonetheless, your words may be trashed on their way to the laptop. The microphone or audio hardware may not be quite right. Or the microphone may have moved when you chugged your coffee. Or your office mates, appliances, or kids may be contributing background garbage of their own to your audio. The result may sound okay to your ears if you play it back, but NaturallySpeaking assistants have very sensitive ears.

It isn't likely that you'll encounter a hardware problem when using NaturallySpeaking, but I include some ideas here in case you do.

Figuring Out Whether You Have an Audio Input Problem

If NaturallySpeaking misinterprets lots of words, your second thought is probably, "Something's wrong with my microphone or sound card." (Your first thought is probably uncharitable toward your new assistant. Shame on you.)

NaturallySpeaking may be messing up for lots of reasons, however. As with a puppy that messes up, one reason may be inadequate training. Before you go looking for an audio input problem, make sure you have completed all the training that the New User Wizard asked you to. (You'll know if you haven't. When you start NaturallySpeaking and choose an incompletely trained user, NaturallySpeaking warns you and gives you a chance to finish the job.) One symptom of a need for additional training or vocabulary building is that NaturallySpeaking makes the same error repeatedly: "cheese" for "trees," for instance. See Chapter 18 for help with that.

If, however, NaturallySpeaking gives you different text each time you say the same thing ("wheeze," "sneeze," and "breeze" for "trees"), you may have an audio input problem. One dead-simple way to test for serious audio input problems is to listen to your PC play back your voice (not available in the Home edition). You can use a Nuance-approved Sound Recorder, if you have one, or you can use the Windows Sound Recorder:

- ✔ For XP, the Windows Sound Recorder is at Start➪Programs➪Accessories➪ Entertainment➪Sound Recorder. Click the red-dot button in Sound Recorder and speak into the microphone to record. Press the button with the line in front of a left-facing arrow to rewind and then press the button with the line after a right-facing arrow to play. If you hear a lot of noise, or your voice is distorted, you may have an audio input problem.

- ✔ For Windows 7, you access the Sound Recorder by going to Start➪ All Programs➪Accessories➪Sound Recorder. Click the red-dot button in Sound Recorder and speak into the microphone to record. Click the red-dot button to stop it and save it to a location of your choice.

The most common cause of recognition errors is muttering through your coffee cup, or otherwise not speaking clearly. See Chapter 17 for tips on speaking clearly. Does your diction qualify you for the British Broadcasting Company? Then read on.

Running the Audio Setup Wizard

If you suspect an audio input problem, the first thing to do is to run the Audio Setup Wizard. The Audio Setup Wizard can do either a complete setup or simply adjust the volume.

If NaturallySpeaking has been working okay to date and only now has begun making errors, your microphone may have moved a bit, or you may be speaking more or less loudly than before. In that case, you only need the wizard to adjust the volume. Choose Audio➪Read Text to Improve Accuracy Wizard from the DragonBar, and follow the instructions. (For detailed instructions on the Audio Setup Wizard, see the discussion of the New User Wizard in Chapter 2.)

Some PCs have more than one sound system installed. For instance, you may have installed a better sound card than the one your PC came with, but the original is still present. If you're using a USB microphone, you almost certainly have two sound systems. If you have more than one sound system, the first screen that the Audio Setup Wizard displays asks you to choose the sound system. You must choose the system your microphone is connected to: USB Audio Device if you're using a USB microphone, for instance. If the choices don't mean anything to you, click Default and proceed. If you choose incorrectly, when the Audio Setup Wizard gets to the Adjust Your Volume screen, it will complain that the sound level is too low. Click Cancel to exit the Audio Setup Wizard, and then restart it and choose the other sound system.

You engineers and serious audio geeks out there can try pressing Alt+1 when the Results screen appears. All kinds of cool, technical displays appear as you talk.

If volume is low, consider speaking a bit louder or moving the microphone slightly closer to your mouth. If you're tired, take a break! I have found that my volume varies considerably over the day and is lower when I'm tired, sitting with poor posture, or sleepy.

Checking your microphone

Many a slip happens between the PC and the lip. Following are some of the problems you may be having on the microphone end of things, and what to do about them:

- ✔ **Your microphone needs adjustment:** Make sure the microphone is off to the side of your mouth, about a half-inch away from one corner of your mouth. You may have to bend the plastic tube that holds the microphone into an S-shape to get this right.

- ✔ **You have chosen the wrong sound system in the Audio Setup Wizard:** Read the preceding section, "Running the Audio Setup Wizard."

- ✔ **You're trying to use the built-in microphone in your laptop computer:** These rarely provide enough quality, and they pick up lots of extraneous noise from the laptop and the surface it lies on. Nearly half of all laptops present an audio input problem to NaturallySpeaking because of their microphones, sound hardware, or both. One good solution is a USB microphone. See the next section for details.

- ✔ **You're trying to use the cheap microphone that came with your PC:** Give it up! Use the one that came with NaturallySpeaking, or buy a serious microphone from the list of Nuance-certified devices on its website in the Support Area.

Being of sound mind, or are you certifiable?

Dragon Systems makes a point of certifying audio (sound) hardware, including microphones and sound cards. Check out Nuance's website at www.Nuance.com for the list of compatible products. While you are at Nuance's website, explore the Knowledgebase in the Support section. You can also go to Facebook. com and type in Dragon Naturally Speaking and go to the discussion link to see what other people have said about various manufacturers' products.

 ✔ **The microphone connection is loose:** Look at where the plug fits the jack in your PC; make sure it isn't wiggly. If you have NaturallySpeaking Premium or higher, try playing back some of your dictation. (Select text and say, **"Play That."**) If it has loud, scratchy noises, you may need to replace the microphone or get someone to test and fix its cable. Some background noise also comes from the PC (not exactly a high-end sound system) and is unavoidable.

 ✔ **The microphone cable is plugged into the wrong jack in the PC:** If the microphone is plugged into a really wrong jack, like the speaker output, it won't work at all. If you have no alternative but to plug it into the IN or LINE-IN jack on your PC (you have no microphone jack), it may work, but the volume may be low. If it's plugged into the IN or LINE-IN jack and doesn't work at all, run a complete setup in the Audio Setup Wizard as the preceding section describes. Volume may still not be high enough, but at least you tried.

 ✔ **A battery is failing in the microphone or adapter:** The microphones that come with NaturallySpeaking don't have batteries, but some microphones do. I'm willing to bet that battery-powered adapters do, too.

Should you get a better microphone than the one that came with NaturallySpeaking? Many voice-recognition professionals swear by getting a better microphone, which can run up to several hundred dollars. A better microphone will generally improve your results, but only up to the limits of your PC's sound card. Both microphone and sound card are links in the chain that brings your voice to your PC, and whichever is the weakest link will limit your sound quality. Those professionals who recommend better microphones also tend to have very good sound cards. Your results will probably not improve in proportion to the money you spend. Check the list of Dragon-certified microphones on Dragon's website for options. But before you go laying out big bucks for a new microphone and sound card, read the next section on USB microphones.

Getting a USB microphone

One great way to get better quality audio and bypass all this microphone/sound-card stuff entirely is to get a USB (Universal Serial Bus) microphone. It's probably the best way to deal with a laptop computer that doesn't have good audio.

A USB microphone plugs into a USB connector on your PC and delivers digital sound right to the PC. You no longer use the audio input features of your PC's sound card. Because the USB mic removes all the variables that the regular microphone and sound-card system present, it's one of the better solutions to audio input problems. Some users have even reported that their words are transcribed faster when they use the USB mic. (Your mileage may differ.)

If you want the very best, a USB solution may not be the answer. Some users report that the NaturallySpeaking USB microphone isn't as good as the combination of a very good separate microphone and a very good sound card.

Playing your best card

Your microphone plugs into a chunk of your PC loosely called the "sound card" or the "audio card." The sound card is responsible for converting what comes out of your microphone into computer bits. Are some sound cards sounder than other sound cards? The answer is a resounding "Yes!"

How do you know whether your sound card is your problem? It's hard to be certain. Because replacing a sound card is a pain, most people try to improve other aspects of their audio first, like speaking more clearly or adjusting the microphone position. If those efforts don't work, they get a new sound card (or buy a USB microphone).

What is a sound card?

Inside your PC is a large board full of electronics that do the essential functions of your computer. Less-essential stuff is on smaller boards, also called cards, whose rear-ends are typically decorated with various connectors. These small boards are designed so that their connectors stick out the back of your PC or laptop, where you plug stuff in. Depending on the whim of the engineers who built your PC, the sound (audio) features may either be on the big ("mother") board or on one of these cards. If your audio features are on a card, changing to a Dragon-certified card is generally easier than if they are on the motherboard. So many sound cards work with NaturallySpeaking that it is unlikely you will have a problem. Make sure to look at the list of compatible sound cards listed on the Nuance.com site in the Support area.

Try all the suggestions first, before buying anything new.

Finding out whether you have a Dragon-certified sound card is a good idea. If you have one, and audio input is poor anyway, you'll know to look elsewhere for the cause.

The manufacturers of some of the sound cards that get good marks from Nuance include top-end cards from Creative Labs (SoundBlaster and Ensoniq cards) and Voyetra Turtle Beach (Santa Cruz), but many lower-cost cards also do just fine. SoundBlaster cards are the "classic" PC sound cards, and NaturallySpeaking works fine with most of them.

The best way to see what you have is to check your PC's or laptop's sound card. Here's the easiest way if you are using Windows XP:

1. **On the Windows taskbar, choose Start⇨Control Panel.**

2. **In the Control Panel, double-click the Sounds, Speech and Audio Devices icon.**

   A dialog box pops up.

3. **Click on the Sounds and Devices Panel icon.**

   A dialog box pops up with tabs.

4. **Click the Audio tab at the top, and see what Default Device is listed for Sound Recording or Playback.**

   The manufacturer's name or telltale initials of the product line appear here.

If you are using Windows 7, do the following:

1. **On the Windows taskbar, choose Start⇨Control Panel.**

2. **In the Control Panel, double-click the Hardware and Sound icon.**

   A screen with several icons pops up.

3. **Click on the Sound icon.**

   A screen pops up showing the volume mixer for your Speakers and System Sounds.

4. **Double-click the icon for System Sounds.**

   You'll see the following tabs at the top: Playback, Recording, Sounds and Communications. See what Default Devices are listed for Recording and Playback. If the ones you want are not the default, click on them to make them the defaults.

What about the rest of you who don't have a Dragon-blessed sound card, or have no idea whether you do and aren't about to spend the money to get one anyway? The best solution is to try to improve your speaking, run the Audio Setup Wizard's volume adjustment regularly, do lots of training and vocabulary building, and make sure you work in a quiet environment.

Ensuring a Quiet Environment

In general, Dragon NaturallySpeaking, like the rest of us, works best in a quiet environment. Noise from an open window, kids, dogs, appliances, fans, air-conditioners, ringing phones, shredders, coffee machines, or a loudly growling stomach can make NaturallySpeaking inaccurate. So this is a perfect excuse to shoo away the dog and kids, shut off the phone, and drink the last of the coffee (and spit out the gum). If you're at work, it's an excuse to close the door to your office. (Lucky you, if you have one.)

Nuance recommends that the best way to do all your training is in the environment in which you plan to use NaturallySpeaking. If it's a loud, busy place, do it there. If you change environments, rerun your audio tests.

Dragon NaturallySpeaking also works best where the environment deadens sound, such as areas with carpets, heavy drapes, or blinds. Hard surfaces such as hard floors, glass windows, granite counters, and metal furniture cause echoes that you don't notice but that Dragon NaturallySpeaking may.

If your environment has become noisier than it was when you trained NaturallySpeaking, you may do well to repeat the training. See the discussion of general training in Chapter 18.

Besides acoustical noise — noise that you can hear — you may be surrounded by the hum of electrical noise. Electrical noise is the result of electricity and magnetic fields zinging around near your microphone or sound card. PCs, laptops, and monitors generate a lot of these fields, so try backing a bit farther away from your PC and monitor when you dictate.

Chapter 20

Having Multiple Computers or Users

*H*eraclitus, the Greek philosopher, is famous for his ideas about change. He is quoted as saying, "You could not step twice into the same river; for other waters are ever flowing on to you." Computer systems change faster than almost any other part of life: If something works, it must be obsolete. If you become a regular user of NaturallySpeaking, you and your NaturallySpeaking assistant will probably go through a number of changes together — new operating systems, new versions of the NaturallySpeaking software, or even whole new hardware. New users may come into your life as family members or officemates decide that they want to start dictating, too.

Some changes have been dealt with elsewhere in this book. In Chapter 19, I talk about hardware upgrades that may improve the performance of NaturallySpeaking: more memory, a better sound card, and a better microphone.

In this chapter, I look at how NaturallySpeaking solves the problem of multiple people, computers, environments, microphones, or hats. I show you how to use these features for better accuracy. (Hold onto your hat!)

Creating and Managing Users

NaturallySpeaking can't understand strangers well, and sometimes it can't even understand you well, if something about you changes: the way you use words or the way you sound. Consider it this way: Many people wear several hats. They are doctors and also administrators; they are accountants by day and poets by night; or they are brain surgeons on weekdays and drill sergeants on weekends. Whichever hat they wear, they write very differently in those roles. They may also sound different because of the environments or microphones they work with at any given time.

If several people use your NaturallySpeaking software, or if you dictate using different words or writing styles, you may need multiple users. Here's why and how to create and manage those users.

One person, different users

NaturallySpeaking understands only those who have officially introduced themselves as *users* and gone through a training process to create *User Profiles*.

Here are four reasons why you may want to make more than one User Profile for yourself:

- ✔ You use different vocabularies or writing styles for different tasks.

- ✔ You use different microphones for different tasks (say, a cordless and a wired microphone).

- ✔ You want to use different NaturallySpeaking options for different tasks. For instance, you may want to turn off certain features to save memory when using NaturallySpeaking with big applications. (See Chapter 3 for instructions.) Option choices are part of the definition of a user.

- ✔ You have a laptop or other hardware and use it in two or more distinct environments (noisy/quiet, outdoors/indoors, in bed/in the pool, and so on).

The drawback of having more than one user per person is the extra training of NaturallySpeaking that the person must do. Each user maintains personal own training and experience, starting with the initial "audio" training that you must repeat for each user. The same holds true for ongoing training. If you use the phrase "boogie-woogie" in both your personal and professional lives, for instance, not only do you have a very interesting life, but you have to train both users so that Dragon NaturallySpeaking recognizes the phrase.

What is a user, really?

The NaturallySpeaking idea of a user is probably not quite the same as yours. To you, a user is . . . you. A human being with dreams and aspirations, hopes and fears. But NaturallySpeaking doesn't know that. All it knows about users is that they make this wiggly electrical signal in its little electronic ear, and that it is responsible for choosing the right words from a vocabulary to match that wiggle.

If you do anything to change that wiggle, NaturallySpeaking won't recognize you. Or if you try to use a word that isn't in the vocabulary that NaturallySpeaking associates with that user, NaturallySpeaking chooses the wrong word.

In other words, a "user" in NaturallySpeaking is more than just you. It's you, plus your microphone or portable recorder, the environment you're speaking in, the sound card in your computer, your laptop, and your vocabulary. (In all editions of NaturallySpeaking except Professional, a user has only one vocabulary. In the Professional edition, a user can have several.) It's also the options you've chosen in Tools➪Options, and the microphone volume set by the Audio Setup Wizard.

You can change or broaden NaturallySpeaking's definition of a user, however. You don't have to have a separate user for, say, when you have a head cold. Instead, you run General Training. NaturallySpeaking will add its "head cold" experience to its previous experience of your voice. (See Chapter 18.) It will do better the next time you are sneezy (or grumpy or both). Likewise, if you run the Audio Setup Wizard, NaturallySpeaking changes the microphone volume to adapt to any change in microphone position. (See Chapter 19.) You can train a single user to broadly cover all the types of writing you do, too. The problem with broadening a user definition is that overall accuracy will go down to the same degree that you have distinctly different situations.

Adding a new user

Setting up a new user is a lot like setting up the original user: You're off to see the New User Wizard. Invoke the wizard's name in either of the following ways:

✔ Click the New button in the Open User dialog box when NaturallySpeaking starts up.

✔ From the NaturallySpeaking DragonBar, choose Profile➪New User Profile from the menu.

After the New User Wizard starts up, it takes you through the same series of steps that you (may) remember from original installation: creating the user speech files, selecting the user type, audio setup, general training, and vocabulary building. Each of these steps is covered in Chapter 2.

You may be able to skip over the most time-consuming part of the New User Wizard (General Training) if you already have NaturallySpeaking user files that you trained on another machine or with another copy of NaturallySpeaking. See "Adding an old user to a different computer," coming up next.

Adding an old user to a different computer

What if the user you want to add isn't really new to NaturallySpeaking but is just new to *that copy* of NaturallySpeaking on a different (or new) computer? Getting a new computer can be fun. Everything runs faster, the hard drive is bigger, it may cause you to get a bunch of fun, new apps that you can play with, and the screen is cleaner than your old screen ever was. But just like moving to a new neighborhood, moving to a new machine means going through a period of uncertainty as you wonder whether all your possessions will make it in one piece or whether you have to leave anything behind.

Or maybe it isn't a brand-spanking-new machine. Maybe you've just decided that your NaturallySpeaking assistant should follow you onto your office computer or home computer, or vice versa.

In either case, the two main possessions that you would like to wrap in plastic and move to the new machine are your NaturallySpeaking software and your user files.

Owning a copy of NaturallySpeaking entitles you to have multiple User Profiles of your own voice (for example, from different sources) on your computer. You can also install it on your other computers if you don't use them simultaneously. You are also allowed to enable two or more people to use NaturallySpeaking on your single computer and keep separate profiles for each person. When you install NaturallySpeaking, the activation process will follow how many computers you install it on. If you run over your allotted amount, you will have to uninstall one to load it onto a new one. See the Nuance website for more information on licensing users and activation.

Transferring your User Profiles to a new computer

DVDs don't remember whether they've been read before, so installing NaturallySpeaking on the new machine is just like installing it the first time. (See Chapter 2.) I assume you have done this.

If you are transferring your User Profiles from the old machine, though, you don't want to redo General Training, so cancel out of the New User Wizard just after you have gone through the first steps that ask you about your age, your accent, and so forth (in other words, right before running Audio Setup). Move on to Import a User Profile. Then you'll be able to go back and set up the rest of the files.

In case you're wondering, a new User Profile requires about 140 MB of hard drive space. One of the easiest ways to transfer the files from one computer to another is to use a USB flash drive. This way, you can easily copy the files from the first computer and move them to another. Of course, if you have a preferred method for moving files, use that. I explain the transferring of files using a USB flash drive later in this chapter.

You always move the User Profile from the original machine you created the profile on to the machine you are moving it to. This means that you use the Export function on the original machine and the Import function on the new machine.

Transferring your user files to a new machine involves a few basic steps. You have to go through this process for each user that you want to move to the new machine. Use the following steps:

1. **Choose Profile➪Manage User Profiles from the DragonBar or say,** "Manage User Profiles on the Original Computer."

   A User Profile window opens up, showing the names of the User Profiles on your computer.

2. **Select your username and click the Advanced button.**

   A submenu displays.

3. **Click the Export menu.**

   A Windows browser screen opens and asks you to click on the location where you want to save the User Profile files you want to move.

4. **If you are using a USB flash drive as recommended earlier, double-click Computer and locate the drive.**

   Make a new folder on the flash drive so you'll have no trouble finding the files you transfer.

5. **Click OK.**

   The files are copied automatically to your flash drive. You should get a message that says the export was successful.

6. **Close the User Profile window. Remove the flash drive and go back to the computer you are moving the profile to.**

7. **With NaturallySpeaking running on that computer, insert the flash drive.**

   You see a message on the DragonBar that says No User Profile Is Loaded.

8. **Choose Profile⇨Manage User Profiles on the DragonBar or say,** "Manage User Profiles on the Original Computer," **and click the Advanced button.**

9. **Choose Import.**

   The browser screen opens and asks you to select the username you just set up when you installed the software in Step 2.

10. **Locate the USB drive and click on the file you copied onto it.**

11. **Click OK.**

   The files are copied and you have successfully moved your User Profile from your original computer to your new computer.

The point of moving the old user files to the new machine is to avoid retraining. You don't want to train the new user files that the wizard sets up. Rather, you just want the file structure to be set up so that you can replace the wizard's generic files with the files you copied from your old machine.

Because you already ran the New User Wizard when you installed NaturallySpeaking on the new machine, you don't need to do it again. The next time you start NaturallySpeaking, it knows about the existence of your newly transferred user. What it hasn't done is calibrate the audio system of this machine for your voice.

Open your new User Profile from the Open User dialog box that appears when NaturallySpeaking starts. (If you don't see the Open User dialog box, it means that your new user is the only one NaturallySpeaking knows about, so it opened that user without asking.)

NaturallySpeaking realizes on its own that the Audio Setup Wizard hasn't been run for this user. When it offers you the opportunity to run Audio Setup, click Yes. For a more detailed look at the Audio Setup Wizard and the screens it presents, see Chapter 2.

Who Are All These Users?

If you aren't sure what users you have, you can find them listed in the Open User dialog box, shown in Figure 20-1. If your copy of NaturallySpeaking has more than one user, the Open User dialog box shows up spontaneously when you open NaturallySpeaking so that you can identify which user you are. You can also ask to see it by choosing Profile⇨Open User Profile from the NaturallySpeaking DragonBar.

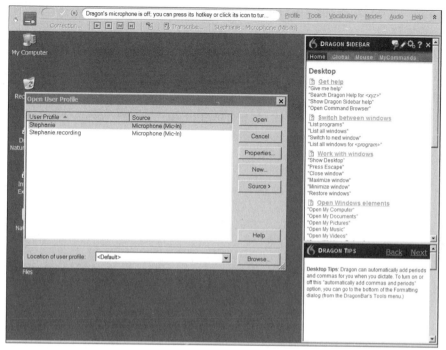

When you look at the Open User dialog box, you may be surprised to realize just how many users you have. Naturally, each person who uses NaturallySpeaking is a different user, but you should also have defined separate users for different input devices (like a mobile recorder), different noise environments (like when you're in the shower), or any other circumstance that may make you sound significantly different to NaturallySpeaking.

Deleting a user

User files take up space on your hard drive, so deleting user files that are no longer needed is good practice. Whatever your reason for wanting to delete a user, however, don't do it rashly. All the backups for that user get deleted, too, so you can't undo it. If you delete your girlfriend's user files when you break up, she'll have to retrain from scratch when you get back together. (She may get annoyed with you all over again.) Perform the following steps to delete a user:

1. **Choose Profile➪Manage User Profiles from the menu in the NaturallySpeaking DragonBar.**

   The Manage User Profiles dialog box appears.

2. **Select the name of the user you want to delete from the list in the dialog box.**

You can't delete *yourself.* That is, you can't delete the current user. Among other things, this safeguard prevents you from deleting the last user on the system. (If you want to do that, you should uninstall NaturallySpeaking.)

3. **Click the Delete button in the Open User dialog box.**

4. **When the confirmation box appears, click Yes.**

Backing up and restoring User Profiles

NaturallySpeaking keeps a backup copy of each user's speech files. It automatically makes this copy every fifth time you save NaturallySpeaking's speech files — which most people do when they are prompted to do so, every time they exit NaturallySpeaking. (You can make this backup more or less frequent by using the Options dialog box discussed in Chapter 3.)

The backup speech files lag behind any changes you make by correcting or training NaturallySpeaking. So, if you make a mistake and save speech files when you shouldn't have (perhaps you vocabulary-trained using the wrong documents), you can restore from an earlier version of those files.

You can tell NaturallySpeaking to update the backup copy at any time by choosing Manage User Profiles⇨Advanced⇨Backup. To restore from the backup copy, choose Profiles⇨Advanced⇨Restore. (The files are located in the folder where you installed NaturallySpeaking, in the Users folder there, in the folder that goes with your particular username.)

Chapter 21

Creating Your Own Commands

· ·

In This Chapter

▶ Creating new commands

▶ Editing custom commands

▶ Using the Command Browser

▶ Deleting commands

· ·

Dragon NaturallySpeaking is a great productivity tool along with its other virtues. In this chapter, you see how to save time when you compose e-mails, reports, and other materials. "How?" you ask. Get your NaturallySpeaking assistant to type all the boilerplate text you normally have to type over and over again!

By working with the Command tools built into the program, you can have your NaturallySpeaking assistant furiously type in all the text you want by stating a simple command. If everything in life was that simple, you would have time to finish all the great literature you keep promising to read.

Creating Commands that Insert Text and Graphics

If you tried counting all the voice commands in NaturallySpeaking's vocabulary, you would be amazed at the final tally. Just browsing the Dragon Sidebar gives you some idea. They are the commands that NaturallySpeaking comes with: the built-in commands and the Natural Language Commands. Even though Dragon provides hundreds, you will still want to add some that are specific to you, either in your job or in your personal life. (Custom commands are not available in the Home edition.)

For example, if you have a long address that you need to put into your business e-mails, you can create a command to do it. If you have more than one signature for your e-mails, you can create them too. How about several paragraphs? It's kind of fun to see how many you can create to save time. Just don't get too carried away!

Creating a new command

Adding a new command is easy using the MyCommands Editor, shown in Figure 21-1. Fill in the dialog boxes and click Save. But, before getting started, there's a more important question you need to ask yourself. "In what application will I use this command?" Consider the following choices:

- ✔ **Global:** If you want to use the same command when working in different applications, you create a Global command.

- ✔ **Application-specific:** If you plan to use the command in a particular application, like Microsoft Word, then you create an Application-specific command.

- ✔ **Window-specific:** If you're going to use the command in a specific window, like your e-mail program, then you create a Window-specific command.

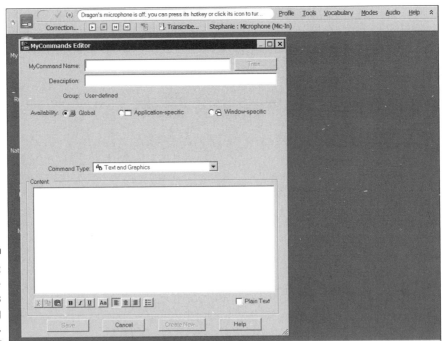

Figure 21-1:
The My-
Commands
Editor dialog
box.

If you're ready with that answer, you're ready to create a command. From the DragonBar, choose Tools⇨Add New Command. Then follow these steps:

1. **Type (or say) the new command name where prompted.**

   In this example, I call it **Catalog Sent.**

   It's best if you name the command something distinctive that you can remember. You may also want to format it using Title Caps or All Caps so that you can spot it easily.

2. **Click the Train button so that your command will be recognized easily.**

   A Train Words screen pops up, as shown in Figure 21-2, so that you can dictate the name.

3. **Click Go.**

4. **Speak the command as you would normally.**

5. **Click Done.**

   Leave the Group as User-Defined. You can only change this if you have the Dragon Professional edition or higher.

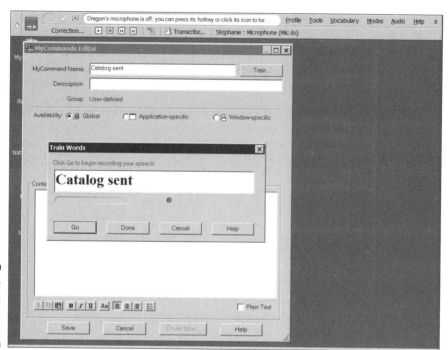

Figure 21-2:
The Train Words dialog box.

6. **If you choose, you can enter a description in the Description box.**

Below that, where you see Availability, select the radio button for the type of command you create. (See the beginning of this section for Global, Application-specific, and Window-specific.)

For this example, choose Application-specific.

You see a drop-down menu with a prompt box to type in your open application (or say it) or click the Browse button to select the application from your hard drive.

7. **Type the application name.**

Leave the Command Type as Text and Graphics.

8. **Type or dictate the content into the large dialog box.**

For this example, I dictated: **"Thanks for your request. We are sending our catalog overnight for your review. We hope this will give you a clear understanding about the value of our products."**

You can also cut and paste boilerplate text into the window of the dialog box or highlight it and say, **"Make that a command."** NaturallySpeaking will automatically pop open the Command Editor and paste it in.

9. **Check the Plain Text check box.**

Putting a check in this check box lets the program know that you want the content to pick up any formatting you are already working with in Word.

If you format it while creating the command, don't check this box.

10. **Click Save.**

You did it! You created a new command. Now every time you want to insert that paragraph in your e-mail, you can do it by saying, **"Catalog Sent."**

Test your new command right after you save it. You don't want to find out you made a mistake when you're in the heat of dictation.

Adding text to your new command

In case you're wondering, you can use the command you just created, with any combination of other commands and dictation. For example, you can dictate a second paragraph on-the-fly that pertains to that specific addressee. In the same e-mail or document, you can put in additional commands, like your signature or address. You can mix and match them to customize it.

Creating commands for new applications

When you create a command, you have to decide what type of command it will be — Global, Application-specific, or Window-specific. But what if you are using a program that hasn't been introduced to your NaturallySpeaking assistant? You need to have them meet! That process is a snap. Follow these steps:

1. **Open the application you want to use.**

2. **From the DragonBar, choose Tools➪Add New Command.**

3. **At the MyCommands Editor dialog box, fill in the name of the new command.**

4. **When you reach the Availability section, select the Application-specific radio button.**

   The name of your new application will be listed in the box, as shown in Figure 21-3.

   Continue to create the new command and remember to select that application from the Command Browser if you want to edit it.

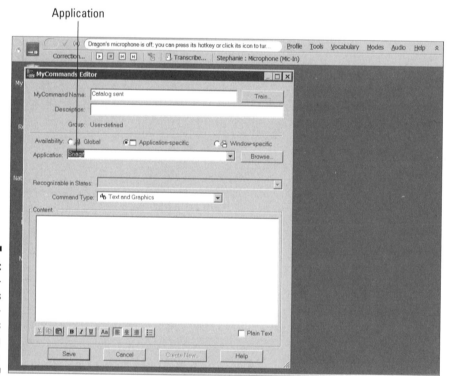

Application

Figure 21-3: The application appears in the My-Commands Editor dialog box.

Introducing the Command Browser

After you create a command, you can edit it with the Command Browser. Don't be intimidated when you open the Command Browser screen. It looks like there is a lot going on. But it's easy to use once you know what you're looking for. (See Chapter 18 for more on the Command Browser.) Let's look around the Command Browser to make it less scary to browse.

Locating commands using the Keyword Filter

Just like searching on the web, you can find commands in the Command Browser by using keywords. The Keyword Filter makes it easy to find the actual command for a function you would like to perform. For example, if you want to locate a footnote in your Word document, your first inclination might be to say, **"Find Footnote."** When you look in the keyword filter, you find the correct command for that action is, **"Open the Footnote,"** as shown in Figure 21-4. Then you know that you should type that exact phrase in the dialog box. This is a good way to find exactly what you want. Of course, you could always use the Dragon Sidebar to find commands, too.

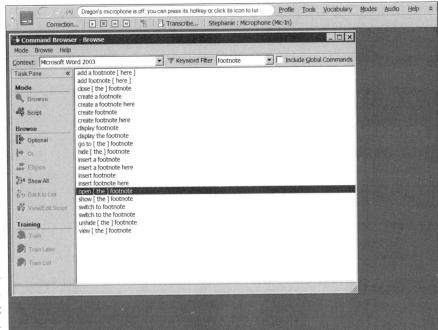

Figure 21-4:
Using the Keyword Filter in the Command Browser to find the correct command.

To use the Keyword Filter to find commands, do the following:

1. **Choose Tools⇨Command Browser from the DragonBar.**

   Look at the Context box in the upper-left corner and make sure you are in the application that applies to this command.

   Use the drop-down menu to pick the application.

2. **Select the Keyword Filter menu option next to the Context box.**

   The Keyword Filter box pops open and you see the list of words along the left side.

3. **Put in words that contain the command you are looking for.**

   In this example, type **Footnote** into the Choose Word dialog box.

4. **After you type in a word(s), click the Add button so that the word is placed on the right side under the current list of filter words.**

5. **Click Done.**

   The Command Browser displays all the commands that pertain to the word *footnote* as shown in Figure 21-5. Now you can choose and use the right one!

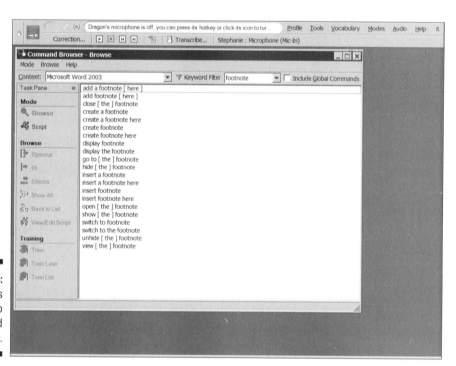

Figure 21-5:
Commands related to the word *footnote.*

Cloning a command to create another

Because you are in a time-saving mood, how about using the command you just created to create another one with a modification? You don't want to start all over again. The Command Browser is a bit different from the Command Editor. Instead of dictating information, you select the command name from a list. To launch the Command Browser, do the following:

1. **Choose Tools⇨Command Browser.**

   You are presented with a big list of commands. Scroll down the list until you find the exact name of your command. Check the Context dialog box to be sure you are in the right type of command. In this case, you need to be in Microsoft Word to edit the command you created for Word. In this example, it is **"Catalog Sent."** See Figure 21-6.

2. **Say or click the name of the command.**

3. **Make sure you are in Script mode, and then choose New Copy.**

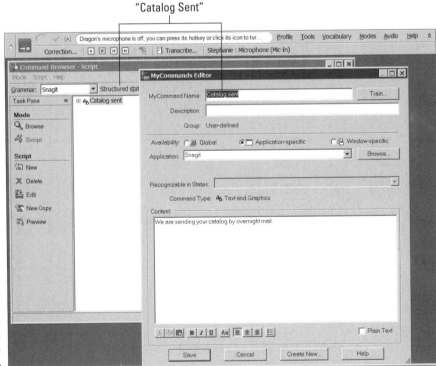

Figure 21-6:
The Command Browser and My-Commands Editor

The Command Editor pops up with the command information you created. You can use the Create New button at the bottom of the dialog box. In this example, use the Create New command as the basis for a new command.

4. **Click the Create New button.**

   Notice that the name is incremented by one. So, for example, if the name was "Catalog Sent," the new one becomes "Catalog Sent 2." You can modify the contents of the command and change the name to something else more memorable. In this example, I changed the MyCommand Name to "Product Docs" and edited the text accordingly by changing "catalog" to "product documents," as shown in Figure 21-7.

5. **Click Save.**

   You now have a new command based on an earlier one, without having to start from scratch.

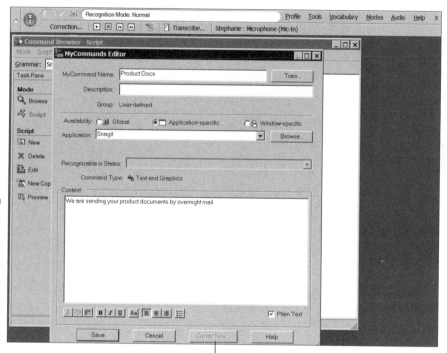

Figure 21-7:
Use the Create New button to modify a previously created command.

Create New button was clicked

Inserting graphics into commands

If you can stand even more time savings, look at how you can insert a graphic with a command. To get started, find a graphic that you want to insert into documents. This could be maps, scanned images, and so forth. For this example, I use a logo.

1. **Copy your logo from your files using Windows, right-click Copy or say,** "Select that," **and then say,** "Copy that."

2. **To create a new command, follow Steps 1 through 6 from the earlier "Creating a New Command" section and choose a memorable name.**

   In this example, call it "Digital Logo."

   When you are at the open window, paste the logo into the window by saying, **"Paste that,"** as shown in Figure 21-8.

3. **Click Save.**

4. **Test the logo command you made by opening a document and saying,** "Insert Digital Logo."

   The logo should be pasted into your document.

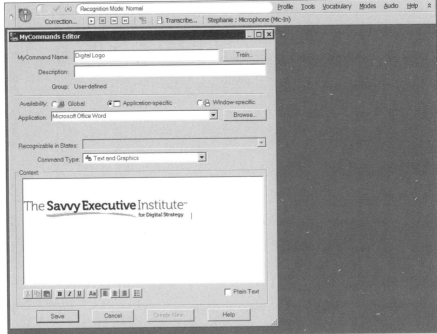

Figure 21-8:
Making a logo available for insertion into documents.

If you are pasting a very large graphic into the window, it helps to enlarge the window into which you are pasting it first, so that you can see the whole item you are pasting.

Deleting commands

If you find you have created a command that doesn't save time or that confuses you, delete it. (Just be sure you want to delete it because you can't get it back. You'll need to create it again.) To delete a command, do the following:

1. **Choose Tools⇨Command Browser.**
2. **Click the Script button under Mode on the left side of the screen.**
3. **Use the drop-down Grammar box to select the application your command is in.**
4. **Click on the name of the command you want to delete.**
5. **Choose the Delete menu item on the left side.**
6. **Click Yes to confirm that you want to delete it.**

   Your command is deleted.

Chapter 22

Getting Help from Your Desktop and Online

*E*very once in a while, you run across a problem that stands head and shoulders above its colleagues. What to do? You can't find anything like it in this book or in the NaturallySpeaking Help files. Even when you bring the problem to your local know-it-all, the one who makes you feel stupid even if you only say hello, he just smiles and says "No kidding? It does that, huh?"

In other words, you need one-on-one attention from somebody who isn't just smart in a general way, but who really knows NaturallySpeaking. Where do you find such people? One obvious place to look is on Nuance.com. You can call or send messages to their Technical Support department.

Another place to look is among other NaturallySpeaking users. By posting a question on a social media site or to an online group that specializes in voice-recognition software, you can get your question to the attention of NaturallySpeaking users all over the world. Some of them are pretty darn smart, and a few of them may have seen exactly the same problem you are encountering.

Getting Help from the DragonBar

Just like any good software product, NaturallySpeaking has Help files that are installed with the software. In addition, Nuance Communications has done quite a bit of work on the interface to provide help for version 11. They also created a Sidebar so that you can see context-sensitive commands when you need them. Here are some of the ways that you can find help directly from the DragonBar on your desktop:

- ✔ **Help menu:** To find help for NaturallySpeaking from the DragonBar itself, start with the Help menu. Here you will find major content areas, an index, and a keyword search area. To reach it from the DragonBar, go to Help⇨Help Topics and type or say what you are looking for. For example, you can say, **"Search Dragon Help For *<topic>*."**

- ✔ **Dragon Sidebar:** The Sidebar is a specific help device that is available whenever you say, **"What can I say?"** (Yes, this is actually a command that NaturallySpeaking responds to.) Because of its importance, I look at it in more detail later in this chapter.

- ✔ **Tutorial:** The tutorial can be accessed both from the Install files when you are setting up and from Help⇨Tutorial.

- ✔ **Help:** This is the place where you can be guided to improve the performance of your software and your total experience. Periodic visits to the menu choice, "Improve my accuracy" are critical, and I devote an entire chapter to it. (See Chapter 18.) Access it from the DragonBar by going to Help⇨Improve My Accuracy.

- ✔ **Performance Assistant:** The Performance Assistant guides you to improve the speed at which NaturallySpeaking can understand your speech. From the DragonBar, go to Help⇨Performance Assistant.

- ✔ **Tip of the Day:** These tips pop up each time you launch NaturallySpeaking. When you are first getting started, they are especially helpful.

The Dragon software includes a Quick Reference Card that shows you how to accomplish some of the common things you will be doing with NaturallySpeaking.

The Sidebar is displayed by default when you launch NaturallySpeaking and open your User Profile. You can choose not to display the Sidebar. Make that setting change by going to the DragonBar, choosing Tools⇨ Options⇨Miscellaneous Tab, and unchecking the box marked Show the Dragon Sidebar. You can always access it when you're dictating. Go to the DragonBar and choose Help⇨Dragon Sidebar, or say, **"Show Dragon Sidebar"** or **"What can I say?"**

The Sidebar provides suggested commands for everything that you are doing while using NaturallySpeaking. This includes both global commands that work in most applications and commands supported only in specific applications, like Microsoft Word.

The Sidebar is divided into two major panes: a Commands pane on the top and a Tips pane at the bottom. You can resize these to suit your needs. It also has several menus and icons. All are shown in Figure 22-1.

Open vocabulary editor   Open Dragon options

Open command browse   Sidebar Help

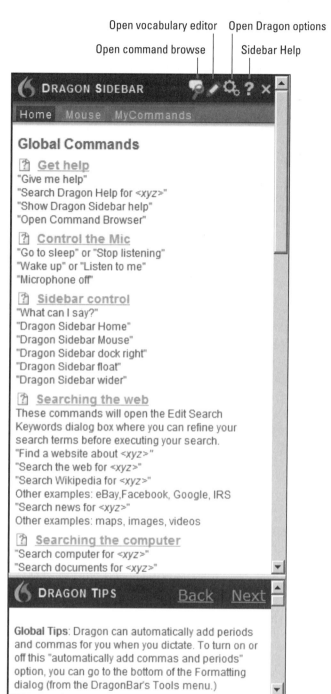

Figure 22-1:
The Dragon
Sidebar.

Let's look at the menu items first:

- **Home:** Try these commands first when you are looking for answers. If you are working in a supported application like Excel, you will see Excel commands. The Sidebar is context sensitive, which means that it displays the most relevant commands for the application or Window you are in.

- **Global:** Displayed here are the Global Commands that can be used anywhere.

- **Mouse:** Click the Mouse menu to see commands specific to moving your mouse, such as, **"Move mouse up"** and **"Move mouse down."**

- **MyCommands:** This section includes the commands that you have created specific to the way you work. For example, if you created a shortcut command for your e-mail signature, you will see it listed when you click here.

Now let's look at what the icons on the Sidebar do. Happily, these are pretty self-explanatory.

- **Open Command Browser:** (Magnifying glass) This icon opens the Command browser so that you can peruse the list of commands available to you. You can also type in keywords for it to search.

- **Open Vocabulary Editor:** (Pencil) Here you can add and train commands that are useful to you.

- **Open Dragon Options:** (Gears) The Option tabs help you control your NaturallySpeaking assistant to do things your way. See Chapter 3.

- **Sidebar Help:** (Question mark) Clicking here will produce the Help files. Alternatively, you can choose Help⇨Help Topics from the DragonBar.

Getting Help on the Web

The web opens up many channels of information, both official and unofficial. Nuance's website contains much technical and troubleshooting information. Other sites also give you information about NaturallySpeaking.

Murphy's Law dictates that companies will reorganize their websites as soon as anyone writes about them, so don't be terribly surprised if particular features of the Dragon website are not exactly where I say they are. (Odds are that the features I mention are still there somewhere.) On the whole, Nuance does a very good job of structuring its website, so if you look around you should be able to find things, even if they've recently moved.

Asking your first question on the Customer Service & Support Portal

To access the Support Portal, you need to set up a free account. From this account, you can register your products, access your stored serial numbers, send a message to the Technical Support department, learn about new Dragon products, or order upgrades.

In general, the better you define your question, the more likely you are to get satisfaction from your e-mail message. If you can say, "When I do this and this and that, I get this error message," the technical support person has a better chance to figure out what's wrong and give you a written answer. They also can do a good job with "How do I make NaturallySpeaking do X?" questions, though I believe I answer almost all of those in this book. And questions like, "Where can I find more about improving my accuracy?" can be easily handled in writing.

For the first 90 days after you register your Naturally Speaking software, you will get your questions answered free. After the 90-day warranty is expired, there is a fee. See the later section, "Talking to Tech Support on the phone," for specifics. In Version 11.5 you will also see a Technical Support link in the Help menu.

To set up an online account and ask your first question, do the following:

1. **Click the Support link on the Nuance.com home page.**

2. **Choose the Get Support link under the picture of Dragon NaturallySpeaking.**

   You are taken to a screen that has a Customer Login box, as shown in Figure 22-2.

3. **Click the Customer Login button.**

   You will be asked to create an account.

4. **Click the Create a New Account button.**

   At the prompts, fill in your information.

5. **Click Submit.**

   A screen appears that says you have created your account successfully and that you should check your e-mail to validate the account.

6. **Go to your e-mail and click the link.**

   You are congratulated for setting up your account and there is a button for you to use if you haven't already registered Dragon NaturallySpeaking.

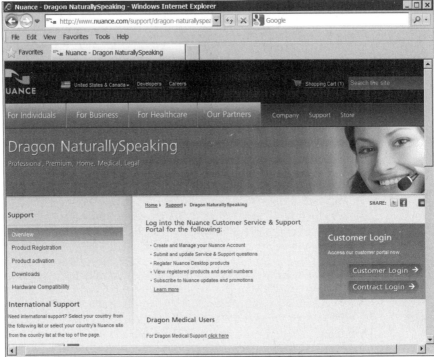

Figure 22-2:
Go to the
Customer
Login box
to create
your free
account.

7. **Repeat Steps 2 and 3. Then log in to your account where prompted.**

   You are taken to the My Stuff area, where you see a list of the questions you asked and information about the products you registered.

8. **Click the Ask A Question button, and then click the Ask A Question button at the next screen.**

   Fill in your question where prompted. You must have a valid serial number if you are asking about your specific situation.

9. **Click Continue until you have answered all the questions.**

   You will arrive at a page that gives you a reference number for your question.

10. **Return to the My Stuff area and click the Notifications button to see the answer to your question.**

    You will also receive an e-mail (at the e-mail address you put on your account) with the answer to your question. If you need to continue the conversation, there is a link to the My Stuff area for you to post a reply.

Talking to Tech Support on the phone

If NaturallySpeaking does something you really don't understand and have a tough time explaining, or if it does something seemingly simple but gives you no information to work with (like failing to install or refusing to respond), you need to talk to a person on the phone.

I don't list pricing for tech support, in case it has changed since this book was published. To determine what you will pay and the parameters under which you may call, go to `http:// nuance. com/product-support/ policy.asp`.

The first thing to understand about Nuance's costs for tech support calls is that they are structured to cost more if you don't first use the question-based system through your free account. (See the preceding section.) Here are your options for speaking directly to a support person:

- ✔ **90-day product support warranty:** Unlimited calls are free during the first 90 days after you register your product or set up your account.

- ✔ **Post 90-day warranty:** There is a fee for this call. And the fee is higher if you don't use the online question-based system first.

- ✔ **Versions bundled with hardware or OEM release:** There is a fee for this call. And again, the fee is higher if you don't use the question-based system first.

- ✔ **Two versions prior to the latest version or one version prior to 2-year-old latest version:** No support available.

- ✔ **Trials and evaluations:** Support not available.

Preparing before you call

A conversation with Technical Support proceeds much more efficiently if you gather the significant information before you call. (Being well-organized has the added benefit of establishing that you are not a complete idiot and there-fore that you may be facing a real problem.)

You should also know what version of NaturallySpeaking you have, both the release number (11.0, say) and the edition (Home, Premium, and so on). This information is displayed from the DragonBar by choosing Help⭥About NaturallySpeaking.

Nuance has taken great pains to handle most system configurations seamlessly. Still, a percentage of the real problems people have with NaturallySpeaking (as opposed to the apparent problems caused by using the product incorrectly) occur from mismatches between the user's hardware and the hardware Dragon had in mind when it created NaturallySpeaking. For this reason, the technical support person will likely want to know the follow-ing information:

✔ **Computer name and model:** They're looking for an answer like Sony VAIO VGN-Z or HP Pavilion 792N (something old, something new). It's probably written on the front of your computer somewhere.

✔ **Processor type and RAM:** If you aren't sure about what you have, right-click Computer from your Start menu and left-click Properties to display the System Properties dialog box. The processor type and RAM should be on the General tab. If you are using Windows 7, choose Start Menu➪Control Panel➪All Control Panel Items➪System.

✔ **Operating system:** Windows XP or Windows 7, for example. Restart your computer and you can't miss it.

✔ **Free hard drive space.** Find your hard drive (C, usually) in either Computer or Windows Explorer. Right-click it and select Properties. On the General tab of the Properties dialog box, you'll find Free Space and some number of megabytes. On Windows 7, double-click the Computer icon and you'll see Free Space displayed for your C drive.

✔ **Sound card name and model:** This is something else to check for in the System Properties dialog box. Right-click Computer and choose Properties, and then select the Device Manager tab. Click the plus sign (+) next to Sound, Video, and Game Controllers. Your sound card should be listed there. In Windows 7, click System Properties after you double-click the Computer icon.

✔ **Microphone name and model:** The obvious place to look is on the microphone. Of course, if you're using the mic that came with NaturallySpeaking, just say that.

Finding your product serial number

The first thing that Nuance wants to establish when you call the technical support department is that you are a bona fide customer. This is why they ask for your product serial number. It isn't a foolproof method, but it does eliminate some of the abuse.

Where can you find your product serial number? Look on the envelope of the software DVD. Do you still have any of that? In Chapter 2, as part of the installation instructions, I tell you to write the serial number on the inside cover of this book or somewhere else where you could find it easily. Maybe you did. Go look. (I'll wait here.) Assuming that you have the number, the call proceeds. (I didn't have the heart to call technical support without a serial number to see what they would do.)

During the call

Take notes. In particular, write down any changes that the technical support person tells you to make. If these changes don't solve the problem (or at least make it better), you may want to undo them later. A difficult problem can take more than one phone call to straighten out, and you may end up dealing with more than one person. This process goes much more smoothly if you can tell the current person you are talking to exactly what the previous person had you do.

Take very good notes if you end up doing something to the Windows Registry. (You'll know because you start using a program called RegEdit.)

This likely will not be the case. Most often, tech support folks will swiftly and professionally handle the issue.

Searching the Nuance Knowledgebase

If you like to look things up yourself rather than ask for help, the Dragon website provides ample reference sources you can look through. If the particular problem you're facing isn't absolutely unique to your system (and most problems aren't), chances are somebody has already asked Dragon's tech support people about it.

If someone has, you can look it up. When the technical support department runs into a new problem, they write down their solutions in their knowledgebase so that their own people can look it up rather than solve the same problem over and over again. Those answers are available to you on the website.

Scanning the knowledgebase

Whenever the technical support people at Dragon figure out how to solve a problem with NaturallySpeaking, they write an answer for the knowledgebase. Follow these steps to scan the latest answers:

1. **From the front page of the Dragon website, click Support.**

2. **Click the Get Support link under the Dragon NaturallySpeaking box.**

   Scroll down to the center of the page and you'll see a Search Nuance Knowledgebase prompt box, as shown in Figure 22-3.

3. **Type in the question for which you want an answer.**

You'll find a list of answers arranged by date, with the most recent on top. It reads like a long troubleshooting guide, with the title of the note being the statement of a problem, such as "Registration reminder continues to appear after successfully registering the product." You can also do a search for a topic by saying, **"Search Nuance support for <topic>.**

Searching for technical information

Sometimes looking through the answers in order can be like searching for a needle in a haystack. Unless you know that the answer you want has been posted to the website in the last few days, you can look at a lot of message titles without finding what you're looking for. Fortunately, Dragon provides an Advanced Search button to help you dig deeper.

Knowledgebase

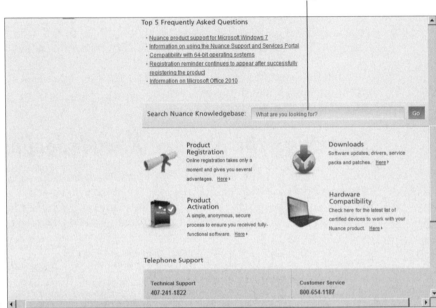

Figure 22-3:
Using the
Nuance
Knowledge-
base.

Accessing the Hardware Compatibility Guide

If you're buying a new system or looking to upgrade part of the system you
have, you can use the site's Hardware Compatibility Guide to check whether
Nuance has tested your system's performance with NaturallySpeaking.

To access the Hardware Compatibility Guide from the Dragon home page
(www.nuance.com), select Support from the menu and click Get Support
under the Dragon NaturallySpeaking box. The Hardware Compatibility link is
on the left side. You can also go there directly by using http://support.
nuance.com/compatibility.

When you arrive at the Hardware Compatibility page, click the kind of hardware you want to check out: microphones, notebook computers, desktop
computers, recorders, sound cards, or miscellaneous to see a list of devices
that Dragon has evaluated in its compatibility labs. (See Chapter 11 for more
information.)

Finding downloads to update your software

On the same Support page (see Step 2 in "Scanning the knowledgebase"), off
the home page is a link to downloads that are available for your software.
Click the Downloads link.

Activating your software

On the same Support page (see Step 2 in "Scanning the knowledgebase"), off the home page you will see the Activations link. Click this if you have questions about the activation process.

Dipping into Product Resources

Nuance provides additional resources to help you learn how to use Dragon NaturallySpeaking. They make it a point to provide a variety of formats because people have different learning styles. You will find the following information at `http://nuance.com/for-business/by-product/dragon/product-resources`:

- ✔ **User Guide and Workbook:** Downloadable user guides help familiarize you with various aspects of the software.

- ✔ **Feature Demos:** See brief videos that focus on specific features of the software, like Correcting Text or Creating Custom Commands.

- ✔ **Edition Comparison:** Here you can access a downloadable feature matrix that shows you how different versions of NaturallySpeaking compare with one another. It will help you decide when and whether to upgrade to a higher version.

- ✔ **Datasheets and White Papers:** This section contains datasheets for all the Dragon products and a list of white papers on a variety of subjects relating to the use of NaturallySpeaking.

- ✔ **Product FAQ:** You know what this is — questions and answers for frequently asked questions.

- ✔ **Microphones:** See the earlier section "Accessing the Hardware Compatibility Guide."

- ✔ **System Requirements:** The listing of system requirements for Dragon Naturally Speaking resides here.

- ✔ **What's new in Version 11:** This area includes a detailed explanation of how version 11 compares to previous editions of NaturallySpeaking.

The following system requirements apply to both the Home and Premium editions of Dragon NaturallySpeaking.

Nuance states that, "The install process checks that your system meets the minimum requirements; if they are not met, Dragon NaturallySpeaking will not be installed." So rest assured that if the software installed, you met the minimum requirements at the time you installed it.

The System Requirements for Dragon NaturallySpeaking are as follows:

- ✓ **CPU:** A minimum 1 GHz Intel Pentium or equivalent AMD processor or 1.66 GHz Intel Atom processor. Nuance recommends a 1.8 GHz Intel Dual Core or equivalent AMD processor. (**Important:** SSE2 instruction set required.)

- ✓ **Processor Cache:** A minimum 512 KB. Nuance recommends 2 MB.

- ✓ **Free hard drive space:** 2.5 GB (2.8 GB for localized non-English versions).

- ✓ **Supported Operating Systems:**

    - Microsoft Windows 7, 32-bit and 64-bit

    - Microsoft Windows Vista SP2, 32-bit and 64-bit

    - Microsoft Windows XP SP2 and SP3, 32-bit only

    - Windows Server 2003 and 2008, SP1, SP2 and R2, 32-bit and 64-bit

- ✓ **RAM:** A minimum 1 GB for Windows XP and Windows Vista, and 2 GB for Windows 7 and Windows Server 2003/2008.

    Nuance recommends 2 GB RAM for Windows XP and Windows Vista, and 4 GB for Windows 7 and Windows Server 2003/2008 64-bit.

- ✓ **Browser:** Microsoft Internet Explorer 6 or higher (free download at www.microsoft.com).

- ✓ **Sound Card:** A Creative Labs Sound Blaster 16 or equivalent sound card supporting 16-bit recording.

- ✓ **Nuance-approved noise-canceling headset microphone:** This may be included in purchase of the software.

A DVD-ROM drive is required for installation, and an Internet connection is required for product activation.

Enhancing Community

In addition to making expert opinions and information available to you, the Internet also gives you ample opportunities to trade information with other users. Through these media, you can find out what problems other users are having; ask questions of your own; answer other users' questions; share experiences; commiserate; speculate about the motivations, intelligence, and personal hygiene of the people who wrote whatever part of NaturallySpeaking you're currently having trouble with; and (most important of all) tell everyone about what a wonderful, readable, insightful book you have found.

Information you get on the Internet — especially from other users — comes without warranty. The vast majority of the users who post messages and comments are well-meaning people who just want to help, and a few of them are downright brilliant. But you should only trust them to the extent that they are making sense. You have no way to verify that they know what they're talking about, so caveat emptor.

Voices of Dragon blog

This blog has been around since December 2010. It's a mix of everything Dragon has to offer. It covers training tips, case studies, web links, and short training videos. It's worth a look. You can sign up for updates if you want to receive them in your e-mail. Find the site, shown in Figure 22-4, at `http://voicesofdragon.com/`.

Figure 22-4:
The Voices of Dragon blog.

Facebook

Like most major consumer software, Dragon NaturallySpeaking has an official Facebook page. Some companies treat their Facebook pages as an afterthought. Nuance is not one of them. They have lots of quality content worth looking at.

You'll find comments from Dragon users along with answers from Nuance staff. You'll also see Customer of the Week highlights and pictures uploaded by Nuance at various tradeshows and other events.

Click on the Discussions link on the left side of the page and jump into the discussions going on. If you're interested, click on the Newsletter sign-up link to get on their list for the next edition. This Facebook page, shown in Figure 22-5, resides at `http://facebook.com/dragonnaturallyspeaking`.

Figure 22-5:
Dragon
Naturally-
Speaking's
Facebook
page.

Twitter

Nuance maintains several feeds on Twitter.com. Two that are pertinent to the topics covered in this book are

- ✔ **@Dragon Tweets:** Nuance has an active Twitter feed that focuses on answering questions, responding to user comments, and tweeting information. This is a great way to quickly get attention for a question that can be answered in 140 characters or less. I'm a big Twitter fan so I use this if I have a question. They also mix in content from their YouTube channel and training tips. This Twitter feed, shown in Figure 22-6, is at `http://twitter.com/#!/dragontweets`.

- ✔ **@Nuance Mobile:** This feed, of course, concentrates on all things mobile. If you use a mobile device like an iPhone, iPad, iPod touch, BlackBerry, or Android, you'll find interesting information here about using them with Dragon NaturallySpeaking. You can find this Twitter feed, shown in Figure 22-7, at `http://twitter.com/#!/NuanceMobile`. For information on using mobile devices with NaturallySpeaking, see Chapter 15.

Figure 22-6:
Nuance on
Twitter.

Figure 22-7:
Nuance
Mobile on
Twitter.

LinkedIn

The Dragon NaturallySpeaking LinkedIn group is more than 350 people strong and requires an invitation. Nuance runs it and has several staffers contributing. I find the wide-ranging discussions most useful. You can find anything from practical tips to hardware discussions to productivity questions or anything you want to share about using NaturallySpeaking, as shown in Figure 22-8. This group's URL is

```
http://linkedin.com/groups?about=&gid=3004295&trk=
anet_ug_grppro.
```

Figure 22-8:
The Dragon Naturally-Speaking group on LinkedIn.

"Ask the Dictator"

If you browse over to Nuance's Dragon NaturallySpeaking channel on YouTube, there's lots to see. At the time of this writing, they have a show called "Ask the Dictator," hosted by Peter Mahoney.

Peter has a nice, easy manner and comes up with interesting things to demonstrate. A recent episode showed how to use Excel with NaturallySpeaking. Nuance's purpose for the channel is to tell you everything you'd like to know about their products and help you find the best ways to put them to use. In addition, you'll see lots of other videos uploaded by fans of the software. Find this, as shown in Figure 22-9, at `http://youtube.com/NuanceDragon`.

Figure 22-9:
Dragon
Naturally-
Speaking
videos on
YouTube.

Table 22-1 shows all the contact information for Nuance Communications, Inc., headquarters.

They didn't do it

The people who answer the phones in technical support departments are the infantry of the software business. They may not be standing in muddy trenches, but they probably are sitting in windowless cubicles with nothing but a phone, a computer, and some reference manuals. They spend their days talking to people who are at best frustrated and at worst totally irate.

Chances are, the person you talk to when you call tech support had nothing to do with designing the product or with creating the mistake (if any) that you are suffering from now. He or she

may well be as annoyed with the design of this particular feature of the product as you are, though it would be unprofessional of him or her to say so.

I know it may be difficult, but try to be pleasant and patient. Figuring out why software does what it does takes time, and the tech support folks are trying to solve in a few minutes something that has probably had you pounding your head against the wall for hours. If they could solve it faster, they would.

Table 22-1	Where to Find Nuance Communications, Inc.
To Contact Them	*Try This*
Customer Service (Phone)	800/654-1187
Technical Support (Online)	Create e-mail account for support
Headquarters Address	1 Wayside Road, Burlington, MA 01803
Phone	781/565-5000
Fax	781/565-5001
Web	www.nuance.com

Part VI
The Part of Tens

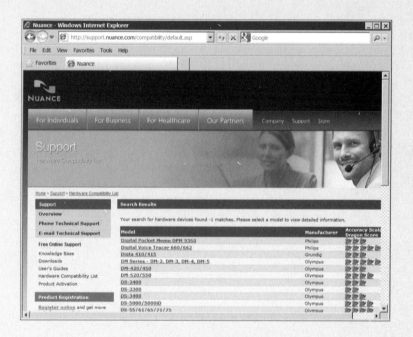

In this part . . .

"The Top Ten Salads of Summer!" "The Ten Top Ski Resorts of Anhedonia!" "The Ten Best-Dressed Celebrities of 2011!" Judging by the popular magazines, it seems like no publisher can resist the number ten.

Just as in the magazines, here is where we cut through the clutter for you and focus on the top ten things in various categories. And there's more at www.dummies.com/go/dragonnaturallyspeaking. Mind boggled by the other pages of this book? Here's the!

Mind boggled by the other pages of this book? Here's the place for you. The Part of Tens. You saw it here first.

Chapter 23

Ten Common Problems

*D*id you ever own something that worked perfectly as soon as you took it out of the box, and never gave you a lick of trouble during its long, productive life? Neither have I. Problems are just part of the experience of owning something. And software problems . . . they are just part of the experience. Period.

So, without further ado, here are ten common problems that NaturallySpeaking users face.

Dictating But Nothing Happens

The words leave your mouth, but they don't appear on the screen. Obviously, they must have taken a wrong turn somewhere. Suppose we follow the path the words should have taken, and see where they may have gotten diverted.

But before we take that trip, are you sure that *nothing* is happening? Say a few words into the microphone and see what happens. Does it say, **"Please say that again."** Okay, back to following the words after they leave your mouth.

- ✔ **First stop: the microphone.** Is it connected to the computer? In the right microphone jack? (The red one is usually the correct one.) Try using the microphone for something else, like the Windows Sound Recorder. If you can record a sound through the microphone, then it isn't the cause.

- ✔ **Second stop: the sound card.** A poor sound card makes for poor recognition, but even poor recognition is a far cry from nothing. The sound card would have to be broken rather than just be poor quality in order to cause NaturallySpeaking to stop dead in its tracks. Seems unlikely.

- ✔ **Third stop: Windows.** Double-click the speaker icon on the taskbar and look at the Microphone Balance. Is the little Mute box checked? Uncheck it, if so.

  Another possibility is that Windows (for its own unfathomable reasons) has changed your device settings — redefined your microphone to be a printer or something equally helpful. (We think we're exaggerating, but it's hard to be sure.) Running through a complete setup with the Audio Setup Wizard will either fix the problem or give you a more specific complaint to take to Dragon Technical Support. (See Chapter 22.)

- ✔ **Fourth stop: microphone icon.** Is NaturallySpeaking asleep? Check the microphone icon on the Windows taskbar or on the NaturallySpeaking toolbar. Is it lying flat on its back? Click it so that it stands at an angle.

  If you are dictating directly into the NaturallySpeaking document window, the preceding are all the obvious sources to check. But if you're dictating into a different application, there are other places to look for problems.

- ✔ **Fifth stop: the application.** Maybe you don't realize which window is active, and text is actually piling up somewhere that you aren't looking. Click in the window you want to dictate into to make sure that it's active. If you use the keyboard to type something, does it appear where you expect it? If not, the problem has nothing to do with NaturallySpeaking.

- ✔ **Sixth stop: the DragonBar.** Look at the DragonBar and see if the check mark is green in color. If it's not green, that means you've lost support for the application you're in or you never had it.

Also, if you're using a nonstandard Microsoft application, it might be a good idea to use the Dictation Box. If this happens inside Microsoft Outlook or Microsoft Word, make sure you close them down along with NaturallySpeaking and then restart them. This usually fixes it. Also, make sure that WinWord.exe or Outlook.exe is not running in the processes tab of the task manager.

Still stumped? That's about as much help as I can give you from this distance in time and space. You need some one-on-one help either from Dragon Technical Support or from other NaturallySpeaking users.

Dealing with Incorrect Results

If NaturallySpeaking just doesn't get it right when you dictate, you're having what's called recognition errors or accuracy problems. Now, don't you feel better, having an official diagnosis of your problem?

No? Then turn to the chapters in Part V of this book. So many different things can affect accuracy that I devote the entire part to them. If that sounds too wearisome, try the following first-aid:

- ✔ Make sure you actually speak each word fully and speak entire phrases. Don't pause between words, and don't skip them, clip them at the end, or slur them to other words.

- ✔ Make sure your microphone is positioned to the side of your mouth, about one-half inch away.

- ✔ Run the Audio Setup wizard again: Choose Audio⇨Check Microphone.

- ✔ Choose Tools⇨Options, and in the Options dialog box that appears, click the Miscellaneous tab. Drag the Speed vs. Accuracy slider more to the right. Click the OK button.

If your problem is that NaturallySpeaking repeatedly gets certain words wrong, make sure you use the Correction dialog box so that NaturallySpeaking learns about its errors. (Say, **"Correct That"** after NaturallySpeaking errs.) If you just select the erroneous text and dictate over it, NaturallySpeaking will never learn.

Speaking Commands That Get Typed as Text

Few things are more frustrating than to select the most important line in your document and say, **"Italicize That"** only to watch the whole line disappear and be replaced with the words *italicize that.* (A quick **"Undo That"** or two usually gets back what you lost.)

This kind of problem can happen for a number of reasons. Here are some things to check or try:

- ✔ **Is the command supposed to work in this application?** I am not sure how many times I've threatened to reprogram my computer with a sledgehammer, only to discover that I had been dictating (well, yelling, actually) a Full Text Control command at an application that wasn't enabled for it or a Natural Language command when Natural Language Commands weren't available.

- ✔ **Get your pauses right.** On multiword commands like **Italicize That** or **Format That Arial Bold 16 Point,** pause briefly before and after the command, but not at all in the middle.

- ✔ **Is NaturallySpeaking hearing you correctly?** Watch the status box, or pay attention to what NaturallySpeaking types instead of doing what you want. If it hears **"Italy sized hat,"** then it isn't going to italicize anything. If this keeps happening, you should do Word training on the particular commands that NaturallySpeaking misinterprets. See Chapter 18.

- ✔ **Hold down the Control key.** Holding down the Control key while you dictate is a way to say "Hey, assistant, this is a command I'm saying!" If this doesn't work, it's time to try to accomplish your purpose another way. For example, you might try saying, **"Press Control I"** instead of **"Italicize That."**

Failing to Control Text with Full Text Control

The most common reason Full Text Control doesn't work is that the application you're dictating into isn't a Full Text Control application. To easily determine if it is, look at the DragonBar on the left side where you see the check mark. If the check mark is green, you are in a Full Text Control application. If the check mark is light gray, you aren't.

Discovering That NaturallySpeaking Inserts Extra Little Words

Some days, you find your documents littered with little words like *in* or *to* or *and.* You are sure you didn't say them. Your NaturallySpeaking assistant just seems to have an overactive imagination today.

These extra little words come from two places. The most likely explanation is that your microphone is positioned badly. If the mic sits in front of your mouth rather than to the side, your words are being punctuated by little bursts of air. Those puffs hit the microphone and make a short, sharp noise that NaturallySpeaking interprets as a short word. It's also possible that the breath coming out of your nostrils is blowing across the microphone. In either case, move the mic farther to the side of your mouth.

The second possibility is that you are trying too hard to enunciate consonants. For example, maybe you had trouble a few lines ago getting NaturallySpeaking to recognize your **Format** command. It heard *formal, form, for Matt,* or some other phrase that wasn't **Format.** Then the next time you needed to format something, you tried too hard to make NaturallySpeaking hear the *t* at the end. And NaturallySpeaking did hear it — a little too well — and so it typed *format to.* The only solution here is to relax; go back to speaking the way you naturally speak. (That's why they call it NaturallySpeaking, you know.)

Dealing with Slow Dictation

You dictate something to NaturallySpeaking, and then you wait. How long is it going to take to figure out what you said? Did it even hear you? Should you repeat? Finally, the words show up.

You can deal with slow response time in the following ways:

- **Ignore it.** I'm serious. Don't wait around for the words to show up on the screen. Keep dictating. NaturallySpeaking remembers as much as a half-hour's worth of dictation, so don't worry if you get a few lines ahead of it.

- **Change the settings.** From the NaturallySpeaking window, say, **"Click Tools, Options."** When the Options dialog box appears, say, **"Click Miscellaneous"** then **"Press Tab"** to select the Speed vs. Accuracy slider. Move the slider toward Fastest Response with the **Move Left <*number*>** command. When you have the slider where you want it, say, **"Click OK."** (You can also do all those steps with your mouse, if you prefer: Choose Tools⇨Options, click the Miscellaneous tab, drag the slider left, and click OK.)

- **Liberate some RAM (memory).** Close any programs you don't need, and turn off background features of those you do need, like automatic spell checking.

- ✔ **Exit all your applications and restart the computer.** If you've been on the computer for several hours and have opened and closed a number of applications, Windows' bookkeeping may have gotten tangled. Restarting may give the computer access to resources it had forgotten about.

- ✔ **Install more RAM.** This isn't going to do you much good in the next 5 minutes, but in the long run it's the best solution.

- ✔ **Turn off natural-language commands.** If you don't need the natural-language commands, just regular old dictation and the dictation commands that work in the NaturallySpeaking window, turn off natural-language commands. Choose Tools⇨Options in the NaturallySpeaking window. In the Options dialog box that appears, click the Command tab, then click the Natural Language Commands button at the bottom. Once there, click to clear the check mark labeled Enable Natural Language Commands. Click OK.

Uncovering Menu Commands That Don't Work

When you say, **"Click"** and nothing happens, the likely problem is that your Use Menus That Are Compatible with Screen Readers check box is unchecked. To check it:

1. **From the NaturallySpeaking window, select Tools⇨Options.**

   There's no point in telling you how to access this by voice, because that's exactly what isn't working!

2. **When the Options dialog box appears, click the Miscellaneous tab.**

3. **Find the Use Menus That Are Compatible with Screen Readers check box and make sure it gets checked.**

Tracking Down Natural-Language Commands That Don't Work

If the Natural Language Commands I describe in Chapter 8 don't work, the two most likely possibilities are

✔ **You aren't dictating into a compatible application.** Natural-language commands don't work in every application you use. Make sure it's enabled for Natural Language Commands.

✔ **Someone has turned off natural-language commands.** To turn them back on:

1. Choose Dragon NaturallySpeaking⇨Tools⇨Options.

2. In the Options dialog box that appears, click the Command tab.

3. Once there, make sure the check box labeled Enable Natural Language Commands has a check mark. If not, click that check box and click OK.

4. On the window still open, click OK again.

Ascertaining That Undo Doesn't Undo

Often, particularly in Word, **Undo That** doesn't fully undo (an under-done undo?). It partially undoes. For example, suppose you highlight some text and speak the command **Format That Arial 14,** but instead of NaturallySpeaking changing the format, it types *Format that aerial for teens* over your selected text. Not what you had in mind. So you say, **"Undo That"** and NaturallySpeaking removes the offending text, but your intended original text is still missing!

In that event, you need to repeat the **Undo That** command. Many NaturallySpeaking actions are actually made up of several Word actions, and **Undo That** only undoes one Word action at a time.

Realizing That Start Doesn't Start

You say, **"Start America Online"** or **"Start Microsoft Works"** or **"Start Quicken"** and nothing happens. What's the deal?

The **Start** command will start any application that is installed on your machine and has either

✔ A shortcut icon on the desktop

✔ An entry on the Programs menu

The catch, however, is that you have to say the name exactly as it appears on the shortcut or menu entry. So if the entry on the Programs menu is Microsoft Word 2010, then you need to say **"Start Microsoft Word twenty ten."**

If the name on the icon or menu entry is too much of a mouthful to be worth pronouncing, or if you can never remember exactly what it says, rename it. Rename a desktop icon by right-clicking it and choosing Rename. You can do the same thing to the Programs menu entries, but you have to find them first. They live in the folder `C:\Windows\Start Menu`.

Another possibility is that you have too many programs on the Start list or on your desktop so it can't open. NaturallySpeaking tracks up to 500 menu and desktop items. If you are beyond that number, you will have a problem opening a program. Cleaning up the list can solve that problem.

Chapter 24

Ten Time-and-Sanity-Saving Tips

. . . .

In This Chapter

▶ Using hotkeys in dialog boxes

▶ Positioning the microphone the same way every time

▶ Changing your mouse habits

▶ Drinking with a straw

▶ Turning off your word processor's automatic spell checking

▶ Working on small pieces of large documents

▶ Using dictation shortcuts

▶ Turning the microphone off when you walk away

▶ Selecting or correcting longer phrases

▶ Using the physical mouse and keyboard

. . . .

Sometimes the difference between doing well and just getting by is a well-placed piece of advice from a wiser and more experienced mentor. Go West, young man. Don't take any wooden nickels. Look before you leap — that kind of thing.

I looked all over for a wiser and more experienced mentor, but I came up short. That's the problem with cutting-edge software: "More experienced" means somebody who installed his copy last Thursday. Anyway, here are ten things I wish somebody had told me last Thursday.

Using Hotkeys in Dialog Boxes

I've become a big fan of hotkeys in general, but they really shine in dialog boxes. The varied features of dialog boxes, the radio buttons, check boxes, and so on, respond unevenly to voice commands. In some dialog boxes, you can say, **"Click *Never Ask Me This Question Again*"** and have a check mark show up in the Never Ask Me This Question Again check box. In other dialog boxes, it doesn't work. But saying, **"Press Alt S"** works every time.

Positioning the Microphone the Same Way Every Time

Misplaced microphones are the number one cause of error. NaturallySpeaking learns best when you sound the same way every time you say a word. And even if you actually *say* the word the same way every time, it *sounds* different if your microphone isn't in quite the same location.

Develop your own precise way of knowing that the microphone is in exactly the right place. Maybe you can just fit a finger between the microphone and the corner of your mouth. If all that is too much trouble, get in the habit of running the Audio Setup Wizard whenever you put your microphone on: Choose Tools⇨Audio Setup Wizard from the NaturallySpeaking menu bar.

Changing Your Mouse Habits

What habits am I talking about? I'm talking about all those things that you might be in the habit of doing with your computer's mouse: clicking toolbar buttons, using scroll bars, dragging and dropping, clicking links on web pages, and relocating the cursor.

NaturallySpeaking has mouse commands, which I describe in Chapter 16. So you *could* keep all your same mouse habits and just use mouse voice commands instead of grabbing the physical object next to your keyboard. But that's not a great idea. The mouse commands (like **MouseGrid**) are usable in a pinch, but they get tedious if you try to do everything with them.

Instead, learn to do the same actions with other commands. Use the web commands with Internet Explorer or Firefox. Say, **"Press Page Down"** or **"Press Page Up"** instead of clicking the scroll bar. Use menu commands instead of toolbar buttons. Cut and paste with hotkeys instead of dragging and dropping. Use the **Move** and **Go** commands to put the cursor where you want. You can also try the 'scroll down' commands to navigate. They work in applications like Microsoft Outlook emails.

Drinking with a Straw

Dictating is thirsty work. You can maintain a clear, steady tone of voice and avoid doing damage to your throat if you keep something to drink close at hand and sip it occasionally. But there is no way to raise a cup to your lips without moving the microphone.

The solution is to drink through a straw! I admit, sipping hot coffee or cold beer through a straw is a weird experience, but most drinks are just fine.

Turning Off Automatic Spell Checking in Word Processors

NaturallySpeaking is incapable of making a spelling error (unless you introduce a misspelled word into its vocabulary through the vocabulary-building process). So spell-checking is a waste of your computer's resources (which NaturallySpeaking may already be stretching near the breaking point). If NaturallySpeaking seems a bit sluggish when you're using a word processor, turn off that word processor's spell checker.

In Word, choose Tools⇨Options from the menu, and then click the Spelling and Grammar tab. Make sure the Check Spelling As You Type check box isn't selected.

While you're there, you can save some RAM by making sure the Check Grammar As You Type check box is unchecked as well. In WordPerfect, choose Tools⇨Proofread⇨Off.

Working on Small Pieces of Large Documents

This tip is another RAM-saver. Large documents take up a lot of your computer's memory, memory that could be better applied to improving the performance of NaturallySpeaking. Don't make your computer keep your whole novel in memory if you really only need to work on one scene. Put the scene in a separate file and work on that file instead.

Using Dictation Shortcuts

You can save a lot of time by teaching NaturallySpeaking some shortcuts. Teach your NaturallySpeaking assistant to type "the Honorable Judge James J. Wackelgoober" when you say **"the boss,"** or to reproduce your full street address when you say **"my address."** See Chapter 18 for details.

You can also use shortcuts to gain some privacy for yourself. If, for example, you have a pet name for your spouse that you would rather not have overheard in the next cubicle when you dictate e-mail, substitute some dull-sounding shortcut.

Turning the Microphone Off When You Stop Dictating

NaturallySpeaking and the microphone that comes with it are usually good enough that they don't pay attention to random noises. The microphone doesn't, however, know that you have just picked up the phone or are talking to the person who just came into your office. I've had some interesting and lengthy gibberish result from such interruptions. It's good to get in the habit of pressing the + key on the keyboard (or clicking the microphone icon) when you are interrupted or otherwise done dictating.

Selecting or Correcting Longer Phrases

When you dictate **"a hippopotamus"** and NaturallySpeaking types "the hippopotamus," don't just say, **"Correct *the*."** NaturallySpeaking may mishear it again, and there's bound to be a "the" in your document somewhere else that it will try to correct instead.

Speak the command, **"Correct *the hippopotamus*."** Chances are good that only one occurrence of "the hippopotamus" is currently displayed and that NaturallySpeaking will pick it out for you right away. Select an even longer phrase, if you can (**"Correct *tickle the hippopotamus*,"** for example).

Using the Physical Mouse and Keyboard

In theory, you can do just about anything with the NaturallySpeaking voice commands. Voice commands like **MouseGrid** and **Click** give you a virtual mouse. The **Press** command gives you a virtual keyboard. So, you should be able to work without the physical mouse and keyboard — in theory. (Theory is a nice place, and I am thinking about relocating there. I hear it has an average temperature all year long.)

Sometimes, however, doing something by voice is simply a pain. Give it up. If you know in your heart that you can do it in three clicks of a mouse's tail, do it. You'll have better days, and you can figure out how to handle the situation with voice commands then. Meanwhile, you stay productive.

Index

• H •

• I •

• *N* •

Notes

Notes

Apple & Macs

iPad For Dummies
978-0-470-58027-1

iPhone For Dummies,
4th Edition
978-0-470-87870-5

MacBook For Dummies, 3rd
Edition
978-0-470-76918-8

Mac OS X Snow Leopard For
Dummies
978-0-470-43543-4

Business

Bookkeeping For Dummies
978-0-7645-9848-7

Job Interviews
For Dummies,
3rd Edition
978-0-470-17748-8

Resumes For Dummies,
5th Edition
978-0-470-08037-5

Starting an
Online Business
For Dummies,
6th Edition
978-0-470-60210-2

Stock Investing
For Dummies,
3rd Edition
978-0-470-40114-9

Successful
Time Management
For Dummies
978-0-470-29034-7

Computer Hardware

BlackBerry
For Dummies,
4th Edition
978-0-470-60700-8

Computers For Seniors
For Dummies,
2nd Edition
978-0-470-53483-0

PCs For Dummies,
Windows
7 Edition
978-0-470-46542-4

Laptops For Dummies,
4th Edition
978-0-470-57829-2

Cooking & Entertaining

Cooking Basics
For Dummies,
3rd Edition
978-0-7645-7206-7

Wine For Dummies,
4th Edition
978-0-470-04579-4

Diet & Nutrition

Dieting For Dummies,
2nd Edition
978-0-7645-4149-0

Nutrition For Dummies,
4th Edition
978-0-471-79868-2

Weight Training
For Dummies,
3rd Edition
978-0-471-76845-6

Digital Photography

Digital SLR Cameras &
Photography For Dummies,
3rd Edition
978-0-470-46606-3

Photoshop Elements 8
For Dummies
978-0-470-52967-6

Gardening

Gardening Basics
For Dummies
978-0-470-03749-2

Organic Gardening
For Dummies,
2nd Edition
978-0-470-43067-5

Green/Sustainable

Raising Chickens
For Dummies
978-0-470-46544-8

Green Cleaning
For Dummies
978-0-470-39106-8

Health

Diabetes For Dummies,
3rd Edition
978-0-470-27086-8

Food Allergies
For Dummies
978-0-470-09584-3

Living Gluten-Free
For Dummies,
2nd Edition
978-0-470-58589-4

Hobbies/General

Chess For Dummies,
2nd Edition
978-0-7645-8404-6

Drawing
Cartoons & Comics
For Dummies
978-0-470-42683-8

Knitting For Dummies,
2nd Edition
978-0-470-28747-7

Organizing
For Dummies
978-0-7645-5300-4

Su Doku For Dummies
978-0-470-01892-7

Home Improvement

Home Maintenance
For Dummies,
2nd Edition
978-0-470-43063-7

Home Theater
For Dummies,
3rd Edition
978-0-470-41189-6

Living the
Country Lifestyle
All-in-One
For Dummies
978-0-470-43061-3

Solar Power Your Home
For Dummies,
2nd Edition
978-0-470-59678-4

Internet

Blogging For Dummies,
3rd Edition
978-0-470-61996-4

eBay For Dummies,
6th Edition
978-0-470-49741-8

Facebook For Dummies,
3rd Edition
978-0-470-87804-0

Web Marketing
For Dummies,
2nd Edition
978-0-470-37181-7

WordPress
For Dummies,
3rd Edition
978-0-470-59274-8

Language & Foreign Language

French For Dummies
978-0-7645-5193-2

Italian Phrases
For Dummies
978-0-7645-7203-6

Spanish For Dummies,
2nd Edition
978-0-470-87855-2

Spanish
For Dummies,
Audio Set
978-0-470-09585-0

Math & Science

Algebra I
For Dummies,
2nd Edition
978-0-470-55964-2

Biology For Dummies,
2nd Edition
978-0-470-59875-7

Calculus For Dummies
978-0-7645-2498-1

Chemistry For Dummies
978-0-7645-5430-8

Microsoft Office

Excel 2010 For Dummies
978-0-470-48953-6

Office 2010 All-in-One
For Dummies
978-0-470-49748-7

Office 2010 For Dummies,
Book + DVD Bundle
978-0-470-62698-6

Word 2010 For Dummies
978-0-470-48772-3

Music

Guitar For Dummies,
2nd Edition
978-0-7645-9904-0

iPod & iTunes For
Dummies, 8th Edition
978-0-470-87871-2

Piano Exercises
For Dummies
978-0-470-38765-8

Parenting & Education

Parenting For Dummies,
2nd Edition
978-0-7645-5418-6

Type 1 Diabetes
For Dummies
978-0-470-17811-9

Pets

Cats For Dummies,
2nd Edition
978-0-7645-5275-5

Dog Training For Dummies,
3rd Edition
978-0-470-60029-0

Puppies For Dummies,
2nd Edition
978-0-470-03717-1

Religion & Inspiration

The Bible For Dummies
978-0-7645-5296-0

Catholicism For Dummies
978-0-7645-5391-2

Women in the Bible
For Dummies
978-0-7645-8475-6

Self-Help & Relationship

Anger Management
For Dummies
978-0-470-03715-7

Overcoming Anxiety
For Dummies,
2nd Edition
978-0-470-57441-6

Sports

Baseball
For Dummies,
3rd Edition
978-0-7645-7537-2

Basketball
For Dummies,
2nd Edition
978-0-7645-5248-9

Golf For Dummies,
3rd Edition
978-0-471-76871-5

Web Development

Web Design
All-in-One
For Dummies
978-0-470-41796-6

Web Sites
Do-It-Yourself
For Dummies,
2nd Edition
978-0-470-56520-9

Windows 7

Windows 7
For Dummies
978-0-470-49743-2

Windows 7
For Dummies,
Book + DVD Bundle
978-0-470-52398-8

Windows 7 All-in-One
For Dummies
978-0-470-48763-1

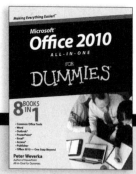

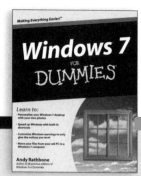

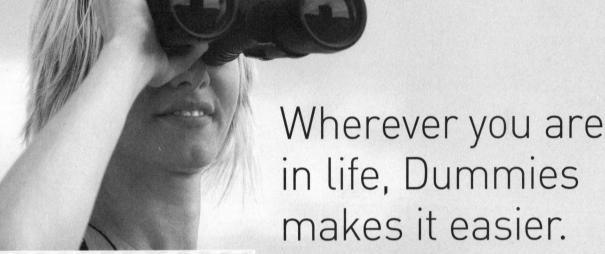

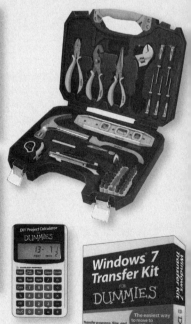